100 Controversial Truths

About Politics and Culture in America

Doug Pancoast

ISBN: 0615793223
ISBN-13: 9780615793221
Library of Congress Control Number: 2013906344
CreateSpace Independent Publishing Platform
North Charleston, South Carolina

Dedication

There are several people I want to thank. Firstly, I want to thank my parents (and my sister), who have put up with so much. They always supported me. They stood by my side through the good times and the bad. I would be nowhere and nobody without my family.

I want to thank those good teachers I had, that inspired me to become the thinker and writer that I am. I want to thank Mrs. Angela Frankhauser, Mr. Robert Bogan, Mr. Gary Wells, Mrs. Eva Arce, Mrs. Andrea Ramirez, Mrs. Joyce Brisco, and Mrs. Jo Sparks. I would not be the person I am without these great teachers. I had some good teachers...and some very bad ones, but teachers like these can help educate students that can change their world.

I also want to thank my friends back in Austin (and actually around the world), especially Smitty. Without them, I am nothing. And although there are countless others I should thank by name, I will certainly have to leave many of them out. However, I specifically dedicate this book to Nandi Cavallaro. He was one of the smartest, strongest, funniest, boldest, most frustrating individuals I've ever met. He was the best friend you could ever have. He taught me more than anybody else I've ever met. He was a genius. And when he died, the world lost a great one. Nandi Cavallaro, like everybody else, would not have agreed with everything in this book. But he taught me how to think outside the box and to question commonly held beliefs. He taught me to watch how people act and to figure out why they act that way. And how to influence them to act differently. Although he also had flaws, he had more strengths than anybody I've ever met. If I ever become 25% of the person he was, I'll be one of the most successful people ever. I dedicate this book to him and his memory, which will live forever.

And it is in his name that 10% of all income I earn from this book will be donated to charities in the United States, half to support education and scholarships and the other half to support the poor and homeless.

A Very Special Thanks

I also want to specifically thank those who financially backed this book, especially my GA professor from my MBA program Art Budolfson. I never could have finished my MBA without his encouragement. To also financially support my book, he has given me so much. Also:

MBA classmates:

Taylor Nelson
DJ Singh.

And other equally important financial contributors:

Eric Fisher
Thomas Vogt
Jacy Johnson
Jeff Ceynar

In addition, special thanks to Robert Salanitro who did an excellent job with the cover design. I'd highly recommend him.

And lastly, but certainly not least, a special thanks to Josh Koblitz for reviewing the book early on and giving me important advice. Eric Fisher also played a very important role in helping me edit one of the chapters. The fact is the book wouldn't be as good without these two guys' help and advice. Although probably none of the people who helped me through their financial support, their writing advice, or through their encouragement agree with every idea in this book, they each still supported me and my dream. They helped make it a reality. I can never thank them enough and without them, this book would not have been possible.

Table of Contents

Foreword and About the Author

This book isn't like any other book out there. Yes, it's a political book. And yes there are some (very) controversial ideas in it. However, this book is NOT a partisan book. This is NOT a book that conservatives will read and agree with almost every word (far from it)...OR a book that liberals will read and agree with every word in it. Instead, there will be some chapters that liberals will love...and some that they will hate. Conservatives, likewise.

However, what *really* makes this book different is that even within individual chapters, conservatives will passionately agree with certain parts of the chapter and be horribly appalled at others. This book is all over the political map. It is not conservative. It is not liberal. It is not libertarian. Or socialist. The number one theme of this book is that both sides are partially right on many of the issues. However, we must be willing to look at an issue and be honest about the real truths...even if they don't coincide with our normal political biases.

Doug Pancoast was born in Macon, Georgia to a white father (who almost always voted Republican) and an Hispanic mother (who always voted Democrat). There, he went to a school that was about two-thirds black and only one-third white. Between school and later mission trips to inner city New Orleans, Doug was able to spend lots of time with both African Americans as well as white Americans. After leaving Macon, Doug moved to Austin, Texas. At first, he attended one of the wealthiest (and whitest) schools in Austin. Later, he moved to a school in a more middle-class area. These experiences allowed him to see how people in all economic classes live and think.

After graduating high school, Doug moved to Tallahassee, Florida to attend Florida State University. There, he majored in International Affairs and continued his active participation in numerous Christian organizations, such as the Baptist Collegiate Ministry, and taught Sunday School in his local Southern Baptist Church. At FSU, he was able to study and learn about different types of cultures and governments throughout the world.

After completing his undergraduate degree in just three years, Doug worked in the insurance and investment industries. He went on to obtain one of the highest certifications in the financial planning industry while learning and educating investors about retirement planning, investing, etc. Doug also completed two Master's degrees, including his MBA, from the WP Carey School of Business at Arizona State University. There, Doug learned about how businesses operate and some of the conditions necessary to have a thriving business environment.

Doug has lived in Korea before and currently lives in Shanghai, China where he writes, works, and is planning to start his own company.

Problems with Conservatism

If there is one key point that I want people to walk away with from this book it's that conservatism is wrong. Just kidding. I want people to walk away realizing that conservatism is right...about some things. And wrong about others. I find it extremely weird to see how many people support basically everything their party and even their ideology believes. Conservatives (or liberals) couldn't possibly be right about everything, could they?

One of the biggest problems with conservatism is that it completely fails to see and acknowledge the link between poverty and violent crime. Or, conservatives just prefer to have large prisons to deal with social problems that always come along with poverty and extreme inequality. We've seen it happen time and time again in history. If the people begin to feel like the rich and powerful elite in their country aren't taking care of them, then they'll fight back...or at least plague society with the major social problems that will always come along with "personal responsibility." What do we do with people who have suffered from bad luck and/ or bad choices? Conservatism basically says, "Screw them." The free market also leads to essential positions (like CEO) getting paid massive premiums and low value-add positions getting paid less and less. The free market does that. And the question is: is that fair? Conservatism says yes. And when it does, it allows for the social problems that come with poverty and inequality.

Another big problem with modern day conservatism, neo-conservatism, is that it is perpetually war prone. It supports having U.S. military presence and bases throughout the world to protect U.S. military interests. It props up certain governments that are U.S. friendly and then is swift to go to war when it is going to benefit the U.S., which creates more enemies and more wars. It's like a Ponzi scheme, but with war. And these wars cost us hundreds of billions of dollars...over a trillion, in fact. And that's our money being given to defense contractors and being spent overseas in these godforsaken places. And that is part of the modern day conservative movement...that we need these wars to make us safer.

Modern day conservatives are right to preach personal responsibility, but wrong not to have a plan in place for those who fail. They are right that we have enemies in the world, but wrong about why. They are right about some of the burdensome regulations America has towards business, but wrong about how to create economic incentives that will help everybody...and not just those at the top (they're also wrong to *completely* trust the free market and oppose certain important financial regulations that protect the American people). They are right on corporate taxes, but wrong on personal income taxes. They are right that family values are needed, but wrong to try and force their beliefs on others...rather than loving and helping those that make bad choices...and then teaching them how to make good choices. Conservatives are right about the national debt, but wrong on many of the ways to fix it. They refuse to raise taxes on the richest Americans no matter what...even if those people don't provide one job for somebody else. Not every rich person is a "job creator." Conservatives are right on free trade, but wrong for not having a better plan in place to help those whose jobs are destroyed by it. They are right about punishing criminals harshly, but wrong for not investing more in programs to help prevent repeat offenders and even first-time offenders. They fail to see how any of their policies contribute to the poverty problem in this country and how violent crime is directly correlated with poverty levels. They claim to hate regulation, but want to regulate marriage. Conservatives are right about many things, but wrong about many things, as well.

Problems with Liberalism

Liberals loved that last chapter. However, their shit stinks, too. It's almost impossible for an ideology to be completely correct...and liberalism certainly is no exception, in both foreign policy and domestic policy. Democrats want to regulate...and tell people how they can live their lives, as well. It may not be morals and religion, but it may be punishing people who eat unhealthy foods. It may be adding taxes that are meant to punish certain activities, but sometimes also come with negative unintended consequences. Liberals also constantly back unions, whose tactics can be borderline criminal and whose demands sometime lead to companies shutting down completely. We should all agree (even though we won't) that the rich enjoy a lot more of America's resources and have a lot more disposable income to help the country invest to make this country better for everybody...and that they *should* be expected to do so. However, if you tax corporations **too** much, they really will just take their ball and go play somewhere else any chance they get. They take their money and their jobs and go somewhere else (yet they still come and sell us what we need even after they eliminated some of our jobs). And everybody loses. But that happened because you taxed them too much. They were able to just go to some other state or country. And Democrats don't realize this. You can't beat the corporations. You have to figure out ways to incentivize them to create jobs here and then tax high personal incomes more. Corporations will go where they can produce cheapest and make the most profit for the company. If we allow them to do that here, the jobs will follow...and then that's where you get the revenue that you need...from the people who corporations pay the most. Another problem is that if liberals demand unrealistic government services, the system will eventually go bankrupt. Furthermore, Keynesian economics (which has extremely high levels of support among liberals) and loose monetary policy have led to asset bubbles and inflation that have punished the poor and lower middle class the most.

Liberals are also wrong on foreign policy, at times. I've lost confidence with the U.N. and international bodies. I think power corrupts and absolute power corrupts absolutely. I think it's important that countries meet and work together to achieve world peace and prosperity. However, much of the U.N. has become about countries trying to politically influence the rest of the world. Yet, like any huge organization with such a diverse constituency, people ultimately do not agree and therefore an organization with weak enforcement resolve and power will be largely ineffective. I think liberals are right to be less obsessed with America's short term advantage and benefit, but wrong to have faith in weak and ineffective institutions (the flip side being that if the institutions were not weak, then the potential for the abuse of that power would be higher).

Many liberals oppose the death penalty and call it cruel and unusual punishment. Frankly, that is ridiculous. The Founding Fathers, who wrote the amendment that forbids cruel and unusual punishment, used hangings and firing squads. How could you seriously argue that our Founding Fathers considered the death penalty to be cruel and unusual? However, to play devil's advocate, the Constitution *has* been proven to have contained problems before (slavery, women suffrage, etc.). At the end of the day, however, the death penalty is much cheaper than locking evil people up for the rest of their lives.

And finally, liberals are wrong for not demanding people learn from their bad choices while wanting to help them. I support welfare for the poor, but I believe it's vital to help teach somebody how to escape poverty. It's great to give people food stamps, but let's figure out how to get people to make good choices and stop making bad ones (assuming they are). Why just offer short-term solutions to these people? Why not teach people how to fish...rather than just advocating giving them a fish?

Tea Partiers vs. Occupiers

When the Tea Party movement first started, it really helped to establish some of the national conversation. It was a little bit kooky at times (ok...more than a little...). However, at times, Tea Partiers seemed to have some valid points. Later, the Occupy Wall Street movement began in New York City. It's hard to know for sure if either of these were actually originally grassroots movements. Certainly, both movements were later funded, and therefore fueled, by behind-the-scenes organizations like the Koch Brothers' "Americans for Prosperity" and (quite possibly) ACORN. And both movements have their fair share of outlandish ideas and whacko participants. However, for all the weirdoes of both movements, each has a core message of truth.

The Tea Party movement was so successful that it ultimately ended up being hijacked by a large percentage of conservatives, each with fairly different views. There is the "Ron Paul" libertarian branch of the Tea Party and then the "Michelle Bachmann" social conservative branch of the Tea Party. The two things that seem to tie all of the various factions of the Tea Party movement together are a desire for a reduction in government spending (and the overall size and influence of government) and the desire for lower taxes. Among these two common goals, the Tea Party is basically half right about each point. Firstly, the Tea Partiers are absolutely correct that both the annual national deficit and the cumulative national debt have spiraled out of control. They have been the leading voice hoping to protect America from its gross overspending. Tea Partiers are also right about the need to make cuts to Medicare and Social Security, as the two programs are unsustainable in their current forms, especially with the changing demographics in America and the rising healthcare costs. However, their methods are often wrong. Some of the ways they wish to cut Social Security and Medicare are very unfair (and bad ideas) and their refusals to touch defense spending or to increase revenues are major sources of political and economic hardship in America. Tea Partiers are also half right on taxes. Corporate tax rates in the U.S. are among the very highest in the world and make American businesses less competitive. However, Tea Party desires for a flat personal income tax would be grossly unfair to lower income earning Americans. Tea Partiers, naturally, are not right about everything...but certainly do have some important points.

The Occupy movement, which seemed to start as a response to the Tea Party movement, focuses on the growing income inequality that exists in America. And they also have a point. While the real median household income in 2011 remained at 1997 levels, the rich's real incomes have grown significantly over the same time period[1]. The top 1% now earn a higher percentage of the total national income and own a greater percentage of the wealth than any time in the last several decades. Furthermore, the movement seeks to protest the secretive connections that exist between the CEO's of some of our country's largest financial institutions and our elected officials. That close and sometimes secretive connection seemed to help lead to the highly deregulated environment that led to the crazy risks that caused the collapse of the American and world economies, as well as the eventual transfer of taxpayer money to these private financial institutions that were deemed "too big to fail." Those are all good points, too. However, some of the Occupiers' ideas and demands are also ridiculous (practically Communist or Anarchist). And some of these Occupiers seemed to be really, really stupid people who probably couldn't do almost any job. Some of them were dirty, smelly, and had no marketable skills. When listening to many of the "Occupiers", you got that same sickening feeling that many people did when watching many of the Tea Party people.

Yet, like many Tea Partiers, Occupiers have a point. And although their political opposition will also try and dismiss their points because of some of their stranger followers, we only continue to hurt our democracy when we do so. Both of these groups may have plenty of weirdoes behind them, some misguided beliefs, and even sketchy funding backing them up. But they both also have some points that need to be listened to if we're going to improve this country together.

24 Hour News Networks

What constitutes "news" these days is really quite amazing sometimes. These networks are just full of excuses (and some of them are valid). It *is* hard to find interesting and informative content to cover 24 hours a day, 7 days a week. And they *are* fighting for viewers and advertising revenue. They are for-profit businesses. They have a product they are selling. And I will give the media credit for occasionally figuring out creative ways to use new technologies to make truth visible to the American people. But some of what they do is so bad and so irresponsible, that it's practically evil.

One thing that amazes me is spending an hour or so watching an average MSNBC program and then spending another hour watching virtually any Fox News show. It is like you literally moved from one planet to another. The way that some of these 24-hour news networks push a consistent leftist or rightist agenda is so disgusting.

But, I can watch either of them and usually hear some story that makes me think, "You know, I probably wouldn't have known about this story without this network." But most of the time, it's just such in-your-face propaganda that it really makes you sad about America. It's unclear how much of it is a real ideological struggle for minds and how much of it is just, "This is the customer base that I am trying to appeal to and this is what they want to hear." And that's the problem with capitalism in the media. I don't believe in having government run newspapers, but whenever news becomes about profit, it puts completely new problems into the mix.

Another one of the problems that comes with the media being for profit is the natural incentive it creates for sensationalism. The real news, and all of the information that would truly help society form reasonable and informed opinions, doesn't sell. People aren't interested in that. Where are the stories about the starving people in Africa? Why can't that get more attention? Or more stories that expose corruption in world governments? Or OUR corrupt government? The modern day media has a particular agenda. Or they want the sensational sex scandal. Or something that's easy to understand. "Quantitative easing? That makes my head hurt. Let's watch Dancing with the Stars." "Sex scandal? That's interesting. I want to hear how they met." What is the media going to spend more time covering: QE3 or Weiner's wiener?

I know that journalists will fight for their reputations until they're blue in the face. And you'd expect that. And there are a few journalists who try their best to put the truth out there. But, I think it's the editors, the producers, and the people even above those people that control the access to what parts of the story get told and which stories even get told at all. But sometimes, even the journalists are corrupt. Many people who have dealt with the media, including myself, have literally seen a story blown up, exaggerated, and distorted in order to sensationalize or promote a certain agenda. And that's what's wrong right now with the 24-hour news networks. They know it. But they won't admit it.

We must get back to a place where there is not liberal news and conservative news. And where the news isn't about scaring you or sensationalizing a story so that you'll watch it. But instead, the news must once again become about informing people of truth, holding our politicians accountable, and providing truly fair coverage of the issues. Until then, it's hard to know if the media is doing more harm than good.

American School System

The American school system is messed up. And there are a ton of reasons why. Conservatives have their opinions on why. And I believe some of them are right. And some of them are wrong. Liberals also have their opinions why. And I believe that some of them are right and some of them are wrong. And this issue is yet another example of how liberals and conservatives each have good ideas and a piece of the (but not the whole) truth.

One of the issues that I believe liberals are dead-on correct about is school funding. It is simply unfair to have schools be primarily locally funded. I know the rich believe that because they make more money and enjoy bigger houses in nicer, more expensive neighborhoods (and pay more in property tax) that they are entitled to nicer schools. As I talk about later, it's astounding the irony of how entitled the rich feel. But it's an obvious cycle of poverty when poor kids grow up in poor neighborhoods and then, on top of all of the other crap they have to deal with in life, have poor and crappy schools, as well. The poor start out, and often run the entire race, with two arms tied behind their back. I know. I went to one school built in 1930. It didn't have air conditioning. All of the books were at least ten years old. And there were gang problems, stabbings, fights, and even students getting caught with guns at school. I moved in the middle of one school year (February) to a very rich school district (my family changed jobs and cities) and found myself literally going from being at the head of my class to being in the back of it (at least in math). Our schools are appallingly unequal. In addition to having the nicest buildings, the newest books, and a much safer learning environment, rich schools also have the best teachers; everybody wants to teach in that district. They have great facilities. They often pay their teachers more. All because the rich parents in that area have more money than the poor people do. I mean, life isn't fair...but how unfair should it be? Is that kind of disparity in educational experiences morally justifiable just because rich people make more money and can afford a more expensive house and pay more in property taxes?

So, there's a money problem. However, there are also cultural problems. Gangs cause fear in poor neighborhoods and often have a very bad influence on many people's decisions. That's not the school's fault and it's not even related to the funding of those schools. There are communities in this country that are full of people who make bad choices. And it's not isolated to any particular race. (However, it is common among poorer economic classes...although it's spreading to other economic classes, as well). One need not forget that many of the school shootings, like the ones in Littleton, CO and more recently in Connecticut, have occurred in very affluent (and white) areas. This is the state of America's schools in the 21st century. And people wonder why we're falling behind the rest of the world. Our kids are messed up. Our society is messed up. "Garbage in. Garbage out." It's true in our culture and society, as a whole, and it's true of our school system. Schools only get the students for eight hours a day. The school can only do so much to overcome all of the influences in students' lives outside of school. And these days, for a lot of kids all over this country, those influences are not good. Teachers should be limited to what extent they teach children right and wrong, but teachers absolutely *should* teach students basic right and wrong and at least try to fight for the hearts and minds of our children.

We owe it to children and to society to help kids, of all economic statuses, understand how education is an investment. Many young kids don't know the statistics about income and educational attainment. Many poor kids don't know anybody who has graduated from college. And they may not even know about grants, loans, or how they could ever pay them back. How can these children know if there is nobody there to tell them? We owe it to all kids to teach them about good choices and bad choices. We have to find a way to help these communities shed themselves of gangs. We have to make them understand the importance of education. We have to give them the skills that they need to be successful. Families must take the lead role in helping their children escape the cycle. But where we, as a government, can reach in and help teach people how to make good choices, I believe we have a responsibility to do so. Some parents simply won't do their jobs. Should the children and society suffer the consequences? I believe investing in children from all economic backgrounds benefits all of society and will save us money down the road, as we'd expect to eventually see a drop in violent crime levels.

So what are the liberal and conservative solutions to our broken school system? Liberals often want to simply throw more money at the problem. And poor schools DO need more money. The disparity in the quality of education that is offered IS unfair. It's morally wrong. (Ironically, conservatives want to get rid of federal money for education and make education even more locally run...AND funded). However, what liberals don't realize is that we can throw all the money in the world at the problems with our schools, but if we don't also start fixing the culture these kids grow up in and go to school in, all the money will go to waste. Kids must be taught the importance of an education and they have to study hard and make good choices. And that is missing in many of our schools.

In addition to changing the way schools are funded and trying to improve the culture at many schools, one final suggestion I'd make is having school year round. In Malcolm Gladwell's book *Outliers*, he discusses studies that show how summer vacations are when poor students fall behind their richer peers. While wealthy, educated parents push and support their kids to study and read during summer vacations, poorer parents often do not.

One exception I'd take to many liberals' approach is their complete support of teachers' unions. Teachers' unions are not always right. For one, they oppose incentive pay. I support certain types of incentive pay. I don't think teachers should be rewarded by performance if you're comparing across different schools, with different students, in different areas. I know teachers also worry about teachers being incentivized to cheat. However, that already happens. There have been major cheating scandals in at least a couple of major cities' public schools. However, I think if you reward teachers using the same kind of balanced scorecard that many private businesses use, it could be successful. Teachers could be judged by students' standardized test scores, their own extra-curricular involvement, student, peer, and administrative evaluations, etc. Currently, many teachers feel like they have no reason to work hard. They will get paid the same whether they do a good job or a poor job. And you wouldn't even *have to* use money to incentivize teachers, either. You could use other rewards and perks instead (or in addition to). Liberal thinking has also led to schools becoming watered down. For a long time, many schools in America "taught towards the middle." For some students, it would be too hard. For some, it would be too easy. But for most students, it would hopefully be the right level of difficulty. However, these days, more and more schools are teaching to the bottom. American primary school students rank horribly low in world rankings. Our schools are just not challenging our students and demanding excellence from them.

Many conservatives in America think that vouchers and school choice are the answer. They want to give parents the option of taking the money that their public school gets for their child enrolling there, and allow them to use it at any school they want...including religious schools. They argue that the best schools will prosper and get more students and the worst schools will eventually close down. However, what about the logistics of when a school (in a poor neighborhood, for example) closes down? Or what if a student in a poor neighborhood's school stays open, but he or she wants to go to a different school, in a different neighborhood? How will he or she get there? What if his or her parents don't have a car? And will schools be allowed to charge *more* than whatever amount the government pays? If so, how will that be fair for the poor? They'll never be able to afford the best schools (that charge more than the government provides) and the gap between the rich and the poor will widen.

American Healthcare System

America's healthcare system, in a way, is quite easy to understand. Everybody who can, makes sure that *they* get rich. And those without lots of money or a good job are left to fend for themselves. The doctors are getting rich. The insurance companies are getting rich. The pharmaceutical and medical device companies are getting rich. And, in their defense, they are also coming up with a lot of great innovations. But, the best innovation comes with a big price tag. Americans spend a higher percentage of GDP on healthcare than any other country...by far. And the question is: do we want to have the best medicine that money can buy, but also have a significant percentage of the population who can't afford it?

Because that's really the dilemma. It is true that the best students will often do what will make them the most money. If that's being a doctor, then they'll become doctors. If it's being an investment banker, then they'll be investment bankers. And if it's being a government official, then they'll try to become government officials. For example, in Korea, many of the best students go into dentistry and plastic surgery. Why? Because those services aren't covered by the national insurance plan and so the government doesn't determine how much they can charge. All Koreans use the same single-payer basic health insurance system. The doctors can really only make more money through more volume (because everybody has the same basic health insurance plan and the reimbursement rate is set). Normal doctors, therefore, try to get patients in and out quickly, and the doctor tries to see two patients practically at one time. But, you walk out paying $5 or $10 out of pocket, the treatment you get is of very high quality, and it's more affordable for everybody. The doctors don't have as many Mercedes, they work longer hours, and there aren't nearly as many rich insurance executives. And the top quality care available in Korea is not as good as the top quality care available in America. But it works.

The current system in the United States simply can't work. What is currently happening is that the supply of doctors and care is being constrained (e.g., by the number of medical schools, which each limit their enrollment). Of course we want the highest quality doctors, but does anybody seriously believe that all of the applicants that get turned down by medical schools couldn't make suitable primary care physicians? They couldn't treat people with flu-like symptoms and runny noses?

Furthermore, employers don't have to offer employees insurance at all (even with Obama's healthcare plan there are many employees that are not required to receive coverage, such as part-time employees). And if they do offer coverage for their employees, the coverage may not be very good. With doctors, hospitals, and everybody charging higher and higher prices, insurance premiums are shooting up, as well. And then both the employers and the insurance plans reduce benefits to partially offset rising costs. As costs become higher and higher, healthcare is becoming more and more unaffordable for Americans. Because the doctors (the AMA), the pharmaceutical companies, and everybody else has bought off our politicians to regulate healthcare so carefully, our access to lower cost options in the free market is prevented...helping keep prices upwards.

Meanwhile, all the people getting rich off of ordinary people fight with each other to get a larger share of the pie and (even more) rich. Insurance companies negotiate lower rates with doctors...if they want to be able to have access to their insureds. So, doctors often try to make up for this reduction in payments by ordering unnecessary tests and procedures. Insurance companies then fight this practice while also raising premiums on insureds. Doctors get courted by pharmaceutical companies to push their medicines to their patients. Medical device companies lure hospitals into buying expensive new equipment and models under the premise that the device will pay for itself...and even generate profits the more they use them. Some people even argue that it seems doctors may have an incentive to keep you unhealthy. It's one big racket. However, certainly many Americans' lifestyles contribute to the massive amounts spent on healthcare. Diabetes, heart problems, joint problems, and many of the other problems that come with many Americans' unhealthy lifestyles drive up healthcare spending even more. Interesting that the national conversation on healthcare costs doesn't include a lot of discussion about living healthier. Just like the national conversation around energy costs doesn't include a lot of discussion on using less energy. We want to use lots of resources but don't think we should have to pay much for it. I'm a huge believer in insurance, but insurance actually exacerbates this problem. Because insured Americans get the feeling (or the message from the doctor) that they're not the ones actually paying for the services, but the insurance company (or Medicare) is, then people approve additional (and sometimes unnecessary) services...and of course those costs get passed back on to insureds through higher premiums.

America really only has two options (or some blended strategy). They can switch to a single-payer system (like in Korea and many other countries) where the government will control costs by establishing rates through a single, government-run health insurance plan. Doctors could still own their own practices, but the government would decide which services are covered and which ones are not (and how much the doctors can charge patients and how much they'd receive from the government insurance company)...as opposed to the insurance companies who usually make those decisions now. I have no problem with the federal government providing a minimum level of national health insurance. However, I think additional private insurance should be available to be sold, as well, to supplement the national government plan. The national plan will help limit the amount of money that doctors make without increasing their volumes. It will also ultimately slow down the rate of innovation in healthcare (because it will limit the profit potential), but the cost of care should go down and access (or at least affordability and demand) should therefore go up.

The other option, and the best option in my opinion, is to deregulate healthcare and allow Physician's Assistants and even Nurse Practitioners to open their own clinics and offer cheap, affordable basic services. If they were uncertain, or if the case was too serious, they could easily then send the patient to a doctor. But, if the most basic services could be offered affordably by PA's and NP's (who could increase the supply of available medical care and compete against MD's in offering basic services), that would help improve both the access to healthcare as well as the cost. There also needs to be more transparency in pricing so that shopping for medical services is more like buying groceries than finding an auto mechanic. Also, if the government allowed us to buy cheaper drugs from overseas it would drive down the prices of drugs sold here. The government has constantly interfered with supply and this is the biggest issue facing healthcare costs...especially with an aging population like ours. And sometimes it seems that it's been done deliberately so that doctors and those in the healthcare industry can profit. And that is my problem with Obama's healthcare plan. It isn't that he wanted to provide more Americans with health insurance coverage. I think that was very noble. Or even that he required them to buy it or face a penalty (that was necessary to cover pre-existing conditions). But by increasing the demand, but doing nothing to also increase the supply of care, prices are almost certain to rise. That's why it would be better to allow for more providers to offer care and require more transparency in pricing (and results), like I have suggested. This should lower costs and make Medicare and a national basic healthcare plan (to cover only the most basic services) much more affordable. Then you could still allow for private insurance that would cover more things and provide better coverage than the basic national plan.

Tort Reform

I remember very distinctly walking up the concrete steps to the subway in South Korea. There was an old woman mopping the steps. This is fairly common part-time work meant to help the elderly earn some money. I looked around. There wasn't a "Caution: Wet Floor" sign anywhere. "That's a lawsuit waiting to happen," I thought. How often do we catch ourselves thinking like that now? I frequently see situations where there is some element of danger, but really should be common sense, but think, "Somebody is going to get sued. And they'll probably win." It's a problem and everybody knows it.

We've all heard the stories. Let me give just a couple of short examples. In 2005, two teenage girls baked cookies for their neighbors and went around delivering the cookies to them. One night, at 10:30 PM, one of the neighbors claims to have experienced extreme anxiety over the girls' late night cookie delivery, and won $900 for medical damages as a result of the stress[2]. Another woman settled with Universal Studios out of court after she sued them because their haunted house was so scary that it caused her emotional distress[3]. We see class action suits where the judgments can be in the billions. There are a lot of problems that can arise in the existing system.

What are the problems caused by these kinds of really frivolous lawsuits? Firstly, there is a cost to business. If somebody sues a business, often even if the business is found not guilty, they still usually suffer from financial and other costs to their business. Perhaps their reputation is unfairly tarnished. Perhaps a small business owner needs to spend his time fighting the lawsuit instead of running his business, which ends up costing him revenue. Maybe a doctor makes a decision or orders a test, not because he thinks it's the best decision but because it will protect him from a lawsuit. You want doctors to be extra careful and to be accountable for acts of negligence. However, doctors also must be shielded from doing unnecessary, expensive, and sometimes possibly dangerous actions just because they want to make sure they cover their ass.

Firstly, we're dealing with the issue of how easy we should make it to sue somebody and have your day in court. Secondly, we're dealing with an issue of how to fairly punish businesses and how to fairly compensate victims. Do all people who suffer from a company's negligence deserve to get rich? Is that the best and fairest way to compensate them and punish the company?

What are some possible solutions? Firstly, we could cap monetary rewards to defendants (and their attorneys) for pain and suffering. Victims of corporations should be taken care of, not made rich. Many people given big lump-sum settlements just blow it anyway. We need to reduce the incentive for people to file these frivolous lawsuits. Secondly, we need to fix a judicial system that sometimes rewards these types of lawsuits. And more judges need to do what some have begun to do and begin forcing people who file frivolous lawsuits to pay the legal costs of the defendants. We can also keep punitive damages to corporations, but use some of the money to invest in education and in low-income areas...instead of just making plaintiffs wealthy. If the cost of putting consumers in harm's way becomes too low, then corporations will simply make calculated decisions, sometimes, to endanger consumers and just pay the lawsuits. Businesses can be ruthless and need to be held in check. However, businesses should also not be overburdened by costly, frivolous lawsuits that also clog up our judicial system. The U.S. has more lawyers, per capita, than any other country in the world. Tens of billions of dollars are awarded in millions of civil suits every year. Litigation is a major business, itself. Capitalism in the courts. We must remove the incentives for profit.

Gay Marriage

Honestly, in 2013, I can't believe this is even still an issue. It's really amazing to me. And I used to be a completely committed evangelical Christian. And yet it *still* amazes me that there are still people against gay marriage. But, then again, it's just bigotry and religious extremism, which is a common phenomenon in many places. I get it. The Bible says homosexuality is wrong. Totally get it. But it says being proud is sinful, too. And even looking at a woman lustfully. Should we really choose laws based on the Bible? It just doesn't make any sense. Regardless of whether or not you believe homosexuality is a sin, Americans should realize that this is not a theocracy and we should not make our laws based on any religion.

I will never totally understand gays. Because I am straight. I can not possibly imagine being attracted to another man's penis. It completely disgusts me. I could understand being attracted to another man's personality. And feeling like you love another man. But, sex? With another man? That's disgusting. Because I'm not gay. This whole idea that most gay people choose to be gay is ridiculous. I think the fact is that many gay men and women, if not most, were born that way. They were born being sexually attracted to people of the same sex. I am a little interested, though, in the relationship between sexual abuse and homosexuality. Many studies seem to show that a very high percentage of homosexuals suffered from sexual abuse, especially at young ages. I have no idea what role this plays, if any.

But I know that no matter what, if a man loves another man, it's not my place to tell him he can't. This is America! Freedom of religion. Land of freedom and equality. How can we tell somebody that you can't get married because my religion says you can't? When did Christianity become more about worrying about the speck in your brother's eye when you have a plank in your own? Speaking of which, why in the world is homosexuality the WORST sin to so many Christians? So weird, isn't it? The Bible doesn't speak against homosexuality nearly as much as it does lying or being proud. Why is homosexuality so horrible? Christians will tell you it's because it's the one sin people condone and promote. That's not true. People promote pre-marital sex. And drinking. And eating too much. And being greedy. And so many other "sinful behaviors." Why is homosexuality SOO bad? Some Christians will argue that sexual sin is, in some ways, worse sin. I think they just hate it because it's the one sin many of them know they've never done. And yet, ironically, many of the loudest gay bashers end up being closet homosexuals.

I think we've got to get religion out of this whole debate. Homosexuals are Americans. As a country, we should not deny homosexual couples equal rights under the law. By doing so, we effectively establish a religion and violate the first amendment. I also support gay adoption. But, I believe there should be a very careful screening process done before allowing gay men to adopt. But not as much because of their sexuality. I would support similar very strict screening measures for single heterosexual men, as well. I am just very disinclined to trust men, unchecked by a woman, with children. Men, both homosexual and heterosexual, have powerful sexual urges. Too many men, both homosexual, and heterosexual, seem to have extremely poor moral fabric and are willing to harm children in order to satisfy their urges. Often sick, unnatural urges. And it destroys children's lives. That is why I support gay adoption, but believe gay men should undergo very strict screening...out of an abundance of caution for our children. But let me end with this: I think that two good gay people can raise a child every bit, or almost every bit, as well as two good heterosexual people. There are many kids out there who are in desperate need of a family and parents who will love them. I can't believe we'd rather leave these kids without a stable family. Crazy.

Affirmative Action

The first African slaves arrived in America around the early 1600's. It was in the early 1860's, about 250 years later, that Abraham Lincoln issued the Emancipation Proclamation. Even after blacks were freed in the South, however, they were still blatantly discriminated against. It was in 1964 and 1965, over 100 years later, that LBJ signed the Civil Rights Act and the Voting Rights Act, finally beginning to really tackle some of the major racial problems. Poll taxes, grandfather clauses, and old-fashioned intimidation were used to keep blacks in the South from voting. Blacks were refused the right to go to the same schools or eat in the same restaurants as whites. It took a long time before our government admitted that separate was not really equal. Blacks may have been free, but their opportunities were severely limited by whites in the South, who truly hated black people. After almost 350 years of either slavery or blatant discrimination in some areas of America, how can people think that things are completely healed less than 50 years later? How can 350 years of oppression magically fix itself in just 50 years?

Blacks today have a million times more opportunities than they did in the South 50 years ago. And people should recognize that. If most African Americans apply themselves, work incredibly hard, make good choices, and stay out of trouble, they can succeed and have a good life. And in this way, America does not have the racial problems it did in the past. However, many blacks were left out of the system for so long. Whites blatantly oppressed blacks for 350 years in some parts of the country and yet they don't seem to feel the responsibility to help pull up a group of people that they kicked down for so long.

While whites were learning about how to practice law, growing their wealth, and teaching their children the importance of education, blacks in the South weren't able to see much gain from education, their opportunities limited by white racism in the South. How can we expect that many blacks will become doctors and lawyers overnight? Plus, there was the study by the National Bureau of Economics Research involving résumés. The study submitted numerous résumés for various jobs in both Chicago and Boston, some résumés with traditionally black sounding names and some with traditionally white sounding names. The study attempted to measure any difference in the likelihood of receiving a call back for an interview. The study found that candidates with similar qualifications and white sounding names were far likelier to receive a call back for an interview. This is simply unfair and a major reason why some type of affirmative action program is still needed.

We must continue to give minorities opportunities to break the cycle of poverty. It's in society's best interest and it's the right thing to do. If we continue to find better ways to help minorities get out of poverty, teach them the importance of education and hard work, and give them opportunities to have good careers, we will continue to see this country improve for everybody. We're not necessarily talking about hiring unqualified, or even lesser qualified people. We're talking about giving one person with similar qualifications the chance over another and could be achieved through incentives offered to businesses who hire minorities (and not through quotas). Having such huge economic inequalities between whites and blacks is bad for the country. It increases the tensions. And such huge disparities point to one of three things: either blacks are genetically inferior to whites, they're being discriminated against, or their culture prevents them from succeeding. Many whites want to say it's *only* black culture holding African Americans back and that affirmative action needs to stop. Many blacks want to say it's *only* discrimination and there are no culture problems. Why can't it be both?

Food Stamps and Taxpayer Funded Abortions

We should help people when they are in trouble and show mercy and love to our fellow man. And I wish that history showed that private citizens, in this country, do a sufficient job of helping those in need. But it doesn't. They didn't do a sufficient job before we had these social programs, like Food Stamps, (which was started by Democrat LBJ)...and they don't do a sufficient job even with them. I do believe that we must be careful with these programs. We must try and use technology to ensure that as little money is wasted as possible. There should be rules prohibiting name brands over store brand items and rules prohibiting certain types of foods (alcohol or other items). And rules for who qualifies. However, we must not turn our back on our fellow man. Private charities just aren't sufficient.

I'm also in favor of welfare and taxpayer funded abortions. But on one condition: if you have kids and you want to go on welfare (or if you want a taxpayer funded abortion), then you must also submit to a taxpayer funded sterilization. These people need help immediately. However, many of them will find themselves in the same situation again. Many have more and more kids and qualify for more and more government assistance. We should make sure that we limit the future costs to taxpayers by demanding the sterilization. Everybody wins. The poor get the assistance they need and the taxpayers' future liabilities have been limited. And from a practicality standpoint, we would be better off as a society with fewer people being born into such conditions.

Christians will certainly protest to the idea of taxpayer funded abortions and argue that many children born into dire circumstances have gone on to do great things. Indeed. But how many more become crackheads and murderers? If a child is likely to be born into a rotten, poisonous environment and world, to poor parents who can't afford the kid, then why subject the child to that? We get it. You think the baby should just deal with it...and would prefer that kind of horrible childhood over a death that they can't ever remember. Do Christians think aborted babies are going to Hell? If not, then what the hell is the problem? Sign me up for the free pass straight to Heaven. I get to bypass this dump? Are you kidding me?

We can't let ourselves be blinded by crazy religion that really doesn't even make sense. I think faith is awesome. But blind faith in something that, if you really think about it, doesn't make any sense...that's just dumb. We must see that society and the world are better off if more children are not born trapped into poverty or with parents who don't really want them. I know some religious people will simply never budge from the position that life begins at conception and therefore you're murdering babies. However, it seems worth noting that most Rabbinic Old Testament scholars argue that the Bible distinguishes between an unborn fetus and a baby.

We cannot allow America to become a theocracy where moral decisions, like when life begins, are decided by the government. This isn't just a women's rights issue. This is an issue of being realistic about what is really in the best interest of children born into families who don't really want them and can't afford them. Counselors should encourage adoption and other options <u>first</u>. But, I think that society should be willing to provide women with this service, if we can also ensure we won't have to do it over and over again (because the woman has been sterilized). Women might say it's unfair, but then just pay for your own abortion (or reversal procedure). And to make it more fair and effective, we can (and perhaps should) force the father to get sterilized, too.

War on Drugs

There is something critical that people need to understand about the War on Drugs, more specifically the war on marijuana. It is becoming increasingly evident that the war on marijuana is largely a ploy to get money from our pockets (through tax dollars) to go to big businesses, many of whom are actually big time lobbyists to the very legislators who maintain the federal drug laws. First listen to how it works: The U.S. government convinces people that marijuana (and some other drugs) are bad enough to be illegal. At that point, they say it is SOOO important, that we should spend billions of (taxpayer) dollars to enforce the law. Where does that money go? Law enforcement, for one. But also to privatized prisons. "What is he talking about?" you might wonder. What do we do with many of these "criminals"? There are tens of thousands of prisoners in our prison systems nationwide who have specifically been incarcerated due to marijuana[4]. It costs more than a billion dollars per year to keep that number of prisoners incarcerated. A billion dollars. Of taxpayer money. And here's the "best" part: with overcrowded prisons throughout the country, who are governments turning to? <u>Private</u> prisons! What is more American than capitalizing the prison system? And who do you think these companies building and running these prisons are owned by? You think they might just be friends of the politicians? One thing is for sure, they spend a fair amount of money on "lobbying." Giving a little back to the government from whence it came.

Now some of you might be left with this overwhelming sense of "but drugs are still bad for you." But ask yourself this: is alcohol good for you? Are cigarettes good for you? No. And yet they are LEGAL. "Cigarettes aren't a mind altering substance." Yes, but alcohol is. And cigarettes are largely addictive and marijuana isn't. It's equally ridiculous when people claim that "we don't need people sitting around and getting high all day." Why is alcohol not (enough of) a threat of people getting drunk all day but marijuana is sure to cause people to get high all day? It's preposterous. Almost every argument against it is preposterous. It's fear mongering to support spending ridiculous amounts of money prosecuting and imprisoning people for using substances the government doesn't think you should. It's wrong. If some of these substances are bad (and some of them are), why don't we create a strategy built around taking that same money and using it to help people break their addictions rather than to prosecute people? And don't they realize that by keeping the drugs illegal and more dangerous to access, they inflate the prices of drugs which plays into the hands of violent gangs who then sell them to get rich? If you legalized drugs, prices would drop, you could sell it and tax it, and then deprive the violent gangs of all that revenue.

But instead, it's all about getting your money and giving it back and forth between the government and their buddies. It's right there in front of us. Do some research on CCA, the GEO Group, and the **American Legislative Exchange Council** (ALEC). Think of what would happen if we took all of the money we spent on the enforcement of draconian and ineffective drug policies and used that money to fight REAL crime and better help addicts with their recoveries? But God knows that would put a lot of college dropouts out of a job. And that's just another part of the problem. The Drug War employs too many people: DEA, Border & Customs, police, even judges, prosecutors, defense attorneys, probation officers, etc...many of whom have no other marketable skills than being a bully with a badge and gun.

That is why drugs are illegal. It makes money for so many people. The government wants to tell you what you can put in your body. Then they will arrest you, lock you up, and people will make money off of it. The drug war is a huge scam. We should be treating people with problems not prosecuting them.

Death Penalty

Every time I think about the death penalty, I think about "A Time to Kill." In the dramatic movie, based on a book by icon John Grisham, a black man by the name of Carl Lee Hailey kills two white men who raped his young daughter. A police officer, a childhood friend of Hailey's, loses a leg in the shooting. Carl Lee goes on trial, likely for his life (as the Prosecutor announces his intent to seek the death penalty). In one particular scene, his white, southern bred attorney tells a young, liberal law student who had been helping him, "The only problem with the death penalty is we do not use it enough."

There are some sick people out there. Some sick. Some evil. Some both. And those hideous people do hideous things. I think some people have been raised in such a bad way, that they are basically animals. They are ruthless. How else can you explain people who kill hundreds of people in bombings? Or people who murder people so violently and ruthlessly? How could you do that to an innocent human being unless you were sick or evil? What do we think society gains by keeping these people alive? The backdoor possibility that they might be rehabilitated one day? Many of them will never become rehabilitated and will rot in prison, costing us millions of dollars over their lifetimes. Some *might* become rehabilitated, they might get out...and then what? Everybody lives happily ever after?

What do death penalty opponents think they are saving? The lives of evil monsters? I think it's fine to say that the death penalty should be used carefully, only when there is absolutely no doubt as to the defendant's guilt. Obviously one of the most important things is that we do not allow innocent people to be executed for crimes that they didn't actually commit. However, there's a big difference between, "Let's not use the death penalty unless there is total certainty as to guilt" and "Let's completely get rid of the death penalty because it's evil." What is the alternative? Free monsters? Pay millions of dollars to keep them locked up? Why?

Some people have argued that the death penalty has a preventative effect. Before a person kills another person, according to the theory, knowing they might face the death penalty deters some people from going ahead and committing murder. Some have argued that statistics disprove that. I'm with those that say, "I'm not in favor of the death penalty because it helps deter some people from murdering people. I'm in favor of the death penalty because it prevents, with 100% effectiveness, murderers from killing again in the future." It may not prevent *other* people from murdering, but it prevents **that guy** from murdering again. That's good enough for me. I don't need any more than that.

Human life is sacred, some would argue. It is. And people have a responsibility to act accordingly. And when they don't, they run the risk of losing their right to live. As a society, sometimes we must do what's in the best interest of the whole. I don't see what positive is gained that offsets the costs that come along with not executing criminals who have committed heinous crimes and have shown no remorse.

And it's shocking to me that people out there try to claim that it violates the Eighth Amendment to the Constitution prohibiting cruel and unusual punishment. Really? The Founding Fathers, who hung people and had firing squads, thought the death penalty was cruel and unusual? Do you know anything about American history whatsoever? On what practical or legal basis can you possibly argue against the death penalty?

Guns

People in America **love** guns. And they love to create all kinds of BS arguments in favor of guns. One thing they love to do is point to one country, such as Switzerland, that is pro-gun and enjoys low crime. Therefore, they conclude... having guns must be good. Then, to add a little punch to the argument, they'll think of one country that has implemented a gun ban, and didn't immediately see a decrease in crime, and conclude, "See: gun control is bad." It's just so obvious to them. Statisticians call these situations having "an *n* of one." It means you've got one example. It's not very smart to draw conclusions from one example. If I can think of a country, such as South Korea, that effectively has a gun ban...and enjoys a low crime rate, does that mean that gun bans are good? Or if I can think of a country that has very lax gun laws and suffers from high crime (hmmm...don't have to think hard about that one do you?), then are lax gun laws bad? Or do we need to look at the totality of countries?

And do we need to look even deeper than that? Do we need to distinguish between countries that have basically always had or (long have had) a gun ban from countries who have somewhat recently implemented one? Does that matter? Could a gun ban work if a country has had it for more than a hundred years, for example (more so than in a country that has just recently implemented one)? I have long argued that implementing a gun ban is analogous to widening a road to increase traffic capacity. At first, during the construction process, traffic actually gets much *worse* as they close lanes, or at least lower the speed limit, due to the construction. However, after a while, once the construction is complete, traffic is much better than before. My argument, to the conservative claim that outlawing guns only leaves guns in the hands of criminals, is that yes...at first, things would get worse. However, as police throughout the country are able to really start getting the old, existing guns off the streets, crime would subside and be much lower than before. If so, then the question is, "How long does the ban need to be in effect before we get to the other side of the parabola, where crime begins decreasing and drops below previous levels?"

Another conservative argument against gun bans is that even if you got the old, existing guns off the street (or most of them), people would still easily gain access to guns. They point to the cities of D.C. and Chicago as proof. Which leads me to my next point: you'd also want to compare countries whose neighbors also had gun bans to those whose neighbors didn't. Take Mexico, for example. About a third (or maybe even twice that) of the guns police confiscate in Mexico likely come from the U.S...a neighbor that allows for easy gun purchases[5]. That doesn't even include the guns that came in from other neighbors that also might have lax gun laws. Of course that's going to affect your ability to successfully implement a gun ban. How are you going to say a national gun ban definitely wouldn't work in the U.S. just because a citywide ban didn't? How effective can a ban in Chicago really be if it's easy for anybody right outside of Chicago city limits to get a gun? Give me a break.

At the end of the day, Republicans are going to make two final arguments in favor of guns. The first is the defense of their personal property and their life. They worry about an intruder breaking into their home with a gun and the police not being able to show up in time. They would prefer to be like the Wild, Wild West and just trust their quick draw. Right. That's the kind of society I want to live in. Plus, the percentage of people that are killed each year by intruders is actually very small. That is a very small threat. It dwarfs in comparison to the number of people who are killed with a gun by somebody they know[6]. I don't want the people I know owning a gun (or the people I don't know). Just one of thousands of great examples of this was the recent murder of one of the greatest snipers in Navy SEAL history, Chris Kyle. Here you have one of the greatest marksmen in the history of the world, at a gun range nonetheless, and his precious gun couldn't save him. Why? Because he had no idea the person he knew was going to shoot him. A gun can't protect you from many of the people who might actually want to do you harm. A gun is far more often a threat to people than it is a source of protection.

The second argument they make is about the ability to defend against tyranny. That is much easier to answer. Do you really think that the people in this country would have any chance against the U.S. military, if they really wanted to fight us? Do you think we could take on their supreme combat training, weaponry, tanks, planes, and nukes? Really? Your shotguns or even semi-automatic weapons are going to take on the entire U.S. military in order to defend against tyranny? If so, then my opinion of the U.S. military just hit rock bottom.

The real reasons why many conservatives are so pro-gun, besides machismo, is they just think they are cool and don't want to give them up...even if they think it might make the country safer. Plus, going back to the machismo thing, they don't trust the police to handle crime. They want to deal with it themselves. It makes them feel more manly. Having several friends who are very enthusiastic gun advocates, I do understand that there are some people who have simply grown up around the weapons, respect them for whatever reasons, and feel that they are responsible gun owners. And many of them are. However, it'd be very hard to convince me that all of the murders and shootings that take place in America on a daily basis are a worthwhile price to pay for whatever benefit gun enthusiasts feel the deadly weapons offer. If you protect the "right" of the 35 year old suburban or rural white male to own a gun, then you do so knowing that some of the guns will always end up in the hands of 14 year old kids in poor urban schools like the one I went to in Macon, Georgia. Is this a net positive for society?

At a bare minimum, I don't understand why Americans allow the NRA to lobby against even the most common sense gun control measures. Why do individuals needs semi-automatic weapons and high capacity magazines that allow for people to fire over 50 rounds per minute? How can that possibly be a good thing to allow people to easily purchase and own such weapons? Why does the government allow "private sellers" to go to gun shows and sell these kinds of weapons to anybody, without any background check whatsoever? Internet companies also. Any gang member, terrorist, crazy person, or straw purchaser can easily purchase a gun this way. Straw purchasers are people who will go and legally buy a gun and then sell it under the table to somebody else. Many straw purchasers go to gun shows along the Mexico border and then turn around and sell those guns to gangs and drugs dealers from Mexico. For those that think law abiding citizens should be allowed to own guns I ask one question: where do you think most criminals get their guns from? I'll tell you: they get them by buying them and stealing them from people who bought them legally[7]. We must try and disarm this country which is becoming more and more of a war zone.

Personal and Corporate Income Taxes

When I was younger, and ignorant, I used to believe that we needed higher corporate taxes and lower personal income taxes. I believed that corporations make lots of money and that individuals make far less money. Therefore, it made sense to tax corporations more and people less. And that's how a lot of people think. However, unfortunately, that line of thinking is based on a very poor understanding of economics and business. In reality, the opposite should likely be true. We should have low corporate taxes and a higher, more progressive personal income tax structure.

In today's global economy, countries are literally competing against one another for jobs. There are some very strong benefits that can come with huge multinational corporations and globalization. However, one of the possible drawbacks is that multinational corporations and globalization make it easy for a company to export jobs to countries with lower costs and/or taxes. And as long as we want this to be a truly free country, we can not force corporations to keep jobs here and prohibit them from sending jobs overseas. So, if a country has a very low corporate tax rate, companies are going to take advantage of that and reward that country by sending jobs to that country (where taxes are cheaper), as opposed to a country with higher taxes.

Plus, you can't really beat these people. If you raise corporate taxes, not only will they likely send more jobs to lower tax countries, they will find loopholes and lobby politicians to get around the taxes (or if all else fails, then they'll just raise prices). Here in the U.S., many companies use techniques to shift profits to lower taxed countries and avoid paying U.S. income taxes entirely. They do that because the taxes in the other country are lower...and so *that* country gets the revenue. And we get stiffed. Corporations will almost always find a way around. But, if you play the game, you can lower taxes in comparison with other countries and attract investment and jobs here.

If you lower corporations' tax rates, they will bring more jobs. However, as a country, we still need revenue. So, in order to raise that revenue, you tax personal incomes (and other methods of passing profits like capital gains)...and tax them at highly progressive rates. Are most rich people REALLY going to leave America? Please. We know that globalization is going to continue to strongly reward those in America with very rare and marketable skills and further punish those that do not have such skills. You can say, "Too bad. So sad." But society is not going to like the result. Instead, we must take more of the rewards that the rich enjoy (as a result of capitalism, globalization, and their skills) and use it to help teach poorer, lower-skilled workers how to fish in the global marketplace.

We've seen why corporate tax rates should be low. But why not also make personal income tax rates low? Having low corporate and personal income tax rates is likely to produce low amounts of revenue. Conservatives talk about the Laffer Curve, where, as tax rates become oppressively high, tax receipts begin to decline as incentives to generate income decline and taxpayers use more tax avoidance techniques. But our new highest marginal rates (for the richest Americans) are still some of the lowest in decades. Raising the top marginal rate further would, by most independent accounts, almost certainly generate more revenue than the current highest bracket for the richest Americans...and we really need revenue right now to invest in education, healthcare, and human capital...as well as to reduce our deficit and pay off our debt.

However, another problem with our current tax code is that nearly half of Americans currently pay no federal income tax at all[21]. This is also a problem. It makes it easy for large groups of Americans to support increasing benefits and federal spending...because they know they aren't really the ones that are going to be paying for it. Perhaps everybody needs at least a little skin in the game. Another way to try and fix this problem would be to tie any future increases in benefits or spending to an increase in taxes...on EVERYBODY. Perhaps then voters would be more hesitant to demand more spending.

Some in America try to argue for a flat tax, where the rich and poor would pay the exact same percentage. They say this system is "fairer" than the current progressive tax system we have now, where higher levels of income are taxed at higher rates. By virtually any account, a flat tax system would raise taxes greatly on the poor and lower taxes on the rich. To suggest that we should switch to a true flat tax system is practically insane. Imagine two people: one person making $20,000 a year and another making $200,000 a year. Which one can afford to pay more? The argument is that under a flat tax, the person making $200,000 still pays more. Sure. But have you ever tried living on $20,000 a year? If you take 10, 15, or even 20 percent...there isn't much left to pay for housing, food, insurance, childcare expenses, and everything else. However, if you take a total of even 30% from the person making $200,000 a year, he still has $140,000 left...seven times more than the person making $20,000 a year and paying no taxes. Taxing the poor (significantly) more will not only make it even harder for the poorest Americans to survive (especially as inflation continues to rise thanks to loose monetary policy that greatly benefits the rich), it will further reduce demand and hurt the economy. No, a flat tax is a terrible idea for America.

What we need in this country are a combination of lower corporate tax rates (to make us more competitive with other countries' lower corporate rates), higher marginal rates for the richest Americans (to make sure that we collect enough revenue to pay our bills), higher capital gains taxes for individuals who derive lots of income from stock and dividends, a minimum income tax for ALL Americans (to make sure everybody at least has *some* skin in the game), and possibly an exemption to the higher marginal rates for those in top brackets that run small businesses and actually do employ people and create jobs. However, not everybody that is rich is a "job creator" that needs lower marginal rates to encourage them to hire more people...like many Republicans try to pretend.

These steps would greatly improve our tax code, but don't look for the two parties to compromise anytime soon.

Social Security and Medicare

There are very few issues that get people (especially middle aged and older) riled up like Social Security and Medicare. They're very complicated issues...and very important ones. America is getting older quickly. In 2011, Baby Boomers began to turn 65. Tens of millions of Americans will begin looking to retire and the country needs to have a financial plan for itself and its people. Considering that three out of four Americans elect to start drawing Social Security at 62[8], many out of necessity, instead of waiting until 65 and getting a bigger benefit, what we do with Social Security and Medicare will help determine what will happen to a huge number of people in this country. I believe strongly in the importance of these programs. However, I also believe we are trying to have Social Security finance a lifestyle that it never was meant to...and one that we can't afford.

Together, over their histories, these programs have been both important and effective. According to the Bureau of Economic Research, "Elderly poverty in the U.S. decreased dramatically during the 20th century. Between 1960 and 1995, the official poverty rate of those aged 65 and above fell from 35 percent to 10 percent, and research has documented declines in poverty among the elderly dating back to at least 1939. While poverty was once far more prevalent among the elderly than among other age groups, today's elderly have a poverty rate similar to that of working-age adults and much lower than that of children." Before Social Security (and Medicare) began, far too many of America's elderly lived in poverty. These programs are absolutely critical, especially with the breakdown of the family in America. People love to talk about personal responsibility. It sounds as theoretically perfect and utopian as Communism. Everybody pulling themselves up by the bootstraps and working hard. "I did it. So can everybody else." Sounds perfect. But it's not. It ignores how unequal opportunities can be. It ignores the human condition and its tendency to make mistakes. It really ignores the social realities that come with letting masses of people fail. We can have a society where we let people be poor and then try to arrest them when they inevitably resort to criminal activity. Or we can try extra hard to help these people and teach them how to make good choices and have a safety net for them if they fail. And they will fail...

However, we must also remember that Social Security was never intended to be a long-term retirement plan. And at the time the mortality tables were created, the average life expectancy was much lower than today. There was a fair percentage of people who lived to an old age, but there was also a large percentage of people who died young and received little in benefits, or even none at all[9]. However, that's often no longer the case. More people are living longer and trying to retire on Social Security for decades. With our large Baby Boomer population, Social Security costs (and Medicare) are eventually expected to go up by more than $500 billion a year...each[10]. Our country, right now, already spends more than a trillion dollars more per year than we're making in revenues. And you're looking at *another* trillion dollars more per year with Social Security and Medicare costs rising? Look. We need to take care of our elderly. Period. But we need to take care of our country, too. We must means test (for income and assets), trim benefits, and raise the normal retirement age...but still remain committed to helping our elderly.

The problem with privatizing Social Security is twofold. Firstly, most people are not qualified to invest their own money. This is people's safety net and you don't want to risk them losing it to bad investment decisions. Not to mention, what if the market were to go through another 25 year period like the one starting in 1929? Where would that leave our seniors? They deserve something more reliable and dependable than that.

Medicare is a far more complicated situation. However, the standard conservative solution of converting Medicare into a voucher program simply isn't good enough. Ultimately what will happen is that the most basic plans offered by insurance companies will provide a very basic level of service, while more comprehensive plans will obviously cost much more than the amount of the voucher and will be outside the reach of poor (and many middle class) seniors. The reality is that rich people enjoy better services than poor people. They can afford better hotels and better restaurants and can afford better medicine. But how much better access to medicine should they really have? And it's not like a lot of people right now are complaining about the quality of coverage under Medicare. That's not the problem. The problem is the total cost to the country. And I believe that the suggestions mentioned in the earlier chapter on healthcare (price transparency, more supply options, etc.) are simply better ways to try and control the costs of healthcare than converting Medicare to a voucher program. We also need to look more carefully at end of life care, which consumes a very disproportionate share of total healthcare expenditures. We can talk about it in scary terms like "death panels" but somebody somewhere (either at the government run Medicare office or the "evil, capitalist" insurance company's office) at some point decides whether or not your medicine/surgery/operation is worth paying and going to be covered. I'd love to extend every senior on Medicare's life for an extra two weeks or even two years, but not if it's going to cost a billion dollars.

America's Addiction to Debt and Spending

One of the biggest problems in this country is that as individuals, and as a government, we have become addicted to spending money that we don't have and accumulating huge amounts of debt. In fact, our entire economy now depends on this debt, which has truly become an addiction. Before the end of 2012, the U.S. federal government became over $16 trillion in debt. Each year, they are spending more than $1 trillion more than they are earning in revenues. It's not just the government of the United States that seems to have no idea how to stay within its budget, however. Americans, cumulatively, possess more than $850 billion in credit card debt. Outstanding mortgage debt is nearly $8 trillion[11]. And there is nearly $1 trillion in outstanding student loans.

Debt is normal. Debt allows you to borrow today so that you can buy things now and pay for them later. And sometimes this is smart. However, you have to make sure that you're going to be able to pay the debts back later. One of the big problems with debt is that as your total debt gets larger and larger, so do your monthly interest payments. Your normal monthly or annual expenses are still there, but now you have to pay interest on your debt (if not some of the principal, as well...) on top of those normal expenses. And eventually, your debt can grow so large that you're unable to pay both your normal expenses plus the interest you owe on your debt. According to Treasury Department statistics, in fiscal year 2011, the United States paid over $450 billion in interest (although some of that was paid to the Federal Reserve who returned some of it to the government). We only raise about $2.2 trillion per year in revenues. The interest on the national debt is now about 20% of our total revenue. With mandatory Social Security costs currently over $700 billion (and rising), defense spending over $600 billion, Medicare and Medicaid costs rising to $800 billion, and the aforementioned interest costs (in addition to the other $1 trillion the U.S. spends each year), the U.S. has long passed the point when it lived within its means.

And the same thing has happened to many Americans. Some bought more houses than they could afford...sometimes speculating they could sell them later, for a big profit, due to the rapidly rising real estate prices (which were mainly rapidly rising due to borrowing being cheap and pure speculation). Some bought a bigger house (singular) than they could afford. Some saw their house rise in value, refinanced, and took a little equity out of their home to enjoy their lives a little more...and took on too much debt in the process. Some bought a house when they couldn't afford it, thanks to lax underwriting standards (pushed mainly by liberals who wanted to make-up to lower and middle class Americans for their stagnant wages while the rich got richer). But now Americans don't know what to do. Their salaries still aren't rising. Inflation is rising thanks to lax monetary policy and cheap credit. And increasingly, Americans are feeling forced to borrow to fund their lifestyles...before eventually filing for bankruptcy.

The government also finds itself addicted to debt. The American government finds itself trapped, with interest rates near zero, but an economy that is still barely moving. Many have said that the Fed has "run out of bullets." In other words, even with the gas on the accelerator, with borrowing costs for government and businesses at rock bottom levels, and even with the government throwing tons of money (it doesn't have) into the economy, it's still barely growing. At the same time, the government faces a debt crisis. The problem is, if the government stops spending money (it doesn't have)...OR if American households stop spending money (that they don't have), then the whole economy will likely just slow further. We seemed to be trapped by our addiction to debt.

In theory, many of these programs seemed like great ideas. Some of them had very good intentions (at least partially). The idea of spurring the economy by encouraging home ownership for all Americans is a very noble goal. So is the goal of trying to ensure that a college education is possible for everybody. I am not against attempts at trying to help more people own homes (including minorities) or to help more people have the ability to go to college. However, we must also think about the long-term feasibility of these programs, as well as potential unintended consequences. Firstly, it'd be great if everybody could buy a home. But it is probably more important that everybody be able to *afford* to own a home. Making it easy for somebody to get a loan that they won't be able to afford isn't a winning long-term economic policy. With college loans, getting a college education is invaluable...if it helps you get the skills you'll need to get a job and earn an income. However, increasingly, students are taking on student loan debt and, either by choice or by accident, failing to obtain skills that will help them get a good job. They took on the liability of the loan, but the asset of the degree was not what they thought it would be. We all know people in this situation. A college degree is only worthwhile if it helps you earn a job and an income. And for a variety of reasons, an increasing number of Americans are taking on student loan debt, going to college, and coming out with no job. Meanwhile, the student loan bubble is growing ever larger.

America must break free from its addiction to debt. Like a physical addition, it will hurt tremendously at first. As spending slows, so will demand and so will the economy. Just think about it. What will happen if we cut Social Security payments to seniors? They'll have less disposable income and they'll spend less money, which will hurt the economy. What if we cut Medicare spending? A few things will happen. Some seniors will simply not be able to afford the care they need (or simply want). This will also affect doctors and the healthcare industry. Other seniors will still get the care they need and want, but will have to pay for more of it out of their own pockets. This will result in them cutting back in other areas like eating out and buying consumer goods...which would also hurt the economy. What will happen to the economy if we make cuts to the military? Companies that make bombs and military planes will lay people off and we've already begun to see this with the sequester. And what will happen if we raise taxes? People will also have less money to spend and economic growth should slow. Reducing the deficit (austerity) hurts the economy. But *not* reducing the deficit puts the next generation in even bigger danger.

We must remember that much of this economy is not real. It's built on money that the American government and its people actually don't have. America has overpromised and overspent and now has a $16 trillion tab to show for it. Americans all over the country, likewise, fuel their unsustainable lifestyles by borrowing from their future. Well, that bill is coming due for America and Americans. Our government's strategy is obviously to continue to borrow more and more money and hope that inflation will eat away at our debt (as we pay back our debt with dollars that simply aren't worth as much). Besides contributing to yet a further rise in prices (especially of imported products), which will put even more pressure on America's middle and working classes, this policy will eventually create problems reminiscent of the 2008 crisis, and I believe, the Great Depression. Eventually, interest rates will rise (causing the amount of interest the government pays annually to balloon with it) and the credit that keeps this country running is going to be turned off as people in the world find alternatives (perhaps the Chinese yuan or a mixture of other currencies) and they stop loaning us money. And when that happens, our country will likely go through some extreme shocks and withdrawals. Just look at Europe. We're next.

The Federal Reserve, Interest Rates, and QEternity

The Federal Reserve, the U.S. central bank, is one of the most powerful forces on the planet. Keynesian economist Paul Krugman once semi-joked that the unemployment rate was whatever Alan Greenspan (the chairman of the Federal Reserve at the time) wanted it to be, plus or minus a random error because he isn't God. Being able to establish the federal funds interest rate is powerful because that rate is the basis for many other borrowing rates. If borrowing costs are low, it is cheaper for governments and businesses to borrow, and it should increase economic activity. The Federal Reserve doesn't actually directly dictate rates (because that would be completely Communist, right?), but instead sets the rate by buying (or selling) bonds from banks in amounts necessary to cause the rate to set at where they want it. To keep interest rates low, they must buy lots of bonds from banks in order to cause the rate to drop. The interest rate has been near zero since 2008 and the Federal Reserve has announced it will remain near zero for quite some time.

There are a few major problems that come with artificially low interest rates. One problem is that it punishes savers and people living on fixed incomes. For example, there are some people who save wisely and then live off of the interest of their savings and investments in retirement. However, due to the artificially low interest rates by the Federal Reserve, elderly people in fixed income get very little income from their safe investments and life savings. Secondly, low interest rates hurt insurance companies and other companies who rely on making money from the safe investment of excess capital. Insurance companies (who I rarely feel sorry for) are often pinched by low interest rates and then are forced to consider investing in riskier assets. I believe this is one of the two secondary goals of the Federal Reserve, in addition to trying to spur economic activity (by making borrowing cheap and creating plenty of liquidity) and participating in a global currency war to devalue currencies to make individual countries' exports cheaper. They want to punish savers and force people to spend their money (which the Fed believes will create jobs now), since saving money at low interest rates will likely result in generating a return that is less than inflation and therefore result in an actual loss of purchasing power. The other secondary goal is to force investors into riskier assets and prop up the stock market. Although the modern day Federal Reserve has never admitted to targeting asset prices, it seems pretty obvious based on past behavior that they lower rates and increase easing measures when stock prices drop.

In addition to the short term problems that low interest rates cause, there are possibly devastating long term consequences from the unprecedented actions being taken by the Federal Reserve. Firstly, if interest rates ever rise, existing bond holders are going to get destroyed. Bonds have both a yield (an amount of interest that they pay) as well as a price people are willing to pay for them. If interest rates rise, the people who hold older, lower yielding bonds will lose a ton of the value of their bonds since people will not want to buy lower yielding bonds when they can buy newer, higher yielding bonds instead. Furthermore, the Federal Reserve has been "expanding its balance sheet" by buying Treasuries and other debt (such as mortgage debt) with electronically created money. If it ever decides to "unwind" its balance sheet, or start to sell its assets, it will flood the market, destroy prices further, and suck up tons of liquidity from the system with the cash it accumulates from the sale of all of the assets it's bought up. It could be a disaster.

The other two risks that come along with the Fed's easy money policies are the creation of asset bubbles and the risk of major inflation at some point in the future. When the Fed makes lending cheap through artificially low interest rates, that excessive money that it dumps into the system has to go somewhere. Quite often, rather than going into productive investments, the money is used to fuel speculation and create short-term asset bubbles. For example, although some of the easy money from the 1990's went into creating long lasting and productive technological investments, much of it went into massively overvalued technology companies. Investors who got in at the right time might have made a fortune while investors who got in at the wrong time lost a fortune. However, ultimately, technology stocks as a whole proved to be a massive short term bubble. In the next decade, easy money from the Fed flowed into real estate. Real estate prices nationwide, especially in certain areas, were bid up. Many people began buying houses as investments, thinking prices would continue to skyrocket forever. Most people knew at least somebody who tried to earn lots of money by "flipping houses" (buying them and then turning around and selling them a short time later, sometimes with some improvements and sometimes not). And, like with the tech stock bubble, those that got in and out at the right time made a fortune. However, those that got in at the wrong time once again lost a fortune, including many individual homeowners who bought their homes right before the crash. As the Federal Reserve continues flooding the system with money through its asset purchases and easy money policies, the question is what will the next bubble be? Many people suspect it will be student loans and even U.S. Treasuries. As mentioned earlier, if rates ever do rise (and if they don't you can almost guarantee the other huge risk will occur: massive amounts of inflation), what will happen to the value of existing, lower yielding U.S. Treasury bonds? Can you say bubble burst?

And then of course there's inflation. The Federal Reserve claims to have a dual mandate from Congress: price stability and employment. Easy money policies are supposed to help drive employment. However, the Federal Reserve says they balance this goal with another primary goal of price stability. Part of price stability, according to the Federal Reserve, is to avoid deflation. Keynesian economists, who seem to largely control the modern day Federal Reserve, are scared to death of deflation. They claim that deflation (the drop in prices) causes people to put off purchases as they choose to wait to buy things until they've become cheaper. "Why buy something now when I can buy it later for cheaper," goes the argument. However, although there may be some very small morsel of truth underlying this way of thinking, I think it also completely ignores the basic laws of supply and demand. As goods become cheaper, demand should rise. At some point, assets would fall to a point where somebody in the market would think they were a bargain and would want to buy them before somebody else beat them to it. However, of course it is true that existing asset holders (homeowners and stockholders) don't want to see a decrease in the value of their assets...and I think this is what the Federal Reserve is *really* worried about: protecting the asset values of people who already own assets.

But their massive pumping of credit and electronic dollars into the system is almost certainly causing inflation. Already. The government has changed the way it calculates inflation, as measured by CPI (consumer price index), more than once already[17]. Although the current government measurement of CPI shows that inflation isn't so bad, I think normal people like you and I can feel it and see it in our daily lives. Why would the government intentionally understate the true measure of inflation? Besides the fact that lying (and "spinning") might be what governments do best, Social Security payments rise with the cost of inflation. If the government reports much lower inflation by using substitute products and other changes to the measurement of CPI, then they can save billions of dollars through lower increases in Social Security payments. In Spain recently, they had riots when the government tried to cap the annual increases to the pension for inflation. The U.S. government can avoid that nasty problem by just changing how inflation is measured so that it's understated. And none of this includes the fact that oil and food prices aren't even included in CPI. Interestingly, oil transactions are denominated in dollars and so although the price of oil in terms of gold has been somewhat steadier, in the last 5-10 years the price of oil in terms of dollars has risen dramatically. And yet few people have thought to associate the value of the dollar with the rising cost of oil. And if the Federal Reserve keeps expanding its balance sheet and electronically creating money to buy bonds and keep interest rates low, with regards to inflation...you ain't seen nothing yet...

The Federal Reserve has little accountability. There is minimal oversight. Much of what they do is done secretly, behind closed doors. Congress is supposed to check their power, but the Fed is also trusted to be smarter and more trustworthy than Congress. The Federal Reserve has created asset bubbles and inflation, engaged in risky currency swaps with Europe[18], and bailed out overseas banks and companies through the creation of TRILLIONS of dollars during the financial crisis in 2008[19]. And yet few people say a word. In 2008, the Chairman of the Federal Reserve Ben Bernanke said that he didn't anticipate any problems in the "large internationally active banks." In June of 2008, he claimed that the threat of a substantial downturn in the market had waned and in July of the same year, he told Congress that Fannie Mae and Freddie Mac would survive and were adequately capitalized, just months before they were taken over by the government[20]. Once again: in July of 2008, Ben Bernanke testified that Fannie and Freddie were adequately capitalized and then two months later they were taken over by the government, and will cost taxpayers around $100 billion. Either Ben Bernanke, who is in charge of the Federal Reserve and is perhaps the most powerful man in the world (at least economically), was completely and totally wrong...or he was lying. Either way, nobody seems to remember that the man, and the entity he resides over (that we put all our faith in), have actually given us little reason to put our faith in them.

The Bailouts

Perhaps the biggest tragedies of the bank bailouts were that those that willfully caused it and majorly profited from it were never held accountable...and that special interests lobbied feverishly to block a lot of the legislation that was needed to ensure that it never happened again. Listen to what happened again. In the past, banks issued mortgages and then collected mortgage payments for income. But that changed when banks began selling mortgages to investment banks who then bundled them and sold them to investors. When mortgages began to be securitized and sold, credit risk was transferred from banks to investors. This created a major moral hazard, where banks and investment banks stopped caring about the creditworthiness of the people to whom they loaned money. They didn't care because the mortgages were coming off of their books and going to investors. Meanwhile, investment banks paid the credit rating agencies, who stamped bundles of crappy mortgages with AAA ratings[12]. At the same time, the Federal Reserve kept interest rates extremely low, making borrowing cheap. This pumped tons of cheap money into the system, which combined with lax underwriting standards by banks (and the practically fraudulent behavior by investment banks and credit rating agencies), created huge asset bubbles. Housing prices skyrocketed and tons of houses were built. However, as it turns out, tons of people couldn't actually pay for all of the things they had borrowed for. The bubble burst. Combine that with the fact that some financial institutions took crazy gambles with their depositors' money (made possible by the Commodity Futures Modernization Act that kept potentially dangerous derivatives unregulated), a few financial institutions hit a gold mine while others were bankrupted. The U.S. government had to step in and bailout some of these huge financial institutions with taxpayer money...or risk bank runs and the potential failure of some of the U.S.' largest financial institutions, many of which really had become too big to fail (partially as a result of the Gramm-Leach-Bliley Act which overturned Glass-Steagall). Glass-Steagall was one of the most important pieces of financial legislation. It separated commercial banks (that take deposits from customers and should safely hold them) and investment banks (which often make risky gambles to try and achieve bigger returns for investors). Signing the Gramm-Leach-Bliley Act and the Commodity Futures Modernization Act were two of the worst things Bill Clinton ever did. It was these four factors: the securitization of mortgages combined with credit rating agencies being paid by investment banks to rate mortgage backed securities, the Gramm-Leach-Bliley Act which repealed Glass-Steagall (allowing companies to do both commercial banking and investment banking and allowed too big to fail), the Commodity Futures Modernization Act (which kept potentially insanely risky derivatives unregulated), and artificially low interest rates by the Fed (among other smaller factors) that caused the financial crisis that led to the bailouts.

I think looking at some of the specific players involved in the financial crisis is also worthwhile. Goldman Sachs and AIG are two of the companies at the very center of the bailouts. AIG wrote many of the derivative products that resulted in Goldman Sachs receiving a huge amount of money. AIG insured that the derivatives would pay out in the event of defaults[13]. When this happened, Goldman Sachs was set to receive billions from AIG...billions AIG apparently didn't have. One of the most interesting questions from the bailout is why did Goldman Sachs get paid out dollar for dollar on these contracts that forced the government to bailout AIG? And what role did Bush's Treasury Secretary Hank Paulson, the previous CEO of Goldman Sachs, play in these decisions? Even more complicated was the bailout of Fannie Mae and Freddie Mac, which will cost taxpayers somewhere in the neighborhood of $100 billion.

However, although we may not like the idea of "too big to fail" and what caused the mess, that doesn't make the mess go away. If we had let these major, major financial institutions run out of liquidity, it could have been a disaster. You can disagree with the details, but I don't think you can argue completely against TARP. The economy could have come to a screeching halt. Many, many businesses need short-term loans these days in order to survive. That is just part of doing business for many companies now. In a developed economy, there needs to be capital that can be lent out. However, during the credit crisis and financial crisis, markets were freezing up. Institutions didn't want to loan anymore. Many of them couldn't afford to because they had so many nonperforming loans and worthless assets on their balance sheets. Many stared bankruptcy, and a potential Great Depression, right in the eye. There was a major threat that some banks could go insolvent, freeze up the credit markets, and severely harm business in this country.

The biggest problem with TARP, by far, is that our politicians did not fully step up and properly regulate the powerful financial interests that caused the financial crisis in the first place in order to try and prevent this from happening again. They did little to change Too Big To Fail. The EXTREMELY powerful banking lobby successfully watered down the Volker Rule and other proposed regulations[14]. The U.S. government has totally been the big banks' and financial industry's bitch. No criminal charges were ever filed. CEOs, who lost billions of dollars and whose companies needed billions in taxpayer money to avoid bankruptcy, left their jobs having made hundreds of millions of dollars. Their companies (and taxpayers) lost billions, yet they made hundreds of millions. And they walked away with all of it. It was a bank heist. But the bankers were the ones who took the money!

The auto industry bailout was a little different. Most people don't think about how a company not only provides jobs for its employees, but also helps other businesses provide jobs (by buying those companies' parts and supplies). One or two major companies going out of business will affect all of the companies upstream from that company that relied on the dead company's business. If GM and Chrysler had gone out of business, it wouldn't have just impacted all of their employees, but also the employees of many of their suppliers. Many conservatives have said that the auto companies should have gone through a structured bankruptcy, but given the financial crisis at the time, it's just simply not clear if the companies could have survived intact. And so the U.S. government loaned Chrysler and GM money and bought some ownership of GM. We infused the money they needed to keep their businesses running, but we also forced them to make changes. The government didn't make all of the decisions for them, but forced a change in leadership and strategy. And it's worked. Taxpayers might lose around $30 billion on the auto bailout, but tens of thousands of jobs were saved, both companies are now profitable and competitive, and the U.S.' auto industry has made a huge recovery[15].

Some people criticize the way the auto unions were given better treatment than most bondholders under the terms of the bailout. However, I actually have no problems with that. Everybody knew the auto companies had massive financial problems and huge legacy costs. People who loaned these companies money knew the risk they were taking. I'd lose a lot less sleep over wiping out rich bondholders who knowingly loaned money to financially troubled companies than if I wiped out lower and middle class autoworkers' benefits that had been promised. One thing that does trouble me, however, is how union workers seemed to get a much better deal under the bailout than many private autoworkers. That definitely has a bad smell to it.

It seems worth noting that the UAW (United Auto Workers) did agree to concessions, such as much lower wages for new hires[16]. It was imperative that the unions not ask for so much that the American auto companies couldn't compete with their foreign competitors. And in fact, UAW labor costs per hour seem to have fallen significantly. The cause of the auto industry's problems was more similar to the causes of the airline industry's problems than the financial industry. The financial industry created its own crisis through what almost appears to be fraudulent intent that was basically just ignored. However, it was a combination of poor management (laziness) and heavy obligations to workers that largely caused the auto companies' problems. Their retirement and wage obligations were making them uncompetitive with global competitors. Once the auto workers union was willing to make major concessions, along with the change in management, auto companies no longer posed a major threat to taxpayers. It's far from certain that the same can be said for financial institutions, who have lobbied and done everything they can to avoid making the kinds of changes that would really ensure that a similar financial crisis would not happen again.

Business and Government in America

I think there is an interesting relationship between the private industry and America. The private industry does (and should) provide the bulk of the jobs that exist in the U.S. The government is typically not in the business of making things... at least not in this country. Typically, the government costs money rather than makes money. And the way it typically "makes" money is through taxes and fees. Some other countries have nationalized some industries, including energy, and use the profits from those businesses in order to fund education, healthcare, or other projects. Would we be better off if a few industries, like oil, generated profits for the people instead of for private shareholders? Or would they be less efficient?

As mentioned, most of the time the government costs money rather than makes money...and usually when they do make money, they don't do it as well as the private sector. And so, especially in this country, when you make government bigger, you're often taking people and instead of having them do something, you're having them regulate something. You're not usually helping something get done, you're making it take longer and cost more. Sometimes you do need that in order to protect consumers. But, we can't forget that businesses provide us with jobs and many of the things we need in our lives.

There's always been debate over exactly to what degree business owners should take care of their workers. You have some people who advocate a completely laissez-faire approach, where the free market has complete control over people's salaries and benefits. If a person's labor isn't important enough for companies to offer health insurance benefits for certain positions...too bad. These advocates for a completely free market also argue against minimum wages. But should people have trouble gaining access to affordable health insurance just because they don't have skills corporations deem important enough to deserve health insurance? Or would the country be a better place if the government tried to help its most precious resource, its human capital, gain some access to quality and affordable care?

Sometimes what is good for business (in general) is good for America...but what is good for one single business is not. We see instances of crony capitalism... where the government basically helps create unfair monopolies that are great for a small number of businesses. Jobs might even be created, but to the benefit of a few lucky companies. Other times, even what's good for businesses as a whole is bad for ordinary Americans. Companies used to make millions while using environmentally unsafe practices. Those companies even created jobs for people.

However, they did it in such a way that the harm that they caused was greater than the benefit they provided. They polluted our natural resources. Or created products that were unsafe and hurt people. Or sent American jobs overseas. All in the name of better profits for their shareholders. In these cases, maybe what is best for business is *not* good for America.

However, America can't afford to make business an enemy that needs to be beaten. Instead, businesses should be looked at as crucial partners who must be incentivized, but still monitored. Nobody would just let a partner walk all over them and take advantage of them. However, partners are also important. The public sector desperately needs a healthy private sector to fund it. The public sector can't overly regulate businesses or overly tax them so that businesses just end up creating tax avoidance schemes and lobbying for loopholes. Once again, this kind of crony capitalism that benefits a few individual businesses is usually bad for Americans. But, instead, the public sector should create policies that are conducive to strong private sector growth...while still holding businesses accountable for safe and fair practices.

Unions

I think few people will deny the importance of unions in the past. But people see the behavior of some union members, and it causes some people to HATE unions. They despise them. And I think the more you talk to people who have had to manage union members, you can begin to see why. Union members will sometimes use thug tactics in the workplace. They team together to try and shield each other from punishment for sometimes pretty ridiculous behavior. They intentionally break things...even very, very expensive things, and then pretend it was an accident. If they do virtually any bad behavior, they'll run and hide behind the union. I think this kind of behavior is immoral, frankly, and reprehensible.

But actions like these do not make unions bad or unnecessary. It makes *those* unions and their members bad. Not all unions engage in such tactics. And furthermore, there is nothing wrong with collective bargaining. There should be some room left to reward individual performance, but I think it's fair to allow a group of workers to fight together for higher wages. If they can't, what power do they have over a wealthy employer? Even collective bargaining can't protect them sometimes.

Unions ultimately go back to the idea of class warfare. There is always an underlying battle for resources. Owners want to be able to rent labor for as cheap as possible and keep as much of the profits for themselves as possible. The employees are always going to want a bigger share of the pie for the fruits of their labor. Unions are the workers' efforts to fight back against owners who, only naturally, are going to try to pay as little as they need to in order to make the maximum amount of profit.

However, you should never have to be in a union to get a certain job. And union members shouldn't be forced to vote a certain way. I think unions should be completely and totally voluntary. And if people voluntarily want to join together to bargain for higher salaries and a greater share of the profit, then that's great. But they must also be careful not to be too greedy. They must first remember that the business they work for has to compete against other businesses. If they demand too much, so that their company can't make a profit, then they've dug their own graves. They killed their own jobs. You'd love to believe your competition will also give higher wages...but they often don't (especially foreign competition). So, the unions must be careful not to ask for *too* much, but work together to make sure that they are taken care of by the company's owners. Greedy unions have destroyed the steel, airline, and auto industries (although U.S. auto companies are coming back after the unions made a lot of concessions)...and so many more.

Ultimately, the number one problem with unions is that they often don't want to allow their members to be held accountable for their actions. Take teachers, for example. I support teachers' attempts to get higher levels of pay. Our children's education is important. Just like conservatives point out that if becoming a doctor begins to pay a lot less, then fewer top students will go into medicine, the same is true of education. If we want great teachers, we must pay teachers a good wage. However, most teachers' unions adamantly oppose any kind of incentive pay...at all. Not just incentives based on performance relative to other schools (which I also oppose), but even incentives based on performance compared with other teachers within the same school, or by comparing it with each teacher's previous years' performance. You get paid the same whether you work hard and are passionate about your students or if you just show up. And it's hard to get fired from being a teacher because the union supports you. Unions should be praised for the good they do, but criticized for the bad.

Unemployment in America

The unemployment rate has stayed high (currently officially at 7.5%) for a long time. That's millions of people who would like to be working but aren't. And there's almost the same amount of people who are either working, but only part-time and not full-time like they would like to, or have just completely given up looking (or they've gone on disability, like millions who have mysteriously become disabled...at unusually high rates...after the financial crisis). This is millions and millions of people who want a good job and need a good job and yet don't have one. Some people want to blame unemployment benefits for causing people to become too lazy to get back to work. They basically tell people who are looking for a job, but can't find one, "You're all f'ing lazy." It's really insulting...and fairly ignorant. In March of 2013, according to the JOLTS (Job Openings and Labor Turnover Survey), there were about 3.8 million jobs that were open, while there were nearly 12 million people looking for jobs but didn't have one[22]. And there was probably another 10 million people not working full-time that would like to. Lazy bums. No, there are serious problems with employment in America...and it's not caused by unemployment benefits.

One major cause of America's new higher unemployment rate is technology. Republicans made fun of President Obama and accused him of claiming that the unemployment rate was caused by ATMs. But Obama's point, that many traditional jobs have been made obsolete and have been replaced by machines, is completely valid. In the past, there were a lot of jobs that would pay a decent wage because, although an idiot could do them, they had to be done. However, we've now replaced a lot of those idiots (with no real skills) with machines. These jobs often don't require thinking, just doing. And the machine can often do the tasks more consistently, and often for a cheaper price...especially with some of our employment laws, costs, and taxes. A machine is now often cheaper than a person. And that's actually okay...if there is another job that person is qualified to do. But, we're running out of jobs that stupid people need to do that a machine can't do...and do it cheaper. This is why programs to promote job retraining are vital if America wants to really begin to tackle its unemployment problems. We must find a way to retrain people who currently don't have the skills they need to find a job (or create their own).

I also think most people don't completely understand the full dynamics of outsourcing. Some ONLY see it as companies being greedy and evil for sending jobs overseas to lower cost countries (or replacing humans with machines). But those people don't know all of the incentives that can cause companies to make those decisions. Companies are in business to make as much profit as possible. That's capitalism 101. That's what firms are designed to do and that's the way our capital markets are set up. Capital (money) is usually given to those who provide the greatest return for it. A company's stock price is, in a way, as much a reflection of the cost of raising money as it is the value of the company. If a company needs to raise more money in the future, a high stock price allows them to issue fewer shares and give away less ownership, in order to raise the money it needs. A low stock price means there is less demand for ownership in a particular company and a company will have to sell a lot more shares of ownership in order to raise the same amount of money. So of course it is in a company's best interest to earn money for its shareholders and target a high stock price.

Part of the unemployment problem in the U.S. *is* caused by greed, but greed by everybody. American companies want to make things as cheaply as possible. Not just because they make more money, but because their shareholders want to make more money. However, greed by corporations and their shareholders sometimes ultimately ends up punishing the American lower and lower-middle classes. It's true that shipping jobs overseas to increase profits may result in lower prices for average consumers (or it may not), but it also punishes the average worker by sending his job overseas. Ironically, as wages stay flat and people are laid off, Americans have less money to buy companies' products. They are also often forced to try and save money by shopping at places like Wal-Mart, which sells them products made by people overseas who took their jobs. Yet even many people who *could* afford to buy American products, made by American workers, don't. And more jobs go overseas. In order to lower unemployment, we must tame the greed of companies, shareholders, and of customers. Americans would need to shop with companies who might charge more, but create jobs in the U.S.

As previously discussed, our high corporate tax rate also does not help the unemployment rate. America has the second highest corporate tax rates in the world and so many companies are simply doing what makes sense: moving jobs overseas to places where they will be taxed less. We seem to really have two choices. We can try and regulate and force companies to keep jobs here. But, you can't beat businesses by regulating them to death and taxing them large amounts. If you try and simply make companies keep jobs here, they'll likely just raise prices to pay the higher costs of salaries and still make their targeted profit. You can pass minimum wage laws to try and help lower income folks deal with rising prices (which I support), but then businesses still just raise the prices more (and lay people off). Business is your friend and your partner. Sometimes, your partner tries to take advantage of the relationship and you have to make it more fair. But, if you ask for too much, you might lose all your friends and they might go be friends with somebody else. And you need your friends because they can create jobs and make your society a better place. The Heritage Foundation (which absolutely has a conservative agenda) did a study that showed that countries with higher levels of "economic freedom" are typically wealthier and more productive. The specific measures of economic freedom that they used (they used ten), and the exact way they measured them, are certainly open for debate. But, I think it's hard not to walk away from the report seeing how countries that promote free and open markets tend to do a lot better than those countries that try and control and antagonize businesses.

Free Trade

I am very much in favor of free trade. I think it can, and will, help balance the amount of wealth in the world. As companies look to make things cheaper and cheaper, they will continue to look to build factories and add jobs in poor parts of the world. And this will almost always result in some transfer of wealth to poorer countries. How much trickles down out of the hands of many of the people running some of these corrupt systems and into the hands of the ordinary citizens will vary. However, free trade has helped many countries lift people out of poverty. And it also opens up our economy to sell high margin, technologically advanced goods to new regions as their citizens work themselves into the middle class. However, for all of the benefits of free trade, it doesn't come without a cost. But it's how you deal with the side effects, so to speak, that come with free trade that determines whether it ends up being successful for the country, as a whole, or only for a smaller number of winners, mostly at the top.

Some people criticize free trade on the basis of the fact that it exploits labor in the third world. But, as free trade proponents argue, it also creates jobs in poor countries that simply weren't there before the factory was built, or whatever job they took showed up. More than exploiting third world countries, free trade pumps capital, resources, and training into developing countries that just wasn't there before. I oppose all cruel treatment that goes on in some of these so called "sweat shops" and I oppose harming workers or putting them in cruel or dangerous environments. However, when it comes to the low wages paid, almost none of these people have better paying options...or they would have taken them. There are very, very few forced labor camps (although there are some) and almost all of these people working at these low wages are choosing to do so of their own free will, because they don't have any better options. Anti-free traders should focus on what is wrong with these poor countries' policies that cause them to be so poor. Several countries, through good planning, fairly honest governance, and hard work have taken their countries with little or no valuable resources and turned them into wealthy countries. These are countries like Hong Kong, Singapore, and even Israel (although they certainly had some help). Free trade was a big part of all of these countries' rapid development.

However, there is also the dark side of free trade. Poor, uneducated workers in rich countries now have to compete with poor, uneducated workers in poor countries who demand a much lower salary. Free trade punishes low-skilled workers in developed countries the most. Developed countries need to establish education systems that have several well-designed programs to give low-skilled workers who have lost their jobs due to the effects of free trade the skills they'll need to find a new job (or create their own) in order to support their families. If a country does this, then free trade will be good for everybody. However, if they do not, free trade will end up severely punishing the poor and will cause a lot of very serious social problems.

And that's exactly what we're seeing in America as a result of free trade. We're seeing a large segment of the society, without marketable skills, having trouble finding work (because it became cheaper to get low-skilled workers overseas) and we see people struggling to get the skills they need in order to get a job. And we see these people becoming burdens on society. The winners of free trade must help the losers. The alternative to free trade, protectionism, causes an increase in prices and can still result in even more jobs lost. Once again, we must combine free trade with a better emphasis on re-training and skills development... but not resort to protectionism.

Illegal Immigration

Illegal immigration is another one of those issues with people on two extremes. You've got one group of people that's like, "We hate Mexicans. They're destroying this great country of ours. We need to build a big wall and if one of them tries to come over, then we shoot 'em." Yee-haw! Another side says, "Let's just let everybody in and then give them all social services and free healthcare, and welfare, and free lollipops." And I find it weird that we haven't been able to meet somewhere between these two positions.

For starters, let's agree that illegal immigration is, in fact, a problem. Firstly, we have a budget crisis. Spending hundreds of millions of dollars on services for people who aren't even from here just doesn't really make a lot of sense. Crime is another issue that comes along with illegal aliens. Some of these illegal aliens are inarguably criminals. They come to the United States planning to support themselves through a life of crime. And these people also cause major problems to Americans.

But I also can't understand why the other side can't realize some other truths. This nation was a nation of immigrants. Did we ask the Natives if it was cool if we came? And wasn't this country supposed to be a place where immigrants from all over the world could find hope? The land of opportunity? Some people would argue that was necessary at the time when we were a new country, looking to build and grow. However, some say that now with 300 million people, we need growth to slow...especially growth from poor countries with people with few skills, like Mexico. But my response to that is that my vision of America is different than yours, but if you really want to do that, then you just take the Statue of Liberty down. Because that statue says, "Give me your tired, your poor, your huddled masses yearning to breathe free."

There would be other benefits of allowing more immigrants to come to this country legally. If we actually recognized their presence here, then we could actually charge them some income tax or Social Security tax. Even a small amount of additional revenue would help during these very difficult times for our country financially. Plus, we have many, many jobs that white, black, and other Americans simply do not want and will not take. In Georgia, after they passed their immigration bill, some farms couldn't find anybody to pick their crops. They lost millions and millions of dollars worth of crops because there simply wasn't enough labor willing to harvest it[23]. It makes sense to allow more Mexicans and other countries' citizens to work in the U.S. and build a path to citizenship. Not to mention that without Chinese, Indian, and other immigrants, there will probably not be enough American students to satisfy our nation's future science and engineering jobs needs...based on current levels of interest and aptitude.

This country should still be the land of opportunity. But, we must also accept several realities. One, there are real security concerns right now with people from certain parts of the world who wish to do us harm. Furthermore, we cannot reasonably accept everybody who would like to live here. That's not realistic. Therefore, I think for several reasons we need to build a big wall across the Mexico border. Grant more visas to Mexican citizens who want to work hard and build a life in America. But we must try harder to keep the dangerous Mexican gang members out. Send people who commit crimes back across to the other side of the wall and don't let them come back. And we must limit the social services that are available for free for those guest workers who are working towards citizenship.

Ultimately, we must increase our level of compassion and let people come to this great country and work hard for a better life. However, we must do it in a very careful, calculated, and responsible way.

Climate Change and the Environment

I don't know why most conservatives (I know why SOME care so much) get so upset about climate change...even more than a lot of other issues. There's a lot of anger around this issue that doesn't really make sense. Take abortion: totally get it. Tax policy: totally get it. I even get the passion about immigration. But I don't know what it is about global warming that pisses conservatives off SO much.

I actually don't care one way or the other. We can heat the Earth up for all I care. Because although I probably SHOULD care about what happens to the people that will have to live on Earth 1,000 years from now (or whenever this is supposed to happen), I don't. That's kind of selfish, but there it is. So, for all I care we can ignore it, whether it's true or not. But I'm also not so passionate about (and fixated on) *disproving* it. I swear some conservatives hate the scientific community. Sometimes, they are almost as anti-science as the radical Islamic leaders in the Middle East.

Conservatives have found some old news clippings of reporters warning of global warming 70 or 80 years ago. They say that those folks were de facto wrong then and therefore this time we are just being lied to again. It seems as if for many conservatives, the case has already been closed that human beings, and their use of carbon emissions, are NOT causing the rising temperatures on the Earth. First of all, I'm not sure we can say, with 100% certainty, that those people 80 years ago were actually wrong about global warming. To use religious terminology, perhaps those scientists many years ago were practically prophets...with knowledge that was ahead of their time. Or perhaps they were false prophets, so to speak, but this time it's the real deal. In fact, the global warming crowd sounds not all so different from the Christian crowd that predicts Armageddon and the end of the world. Hell, maybe global warming is the Armageddon that Christians believe Revelation is talking about. How would that be for some cosmic irony??? I can understand why many conservatives have their doubts about the cause of global warming, but I don't know why many are so opposed to the possibility that it *could* be manmade carbon emissions. Why is that not even possible...especially when something like 90% of experts claim it's true? Just because it might interfere with your precious businesses?

However, I also think much of the pro-environment crowd cares more about plants and animals than they do about people. When it comes down to saving some rare, obscure animal or saving millions of dollars, they are quick to advocate businesses and government spend the millions. And I do think human beings need to be careful not to create major disruptions in the food chain of important animals. But, I think when we have to balance taking care of the environment with taking care of human beings, human beings should take priority. Furthermore, sometimes the environmentalists actually do more harm than good. Some scholars argue that environmentalists' stance against DDT cost millions of children's lives, when mosquitoes carrying malaria were not contained as well without using DDT. As usual, environmentalists deny these claims, but they are accepted by many experts.

I think we need to get to a point where we try to balance not destroying the environment with not caring about it more than we care about people. We must value human beings more than animals and nature. Many animal groups, for example, also seem to care a lot more about the spotted owl than the hungry homeless guy downtown. We must find a balance on these issues somehow, without basically denying science.

America's Addiction to Oil

I think one of the reasons you see this insistence on being the world's police and spending hundreds of billions of dollars on defense (multiples of any other nation's military spending), is to protect our financial interests in the world. Especially our oil interests. The U.S. spends tens of billions of dollars per month, importing hundreds of millions of barrels of foreign oil. That amount, which we have to spend to keep our economy running and our cars on the road, goes up significantly as the price of oil goes up. The U.S. has a major financial interest in keeping the price of oil down.

In 1945, the U.S. was a net oil exporter. By 1950, however, we were importing a million barrels a day. Today we import about 7 million barrels of oil per day[24]. That oil costs money. Right now we need it to run our cars, heat our homes, dry our clothes, and (maybe most importantly) run the machines we use in our businesses and factories. In other countries, they use public transportation to save energy. And they hang dry their clothes. Because a lot of governments don't give tax subsidies to oil companies, in the billions, to help keep the price of gas down.

Here in this country, many think private industry is always better and the government always does things worse. We feel like the motivations for profit and competition will help us discover new oil supplies faster and better than a government run oil company. Therefore, we let private companies reap billions off the top in profits (plus give them tax credits) to go and get the oil. We hope that they do it that much more effectively and efficiently than the government would. But somehow, we need the oil. We have to have it.

The question is: what are we going to do? We have a huge annual trade deficit at the same time we spend hundreds of billions of dollars a year importing foreign oil. And if the price of oil goes up, like in 2008 when the price was nearly $150 per barrel, then we'll have to either buy less oil or transfer even more money to pay for it. And you can see where the military-industrial complex comes in. We have supported and armed ruthless and evil dictators in the Middle East for decades in our quest for cheap oil.

In the 1970's, we propped up the Shah in Iran. He was corrupt and he treated his political enemies horribly. Eventually, he was overthrown and then the Islamic government that was established in his place had very anti-U.S. policies. They shut off some of the supply of oil and sent prices skyrocketing. Conservatives have largely focused their efforts in our energy crisis on securing more oil. They realize that we shouldn't feed our addiction to debt with more debt, but they think we should feed our addiction to oil with more oil. They use the military and interfere with other countries' affairs, in an effort to feed our oil addiction. They provide arms to ruthless regimes like in Saudi Arabia so we can have access to oil[25].

We must create new sources of energy or use less energy. It's a big part of our dangerous trade deficit. It's a big driver of our foreign policy and our wars. We must find a solution. Some people believe that there is plenty of oil...we just have to find it. Others believe that fossil fuels are literally running out and that we're approaching a global energy crisis. If that's the case, things would get horribly ugly very quickly. We must find answers. We must find ways like renewable energies (e.g. solar), natural gas, and safer nuclear energy so that we can get the power we need, but do it in an affordable way that doesn't force us to rely on the extremely politically volatile countries in the Middle East. Each alternative energy source has some problems, and countries (especially the U.S.) will need to tailor a strategy that likely uses some combination of the various options. Renewable energies (like solar, wind, and water) are great ideas, but have severe limitations. Some areas of the U.S. might not enjoy as much sunlight (or wind or water) as others. Solar and wind technologies are also still too expensive without government subsidies. I think nuclear power is one of the most promising, but after the Fukushima disaster (and the others before it)...and with the threats posed by terrorism...I could understand people's reluctance to have a nuclear powered plant near their home. Sales of battery powered cars have been extremely disappointing. Based on the current technology, who wants to pay significantly more for a car that can only go limited distances before it needs a charge (and when there are a limited number of charging stations)? It seems that hydrogen and abundant natural gas are the most likely solution for cars, but even those cars are more expensive and lack an acceptable number of refueling stations.

The Military-Industrial Complex

In his farewell address to Americans as President, Dwight Eisenhower spent some time talking about the rising importance of a strong U.S. military. There were grave threats in the world. America needed to be ready. It needed to invest in permanent military production, so that we'd have the bombs and weapons we would need, should we have to go to war. We've got both private companies (Lockheed Martin, American Defense, BAE Systems Land and Armaments, Northrop Grumman Corporation, Boeing, etc.) and federal employees whose livelihoods are dependent upon us building more weapons. The U.S. has been spending over $500 billion every year on defense. And that doesn't include the money we spent in Iraq and Afghanistan, which has grown to more than $1 trillion since we first attacked Afghanistan after 9/11.

There are real problems in the world. Real evils. Real threats. But, I think it's reasonable to step back and take a look at the best ways to deal with those threats, as well as what might be causing those threats. The U.S. has been spending over $500 billion a year on defense. The next closest country is China, which is somewhere close to $150 billion[26]. Is the United States' defense strategy working? Is it sustainable? Are there any financial interests that might be contributing to some of this crazy level of spending? The U.S. has military bases in over 60 countries. How would we like it if China or some other country put up a base in our country? Or a country neighboring us?

We have to have some amount of military spending. There is no question. We need a military in order to protect our citizens from some of the evil threats that exist in the world. There are countries and people that would like to harm the American people. That is real. Granted, some of those people might actually have a reason...but that still doesn't make it okay. Killing innocent people is never the answer. However, there may be a reason why people hate us and want to harm us. I don't think they just "hate our freedom," or that there are a large percentage of people actually trying to pursue a worldwide Islamic revolution, or that any nation plans to invade the United States. Which country is a real threat to attack us on our soil? Why do we need to spend three to four times more on the military than the next closest nation? And I am not convinced that spending over $500 billion a year, the way we're spending it, is the best way to deal with the threats that we face. I think the military should be, as Robert Gates envisioned, small and nimble. Less heavy infrastructure used in land battles and more high tech, expensive, cutting edge weaponry (and a smaller force).

Take one look at Iraq. CEOs at top defense contractors reaped annual pay gains of 200% to 688% in the years after the Sept. 11 terror attacks in 2001. In September of 2007, journalist Michael Brush wrote an excellent article called "War Means a Windfall for CEOs." In it, he points out several amazing statistics. "The chief executives at the seven defense contractors whose bosses made the most pocketed nearly a half-billion dollars from 2002 through last year...Sales at General Dynamics increased 76% from 2002 to 2006, with significant help from Department of Defense spending. Overall sales increased to $24.1 billion from $13.6 billion, and at least a third of that increase came from higher Department of Defense spending. Those contract awards helped General Dynamics' stock more than double to $80 a share from $39 at the start of 2002...David Lesar at Halliburton (Dickey Cheney's old company) made $79.8 million, or nearly $16 million a year, from 2002-2006. During this time, Defense Department revenue at his company grew from just 4% in 2001 to 40% in 2004. That year, the company got nearly $8 billion in defense contracts out of total revenue of $19.9 billion. The gains allowed Lesar to reap $13.6 million just by cashing in options last year, and $14.7 million the year before...Lockheed Martin Chief Executives Vance Coffman and Robert Stevens together earned $64.8 million from 2002 to 2006. Lockheed Martin's Defense Department-related revenue increased from $17 billion in 2002 to $26.6 billion in 2006, a 57% increase. The stock has more than doubled to $100 from $47 at the start of 2002. Lockheed Martin was the top Defense Department contractor last year."[27] The Iraq War made a lot of people filthy rich. And it represents precisely how the military industrial complex works. That war was one of the greatest wealth transfers in the history of the world. Right from our pockets, the taxpayers, into the hands of private defense contractors and their CEOs. War is about money.

On one hand, weapons have been around since the beginning of time. Even the cavemen created clubs they could use as weapons. Rocks, knives, and all sorts of prehistoric weapons were used for thousands of years. However, this first begs the question, what is man's obsession with murder and destruction? Why can't man be satisfied to simply build and help others?

But here's what's different: now, we don't *just* have the ability to kill. Man has now begun to *master* death and destruction. Now, rather than just being able to kill another person, we are able to kill thousands and even hundreds of thousands of people at one time by pulling one trigger in one plane...high up in the sky. Furthermore, for many years now, we have had the ability to destroy everybody and everything. With the invention and expansion of nuclear arsenals, we have achieved the ability to completely eradicate ourselves and everything on the planet.

What must happen for the world to reverse course? Many conservatives, especially in America, would consider this kind of thought to be overly idealistic. (But isn't that what we should all want and strive for: the ideal? Why do we always settle for less than the best?) And maybe a world without weapons is a little unrealistic. But how will the world ever reverse the march towards potential annihilation if nobody ever makes the suggestion to disarm? Why would anybody ever disarm unless somebody at least suggested it and talked about it? Not to mention put it into action. I give President Obama a little bit of credit on this front, especially regarding his efforts to pass the new START treaty with Russia.

But the world still marches onward with plans to arm more people and to find new ways to kill even more people. Even though Russia is also a major supplier of weapons, nobody even comes CLOSE to selling as much weapons to other countries as the U.S. Then other countries try to catch up. Everybody wants the best guns, the best planes, the best bombs. And I think many begin to think of these weapons like they're toys and so cool. But, in reality, these are weapons of war and murder and destruction. We should begin to try and work towards a world where we see weapons for what they are. Teddy Roosevelt is famous for saying we should, "Speak softly and carry a big stick." And I agree with that. However, I think because of the military industrial complex, you have to make sure that you're stick doesn't become so big and so economically important, that you might gain extra incentive to use it.

We are the largest military in the world, by far. We have more weapons for war than any other country. Our technology is by far the most superior. We could single-handedly destroy the entire world if we wanted to. And yet we're always told we need more weapons. A bigger edge. We have all of these enemies that we need to be worried about. When does it stop? It never stops. And at the same time we'll probably continue to sell weapons to our "friends" (like Bin Laden, Saddam Hussein, Saudi Arabia, the Egyptian government, etc.)...who will eventually become our enemies. Again. It's like a war Ponzi scheme.

Terrorism

Al Qaeda is an organized crime group. They are actually half organized crime...half special interest group. For example, do you really think *all* of the people who work for Greenpeace really care about the environment? Hell no. For many people, it's only about raising money, just like many other nonprofits. "What can we draw people around that will make them give us money?" In America, it's the NRA and the environment. In the Middle East, it's hating the U.S. and Israel. At least some Al Qaeda members probably don't care about the U.S. that much more than some in Greenpeace care about the environment. It's a marketing tool they are using to capitalize on people's dislike of U.S. foreign policies...so that they can make money. They are fighting to raise money. They sell drugs to make money. Interestingly, they then take some of that money, give some back to the community to gain favor...AND to market for more hatred of the U.S. Not that the U.S. needs much help causing people to hate them.

Many Americans believe that there is a huge existential threat posed by Muslims, who are trying to take over the world. But a lot of these people are out there living with goats and shit. They aren't taking over any world any time soon. Terrorism *is* real and certain radical Islamic sects *do* pose a major threat. But there is simply not a real threat that <u>most</u> Muslims are trying to take over the world and instill Sharia law. That is fictional garbage. A small group of radical Islamic terrorists have made such audacious claims, but it'd be like the U.S. Mafia saying they were plotting for world domination. It's a little silly. That's Baghdad Bob talk. Nonsense. These are mostly just highly organized gangsters who can do damage. The only real motivation for many of these terrorists is simply to steal, kill, and destroy. They falsely use Islam, like the KKK uses Christianity, to promote their very non-Islamic desires (killing). Many are monsters who only care about money and have no regard for human life. (Others are just hungry and pissed at their corrupt rulers, many of whom the U.S. government supports and props up...some of the terrorists are pretty mad about that). But most of these terrorists are not true Muslims...only people who use it for their own sick ambitions.

Interestingly, in some ways, terrorism has actually helped conservatives promote their desired agenda. Terrorism has successfully distracted our citizens from our own deficiencies and instead focused our attention on a common threat from "outsiders" or "foreigners." It served as a great pretext to go to war. Many of the conservative-friendly defense companies and oil companies (like Haliburton, where Dick Cheney had served as CEO) made billions. It also helped us go over there and try and install some U.S. friendly governments in the region who will hopefully help us get cheap oil along the way.

And here's the *really* fascinating thing: President Ronald Reagan armed the mujahidin in Afghanistan and many believe his administration funded Bin Laden himself! He called them freedom fighters. Conservatives somehow conveniently forget this fact when they fawn over Reagan like some kind of immortal. We armed the Taliban because we were fighting our other mortal enemy, the Soviets, and we ended up helping the very terrorists that we're fighting now. We let the Muslims in Afghanistan (and Iraq) fight our enemies the Soviets (and the Iranians)...and then declared them the enemy. We're like the Joker in the opening scene of the Dark Knight when each bank robber gets killed after he isn't needed anymore. Rather than messing with these people over there, some of whom are indeed terrorists and now kill our troops which are conveniently based on their land, we need to get out of there. We lost 3,000 people on 9-11. But we've lost more than twice as many troops in these wars. The wars are *not* making us safer from terrorism. Many in these countries do NOT want us over there on their land. We need to bring our soldiers home, close our bases in the Middle East, and protect our borders. We are spending trillions of dollars and losing thousands of lives "fighting" (fueling) terrorism.

TSA and Airport Security

It probably shouldn't surprise you that I am not a big fan of the TSA. Like police, I have met some very, very professional, polite, and courteous TSA officers. Most of the agents at the airports in Phoenix and Austin are great. But, in many other airports, they aren't very professional, polite, or courteous. And we increasingly grow tired of them groping us, our children, and our elderly in the name of safety.

This issue is an extremely complex one. The reality is that there are evil people in this world who would like to do evil things and kill innocent people. That's real. But, I think it's not unreasonable to step back and ask, "Are the things that you're asking us to do *actually* making us safer?" It's true that there are dangerous terrorists plotting to kill Americans who could use planes again as a means to do so. But, if I asked you to stand on your head in order to keep the terrorists away, surely you wouldn't just do it, would you? Isn't it reasonable to ask whether or not the things our government asks us to do actually make us safer and then, even if they do, are they worth it? And then with limited resources, I think it's fair to ask if the resources being spent on keeping Americans safe are being spent in the best way. I also think some liberal Americans feel resentment that it's the government's policies that sometimes help cause these people to hate us and then *our* comforts and civil liberties are what suffer the most.

I question whether patting down 90 year old women in wheel chairs makes us safer. I question whether patting down little children makes us safer. I question whether it's necessary for TSA agents to be so rude and abrasive. I don't think it is since some of them seem to manage to do their job and do it with a smile. And that's just it: some of them are just doing a job to earn a paycheck. They understand travelers' frustrations and try to make it painless on them. Others, however, seem to feel like they're on some holy mission that everybody should just accept. They're rude and abrasive. How does that make us safer?

And is any of this stuff *really* making us safer? Sure, there will always be holes in security. That shouldn't cause someone to advocate just making more holes. But look at how many people have managed to get guns, stun guns, and other dangerous items through our security. We're pouring billions of dollars into TSA, which has advocated all of these invasive procedures like groping and naked photos, and yet there are still holes. How much safer do these intrusive measures make us?

And is it worth the cost to our civil liberties? It might be. After a major terrorist attack, travel halts, the stock market plunges, and...oh yeah...lives are lost. The consequences of even one major attack are so great, it might be worth doing anything possible to try and prevent it. People bitched recently about being photographed naked. But airline travel in August of 2001 was over 60 million and then, in September of 2001, it dropped to under 40 million...a one-third drop in passengers[28]. Smaller airlines went out of business. The market consolidated into the hands of a smaller number of bigger players. Annual revenues in the airline industry worldwide fell by about $20 billion between 2000 and 2002, creating huge losses for airlines[29]. And so these are the kinds of things (including jobs... and human lives) that the government is worried about. It's too bad human nature leads to such extreme reactions following traumatic terrorist attacks on planes. It's going to lead to the kind of heavy-handed approaches to air travel safety that we're seeing. Because, despite all of the bitching, air passenger travel is still far higher than just after 9-11. Americans say they hate all of the security procedures, but as long as the revenues are still there, the U.S. will do whatever they feel like they need to do to prevent another attack. The risks are just so large.

Snowden, Manning, and the U.S. Government's Spying

What an incredible story. This story broke literally RIGHT after I sent this book off for print. I just couldn't believe it. This is easily one of the most amazing stories of my lifetime. Here you have the government of the United States, "the free-est country in the word", where we are more free than everybody else (Thank God for those freedoms, right?), was collecting our e-mails and the data on who we were calling. If that was the entire story that would have been a pretty big bomb shell. That wasn't even hardly the beginning of the story.

It's hard to know where to begin but you'd think it is only appropriate to begin with the source of the story, Edward Snowden. A traitor to some (an opinion that I frankly have no respect for), a hero to others (certainly a hero of mine), but perhaps an enigma to most, Edward Snowden decided to fuck with the most powerful country on the planet and reveal their dirty secrets and tyranny. And make no mistake about it, that country (the U.S., of course) was fucking pissed (the second half of this book will discuss profanity, but make no mistake about it, the U.S. government was more than just a little angry that this gentleman decided that the American people deserved to know that their government was collecting data on them...and so, so much more).

And Snowden was smart to get the hell out of Dodge. Obviously he'd be in jail right now, sitting and waiting for God knows how long before they put him on some kind of secret trial (for "state security reasons" "to protect classified information" of course). I'm not sure Russia is heaven, but freedom beats a U.S. government supermax prison most days. His journey was amazing. He fled to Hong Kong hoping that they would protect him. There was much speculation as to why he chose Hong Kong. I really believe he thought he had three possible layers of protection there (all of which ended up failing him). One hope was that the Hong Kong people and their values would protect him. Historically, Hong Kong has been an advocate of freedom of speech (and have had their own battles with the Mainland over free speech and privacy issues) and I am quite sure that Snowden hoped the people would come to his defense. And they did, but he also needed them to sway the local politicians' and officials' minds. And make no mistake about it, the U.S. government applied every bit of pressure they could, to everybody they were able to, in order to try to arrest Mr. Snowden. They were trying to smoke him out of any possible hole that he might climb in. On top of Hong Kong's historic support of free speech, I believe Snowden hoped that the Hong Kong and Beijing governments (Beijing has final say on Hong Kong's foreign policy decisions) would protect him because he had evidence that the U.S. government was spying on them. Now, certainly that caused those governments a loss of face that they'd have to decide how to deal with. But, it's not like those governments didn't already know the U.S. government was spying on them. Most intelligent people knew. Countries spy on each other...even friends (as Snowden would later help prove). Hell, Israel has been caught spying on the U.S. several times. And they're like supposedly our BFF. The final reason I really believe Snowden was hoping that the Chinese government would offer him safe harbor is that Snowden knew that the U.S. government had offered asylum to Chinese dissident Chen Guangcheng. When blind Chinese political activist Chen Guangcheng escaped his village in eastern China and fled to the American embassy in Beijing (claiming political asylum), the U.S. government embarrassed China by offering him a chance to study in the U.S. They protected China's political escapee. I think Snowden was really hoping China would decide it was worth returning the favor to the U.S. But I think he underestimated America's resolve to get him and the importance of the Chinese-U.S. relationship.

But China let him slip out the backdoor, even if they didn't let him stay in Hong Kong, and he ended up taking a trip to Russia. Now, this was supposed to be just a short-term stop in the airport. You see, he had to fly on routes that didn't stop in U.S. friendly countries (where he'd immediately be arrested) and couldn't even fly *over* U.S. friendly countries (because the U.S. was actually demanding friendly countries pull any plane suspected of carrying Snowden over their territories out of the sky so they could arrest him immediately. They even forced the plane of the Bolivian President to land in Austria after it was suspected...falsely... of carrying Mr. Snowden). The U.S. was desperate to arrest Mr. Snowden, no matter what extreme measures had to be taken. Letting the American people and the world know to what extent the U.S. government was spying on them sometimes seemed to make Edward Snowden more wanted by the U.S. government than even Osama Bin Laden was back in the waning years of the Bush administration. Isn't that interesting? Well, after weeks in limbo as a ping pong ball in a match between Russian President Vladimir Putin and U.S. President Barack Obama, Putin offered to give Snowden asylum, at least for now.

One thing that I think is fascinating to contemplate is the comparison between Edward Snowden's story and the story of a man by the name of Robert Seldon Lady. Around the same time the Snowden story was just everywhere, I was up late one night and noticed a small note at the top of every single news website that I scan that announced that ex-CIA agent Robert Seldon Lady had appeared and been taken into custody by Panama. Well, now that sounded like an interesting story. So, I did a little research. As it turns out, Robert Seldon

Lady was an Italy-based American CIA agent, who in 2003 was ordered to kidnap an Egyptian-born radical Islamic cleric off the streets of Milan, fly him to (ironically) his home country of Egypt (who was a U.S. ally and, 10 years later, would experience a second revolution in less than two years), where he was interrogated and tortured by the U.S. CIA. Wow. And Italy (who some claim knew about the operation in advance...though the government denied it) went on to convict Robert Seldon Lady even though he had since fled the country and literally completely fucking disappeared. It's amazing how those CIA guys do that. And then ten years later, this guy appears out of nowhere in Panama, where he was taken into custody. This guy disappeared for ten years and then magically reappeared in U.S. friendly Panama (and then strangely disappeared again...how do they DO that?).

Now, Italy had long had an international request out for this guy. He was a convicted criminal in Italy. The U.S. was PISSED when Hong Kong (China) had let Snowden leave for Russia (and Russia was protecting him) despite a legal Interpol request for his arrest. Well...who do you think Panama, one of the U.S. government's closest regional allies, sent Mr. Lady to? Italy? Or the U.S.? That's right, my friends. They sent him home. You think the U.S. government will ever send Mr. Lady back to Italy to go to prison for the crimes he was convicted of and for which there's an Interpol request out for his arrest and extradition to Italy? Hell no. And not only does that just reek of hypocrisy, what is the lesson that can really be learned from this? If you dare let the American people know to what extent the U.S. government reads their e-mails and spies on them, then the U.S. government will fucking crush you and chase you around the world for the rest of your life. But if you kidnap (radical) Islamic clerics and torture them in Egypt at the request of the U.S. government...then they've got your back. "America, America. God shed his grace on thee. And crown thy good with brotherhood from sea to shining sea!"

And we can not have a chapter discussing this issue of classified information and the U.S. government's attempts to keep embarrassing information out of the hands of the public without also mentioning the case of whistleblower Bradley Manning (I apologize to Mr. Manning in that I am a HUGE supporter of his, I hope with all of my heart that the U.S. government will free him, and that he'll have the ability one day to find a man he loves and marry him...but I ain't calling him Chelsea. Sorry, man...). Here you have another guy who has become an enemy of the state and will spend decades behind bars because he told the U.S. government's dirty little secrets (including releasing information about the carnage going on in Iraq and videos like the one with the U.S. militarily somewhat carelessly attacking and killing what turned out to be journalists). Are we sure that this is about supposedly protecting our troops and keeping America safe and not protecting Uncle Sam's reputation and interests?

Because there's still more to these stories than just Mr. Snowden's amazing journey (and the complex reactions it set off from various countries with their own interests and values) or Bradley Manning's imprisonment (and gender identity). There are also the questions about whether what they did was right or not...and also the question of whether what the U.S. government is doing is right or not. First, we must ask what exactly their crime was. Their crime, we're told, was illegally releasing classified information. Well, first of all, why did they do that? They both said that they legitimately believed that the programs of the U.S. military and the intelligence machine were wrong and illegal and that the American people had a right to know. Given what has since come to light about the full extent of the programs, I think that seems quite reasonable. The U.S. government argues that there were other channels they both could have used to express their concerns without illegally releasing classified information to the public. That seems very hard to say. You're having judges and civilian defense department employees, who are often appointed by the President, making the ultimate decision (in secret) as to whether or not the Executive branch (via the CIA and NSA) is legally allowed to collect e-mail, phone, and internet data on American citizens. I would argue the system had already failed (at a bare minimum with regards to the lack of transparency and the inability of Americans to have a voice in the decision) and that there was no reason to believe anything short of pressure from the American people would ever be effective in reducing or limiting the expansion of these top secret programs. Honestly, Americans just deserve to know. Not to mention that the Fourth Amendment (remember that one?) is nearly dead (thanks to both Bush AND Obama).

An old friend of mine from high school, who really did play a very important role in making this book become a reality, really pressed me about an assumption I'd been making in this chapter up until this point: that the U.S. government spying on us is actually bad. Up until now, I've basically ignored that narrative out there that says: "these things are for your protection and if you're not doing anything wrong then you have nothing to worry about." As an aside, it absolutely amazes me that the vast majority of people who take this position are the very first people to talk about the government boogeyman stealing their tax money. How they reconcile the fact that the government is evil, political, and incompetent with, "But we do want them spying on our phone calls to keep us safe," is beyond me. But besides this strange cognitive dissonance, there certainly still is some amount of truth to the fact that there are evil people that want to do us harm and the government should have the ability to take at least some reasonable steps in order to protect us. So, what's the harm of these programs really? Well, for that, let's recall what Edward Snowden claimed the risks were during that first interview that he gave in Hong Kong:

"Because even if you're not doing anything wrong, you're being watched and recorded. And the storage capability of these systems increases every year, consistently, by orders of magnitude. It's getting to the point where you don't have to have done anything wrong, you just eventually have to fall under suspicion from somebody, even if it's by a wrong call, and then they can use the system to go back in time and scrutinize every decision you've ever made, every friend you've ever discussed something with, and attack you on that basis to sort of derive suspicion from an innocent life and paint anyone in the context of a wrong-doer." Later in the interview he says, "And the months ahead, the years ahead, it's only going to get worse until, eventually, there will be a time when policies will change, because the only thing that restricts the activities of the surveillance state is policy. Even our agreements with foreign governments, we consider that to be a stipulation of policy rather than a stipulation of law. And, because of that, a new leader will be elected, they'll flip the switch, say that because of the crisis, because of the dangers that we face in the world--some new and unpredicted threat-- we need more authority, we need more power. And there will be nothing the people can do at that point to oppose it and it will be turnkey tyranny."

Now God knows I hate slippery slope arguments. Slippery slope arguments are often straight out of the Logical Fallacies 101 Textbook and state that a fairly small action will cause a chain of events leading to a much bigger effect. For example, some crazy people on the right claim that if we allow two adult people of the same sex to marry then the next step is to eventually allow pedophilia and bestiality. Some people believe that. Because they're crazy, dishonest, and/or idiotic. But this is a textbook slippery slope argument.

Yet, are all slippery slope arguments fallacies? Do small events sometimes lead down paths that don't ever seem to turn around or even stabilize? For those conservatives on the right, would you agree that once you start a government program, it seems difficult or impossible to end it? That government tends to get bigger on its own and not smaller? That as people become dependent (on the government, for example), that it can lead to a real risk of a lifetime of dependency (in some cases)? If you agreed with all of those things (and to a limited degree so do I), how can conservatives on the right not also see how when you give the government sweeping powers to do whatever they want to do as long as they say it will keep us safe...that the government (yes, that "evil" government that conservatives say they hate) might one day abuse those powers in the future? Many of these same right wingers who are convinced that the IRS and the Obama administration was politically targeting them (I have no idea what to make of it personally, but I haven't been impressed at all with the administration's transparency on the issue) want the government to have the ability to monitor everything we do. That is an incredible amount of trust in government that I really can't imagine how anybody feels like they've earned it. The truth is that Americans enjoy great freedom now. But the spying programs give the government an easy, easy way of taking away many of those freedoms overnight should they want to (or say they need to).

The potential for abuse is high and the government often seems to allow Americans to be the frogs in boiling water, by gradually taking their rights away over time so that they don't even notice.

So, those are the risks. Those seem like pretty big risks. Let's re-acknowledge a couple of things. First, once again, the threats (from terrorists) are real. The Oklahoma City Bombing really happened. 9-11 really happened. There are evil people out there who want to kill lots of other people. And they cause death and fear and financial damage and all of those things. But there are also major risks associated with granting government the power to monitor everything we do. Plus, as alluded to in the TSA chapter: we should also ask if the actions that the government is taking are REALLY making us safer...AND if they're worth it.

So, let's start with the question of whether the government spy programs are actually making us safer. The reason this is so important is that if the government is asking to collect and analyze our phone data and to have the power and ability to monitor our phone calls and e-mails, then those activities should result in keeping us significantly safer in order for them to be worthwhile. For example, if the government told everybody to chew gum or carry around garlic and crosses to keep the terrorists away surely everybody wouldn't just do it, would they? (Would they?) So, the question is: are all of the government's spy programs actually making us safer? Well, first of all, we can't really know because we pretty much just have to take their word for it (and I'm sure they don't have any incentive to lie or stretch the truth in order to keep their budgets and powers. Remember, it's a scary world out there...lucky for them). Don't you see? If they tell you about how the programs helped keep us safe, then that will help the terrorists. So you sit down, be quiet, and trust that they've got your best interests in mind, sweetheart. It won't hurt. They promise. The number of attacks prevented has been exaggerated as high as 54, but the reality seems to be closer to low single digits. But how can we ever really know since they can't/won't tell us or prove it?

In addition to asking whether the government's spy programs are actually effective, the other key question that we need to ask ourselves is: are they worth it? Believe it or not, a prison can be a very safe place (assuming you're not in a cell, I guess). Lots of armed guards. Everybody who goes in gets screened (well, they're supposed to). Airports are actually very safe places. But I wouldn't want to live in those places. There's no doubt that there must be some balance struck between being willing to give up some minor amount of privacy in order to effectively protect people from modern day threats and demanding that we retain a free society (although people would certainly be wise to consider the words of Benjamin Franklin: "Those who would give up essential Liberty, to purchase a little temporary Safety, deserve neither Liberty nor Safety"). Ultimately, do I want to live in a terrorism-free society if that means I have to allow the government to monitor everything I do? For me, it's not worth it but I guess everybody has to make that decision for themselves. It really seems worth pointing out, even if only for a brief second, that countries like Switzerland, who do not support Israel's occupation or have bases in the Middle East, seem to stay relatively safe from terrorism without spying on their own citizens. Strange how they manage to pull something like that off.

This government, our government, has basically been acting like a mafia boss whose secret records have been stolen. They've pulled a South American head of state's plane out of the sky to try and find Snowden. They had a reporter's partner detained and harassed at the airport in the U.K. and have basically trapped Edward Snowden in Russia. All because they didn't want Americans and world leaders to know the extent to which the U.S. government was spying on them. The U.S. government has imprisoned a member of the military who released details about the violent, accidental, and arguably careless killing of journalists by the U.S. military. They say these actions protect us. But they mainly seem to protect the U.S. government. Do these seem like the actions of a benevolent government solely concerned with the protection of its citizens? Or the actions of a government and intelligence machine that has gotten too big to control? Are we certain these are the people we want to be giving all of these powers to?

I want to simply end with one more quote from Edward Snowden, the man who was making six figures, living in Hawaii with his girlfriend, when he decided that he was willing to throw it all away because he felt like people deserved the right to know that the government was watching them. He said, "The greatest fear that I have regarding the outcome, for America, of these disclosures is that nothing will change. People will see in the media all of these disclosures, they'll see the lengths the government's going to grant themselves powers unilaterally to create greater control over American society and global society, but they won't be willing to take the risks necessary to stand up and fight to change things, to force their representatives to actually take a stand in their interests."

The Middle East

Our "friends," the Saudis (and the Egyptians), HATE the Iranians. And many Iranians *are* kind of elitist Persian a-holes. *And* they fight dirty. But then so do most of the Middle Eastern countries. But Iran *is* probably the worst. However, it is also worth noting that the war propaganda against Iran is absurd.

There's really, in some ways, a modern day Cold War going on in the Middle East. For years, Russia had been making millions of dollars selling Iran military weapons and uranium. Russia is also close allies with Syria, who is a huge ally of Iran. In fact, when the old Soviet Union chose to arm Saddam and Iraq during Iraq's conflict with Iran, Iran was still able to obtain Soviet weapons via Syria. Syria and Iran both try to exert influence on Syria's neighbor Lebanon. Without Syria and Iran's support and influence, Hezbollah would not have as much power as they do in Lebanon. So these three countries: Iran, Syria, and Lebanon have very close ties and there is at least some connection with this group and Russia.

Iraq, which we will come back to later in the chapter, was previously controlled by Saddam, who was an Arab Sunni Muslim. Iran, meanwhile, is mostly Persian Shia Muslims. However, interestingly, Iraq is predominantly an Arab Shia country and their Prime Minister, post US-invasion, is an Arab Shia Muslim with ties to Iran. The new Iraqi government is *much* friendlier with Iran, who is the greatest evil in the region, than Saddam ever was. Saddam *hated* Iran and, as alluded to previously, even went to war with them. Syria, with their connection to the bloc with Iran, had a very strained relationship with Iraq. And both Iran and Syria border Iraq. Interestingly, now that Iraq is led by a Shia Muslim, their leaders greatly worry about what will happen in the country if Sunni Muslim rebels successfully win control of Syria. How might the Sunnis in Iraq respond or would the rebels then look next door? So by overthrowing Saddam's government, we made Iraq much more vulnerable and drove it closer to the most dangerous countries in the region.

Running counter to the group centered around Iran, Syria, and Russia is a group that is led by Saudi Arabia, the U.S., and with Israel in the background. The dynamics of the relationship between those three countries is just remarkable. Basically, America is the Saudis' biggest customer. To keep us happy, Saudi Arabia, along with Turkey, provide Israel with the Middle Eastern support they need to help keep them from being attacked (even though both countries actually really detest Israel, but not as much as they both hate and fear Iran).. This bloc, which also contained Egypt, includes several Middle Eastern monarchies that we help support (such as Kuwait, Jordan, Bahrain, etc.). This bloc is one reason why America turning their back on Mubarak in Egypt upset the Saudis so much: because it made the Saudis worry that the Americans might be willing to leave them out to dry, too. The United States supports (and even helps establish) kings and evil dictators in the Middle East that we think will be friendly to us and sell us cheap oil. That is a fact. Minus the alleged sinister nuclear goals, the Saudi regime is every bit as backwards and despotic as the Iranian regime. And yet Americans don't have any problems with seeing pictures of George W. Bush holding hands with their king. Is it any surprise that many Arabs in the Middle East hate the U.S. when we prop up the dictators who oppress them?

The role of religion and ethnicity in the politics of Middle Eastern countries is often fascinating. Some countries, like Iran and Saudi Arabia, are at least partially controlled by religious extremists who enforce extremely harsh religious laws. However, most of the people want more freedoms than they have. Other countries, like Turkey and Egypt, have traditionally had more secular governments lately, while much of their populations have wanted religion to play a bigger role in their government. The diversity in many of these countries is also fascinating. Iraq has three major ethnic groups: the Kurds in the north, the Shias in the south (the largest group), and the Sunnis. Turkey also has Kurds in the southern part of its country, bordering Iraq. The Kurds in Turkey's south and the Kurds in Iraq's north both would like to have their own country, but of course neither Turkey nor Iraq wants to give up their land for such a state. And the U.S., which claims to support people's freedom and autonomy, has chosen to appease the Turkish and Iraqi governments rather than supporting the creation of an independent Kurdish state. Syria, which borders Iraq and is currently going through a civil war, is also an interesting case. Syria is very diverse. Although Sunni Muslims are nearly 75% of the population, Syria also has Alawites (who currently control the country and are fighting to the death to maintain that control) as well as Christians. Neighboring Lebanon is also a diverse country, with a little more than half the country being Muslim (with half of the Muslims being Sunni and half Shia) and another large portion being Christian. Syria and Iran constantly try to influence Lebanon, especially through their support of Hezbollah.

This is an extremely basic look at the political landscape of the Middle East right now. However, if there is a continued Arab Spring, and more states follow the way of Egypt, Yemen, Libya, and likely Syria...well, the political landscape in the Middle East has historically been pretty fluid. The U.S. backed Saddam and then turned on him. They supported the Taliban and then turned on them. You know the U.S. will do what they think is in their best interest, but I think what is *really* in the U.S.' best interest is to take their bases out of that place, try to trade with those countries, and otherwise mind their own business. The U.S. has bases over there to protect its oil interests and supports evil monarchs...and then acts surprised when they aren't liked there.

Peace in Israel

I think this problem is obviously extremely complicated. To some degree, it is obviously silly to compare the moral positions of extremist Muslims and most Jews. Incredibly silly. But I also don't believe it's even remotely close to as simple as, "Israel is right and wants peace and Muslims are wrong and want war." I think it's way, way, way more complicated than that. Obviously most people have never been to Gaza or the West Bank. And let's be honest, MOST Americans haven't ever been to Israel, either...or probably even talked to anybody FROM Israel. I was lucky at Shabbat services to talk to a few Israelis who were studying in the U.S. and they definitely give you some unique insights into their daily lives and how the threats affect them.

However, I've also been fortunate to talk to some people from Gaza and the West Bank. Compared to the average Israeli, the things they see from day to day are very different. I think Israelis obviously put the majority of the blame for the Palestinians' plight on the Palestinians' own leaders. And there's probably a lot of truth to that. *And* there's probably some truth to the fact that the reason Israel treats them like shit, frankly, is because they legitimately must worry about the Palestinians attacking them. But, Israel has occupied Palestinian territory for decades now. They continue to expand their settlements. They've been stalling and refusing to allow for a Palestinian state for decades, as well. I never advocate violence, but whatever peace the Palestinians have offered has never worked. And then, Israel frequently responds to attacks disproportionately, basically bulldozing entire neighborhoods in Gaza and the West Bank after rocket attacks and suicide bombs. Israel's treatment of the Palestinian people has been ruthless at times, not only occupying Palestinian land, but restricting their economic opportunities, as well. Palestinians live like caged prisoners in their land, unable to freely come and go or buy and sell goods. And yet the U.S. has consistently unilaterally supported Israel almost no matter what they have done.

There is no good side in this fight. Only bad sides. Just one side (Hamas) is probably worse than the other. Israel really has little morally defensible ground to stand on, if you've spoken to enough Palestinians. If you disagree, how many Palestinian citizens have you spoken to? The leaders of Hamas ARE evil. They ARE corrupt and they DO help cause their people to live in poverty. They DO lie to them and inflame tensions in the region. That keeps them in power.

But what about the average Palestinian? "Why would they vote for Hamas?" Well, why WOULDN'T they vote for Hamas? Not only has peace failed to deliver the Palestinians their own state, Hamas takes the money they make from illegal drug and weapons sales and gives some of it back to the people to build schools and hospitals. The whole "kill the Jews" agenda, for the average Palestinian, is either something they tolerate, or an added bonus as a response to the oppression they've experienced at the hands of Israel. It happens after somebody kicks you off your land and then comes in and bulldozes your neighborhoods. Sure I understand why Israel does things like that, but you HAVE to try and see things from the other perspective. You have to try. And one of Israel's biggest faults lies there: they never try and see anything from the Palestinian perspective. Only their own. True negotiation can never work like that. Their brutal actions and mistreatment of Palestinians only ensures the conflict will never end.

Most people feel like "if A is true, then B can not be true." One of these two groups must be "right"...or at least "almost right." But I don't think either side is right. They both disgust me, frankly. I think when you talk to secular Jews or even some religious Zionist Jews who support the nation of Israel, you will find that some of them are also frustrated with the Israeli government and the way they have handled "the peace process." And many of those have been to Israel. Everybody knows Hamas commits terrorist acts. But how many know about the terrorist-like actions and land grabs done by Netanyahu and other Israeli leaders like him in the past? The only solution to the violence in Israel is a real exchange of land for peace and the creation of a Palestinian state. However, densely populated Israel will almost certainly never agree to this, under the guise of security concerns, even though they'd always be stronger than any Palestinian state. But honestly, they want that land. More than they want peace.

China

I love China and I love Chinese people. I have little doubt that they are the greatest civilization ever. However, they have often suffered at the hands of bad rulers. The Chinese people have not had it easy, by any means. And yet their traditional culture, their grace, and the way about many of them are so great. Many people have this same experience when they interact with China. Yet, we also know that China is far from perfect. For one, China has for centuries (and perhaps millennia) suffered from a dangerous subculture of cheating. There are a very large number of Chinese people (a minority but a large enough minority) who are just simply cheaters and crooks. They'd probably cheat their own mother. And it's not just lower class people cheating to survive. This cheating subculture shows up in the way they do business and the way they govern. And there are no limits to how far people will sink in order to cheat others out of their money. One company went as far as to sell milk for babies...that was actually toxic. The Chinese people like this have absolutely no conscience or morals.

China is a country that, as I mentioned, has suffered. I would first argue that Mao was a pretty terrible leader. He did a few good things. China had long suffered from warring factions. China, in many ways, was just another country plagued by civil wars and coups. China endured many kings and many dynasties. Sometimes, they would enjoy success under the rule of a good king. However, inevitably a corrupt king would take power and the dynasty would get overthrown. Or China would be invaded by outsiders, including Japan. Mao, quite ruthlessly, united and protected China from foreign enemies. He did it violently, at times. And he did a terrible job of governing that unified China. But he did unify it. Mao also saw the corruption that existed in the previous system that he fought against. It's just unfortunate that Mao also craved power and had completely disastrous policies.

And brave men like Deng Xiaoping, and even more so Zhao Ziyang, suffered at the hands of Mao. Yet they endured and fought their way back to be able to take control and lead China out of those dark times. Deng was like a better version of Gerald Ford, helping the country move forward and heal from the painful Mao years. And men like Zhao Ziyang stood by the side of the Chinese people and tried to bring them the political reforms that they deserved. Unfortunately, too many powerful people were not ready for that. And Zhao Ziyang lost. And Jiang Zemin and Li Peng later came in and really slowed down China's true progress. Sure foreign investment and GDP increased, but Jiang and Li really damaged the rural areas in a country that is still heavily rural. They shut them out of the economy. And it was wrong. They also slowed down the growth of the private sector and increased the influence of the state on the economy.

Most recently, China had been under the leadership of Hu Jintao and Wen Jiabao. I think these men did a pretty good job of easing into reforms: primarily economic, but also some political. However, the reforms haven't come as quickly as anybody wants, or even as quickly as they are needed. But people must also try and understand the very complex political situation in China. Nobody controls that country alone; it is very much an oligarchy. There are some very rich and powerful interests that try and keep the status quo: because that is what is best for those people, personally. There is tons of corruption. And it's threatening the entire People's Republic. However, I think China's new leaders seem to be trying to walk that delicate tight rope act towards reforms. The Chinese people need their leaders to have the courage necessary to make the changes needed to save the People's Republic.

Part of those reforms should allow local businesses to raise capital and start businesses more freely. So far, China has still too heavily relied on foreign investment, foreign technology, and foreign demand (and government directed investment). China's position in the world economy has been, "Come and rent our cheap labor and buy our cheap goods and supplies." However, those are "low value-add" activities. They don't create high margins of profits. They typically earn little money in comparison to the businesses who design the products that China manufactures. They also need to break up state monopolies and reform the financial sector so that private businesses have better access to capital, compared with many inefficient state-owned companies and local provincial governments. Finally, they must hold local and national government officials accountable.

Another problem is that China has made tons of money, but much of it is in the form of IOU's. They own over $3 trillion in foreign currency...much of it in the form of loans they made to the U.S. (by buying U.S. Treasuries our government issues). It's a vicious cycle for China. They loan us money that we use (often indirectly) to buy more of their stuff. If we stop buying their stuff, then they don't have the internal demand to keep their economy going (because a relatively small number of Chinese have gotten rich, while many poor have stopped seeing real wage increases since the 80's...keeping Chinese demand for goods relatively low). But if they keep loaning the U.S. and Europe money through the purchase of sovereign bonds, they run the risk of one day not getting paid back if these countries default. That is why China has been using their foreign currency holdings the last several years to buy commodities, such as oil and minerals. Although the U.S.' total trade deficit with China from October of 2010 until September of 2012 was about $500 billion, China's U.S. Treasury holdings stayed the same at around $1.1

trillion[30]. That tells me they've been taking the money they earn from selling stuff to us and are using it to fund these big commodity purchases in Africa, South America, and Australia. Dambisa Moya's recent book, entitled *Winner Takes All: China's Race for Resources and What it Means for the World*, is an excellent resource for learning more about how smart the Chinese government has been acquiring these resources.

The relationship between the U.S. and China is a very interesting one. Over the last couple of decades, the two countries have really depended on each other... but also took advantage of one another. The U.S. needed the Chinese to lend it the money it needed (through Treasury purchases) to fund its wars and massive deficits. The U.S. also needed cheap Chinese goods to help keep prices down for consumers. However, those cheap Chinese goods came at the expense of many Americans' jobs. The U.S. also accused China of manipulating its currency (keeping it artificially low to make their exported goods cheaper) at the same time that the U.S. was expanding its own monetary base (devaluing its own currency)...and also at the same time that the U.S. was doing everything short of begging China to lend it more money by buying more Treasuries. Recently, China has made headlines for hacking many U.S. government agencies (and even private corporations). But the U.S. made headlines a decade ago when a U.S. spy plane crashed off the coast of China (probably China intentionally bumped the plane out of the sky). Can you imagine if Chinese spy planes were flying off the coast of California? What kind of outrage and paranoid fear would Americans display? But it's okay when we spy on them. Listen, countries spy on each other. That's what countries do. I'm not excusing it, but Americans who didn't already think that our country was trying to hack into Chinese government computers before Snowden leaked the documents showing that the U.S. government was, in fact, spying on pretty much everybody were either being dishonest or were retarded.

The question is going to be what does the future relationship between the two countries look like. President Obama has already made a pivot with his military strategy, putting more focus on the Asia-Pacific region. The U.S. is sending clear messages that they are keeping their eye on China. And one could argue that these aren't friendly messages. How would Americans feel if Chinese warships were traveling closer and closer to the U.S. Pacific coast? The two countries have long been considered "frenemies." Part friends. Part enemies. Personally, I think it's much better for the world if both countries stay closer to friends than enemies. However, it seems quite clear the U.S. feels threatened by China's rise. It'll be interesting to watch how several things play out between the two countries. One is the Diaoyu Islands conflict. The U.S. put the disputed islands under the control of Japan after World War II, despite the fact that historically they had belonged to China (prior to when they were "annexed" by Japan after the Sino-Japanese War). And as the two countries both increasingly look to claim control over the islands and their resources (not to mention stir up nationalism in their respective countries), the U.S. has vowed to support Japan in any conflict. Another thing to watch is how much the yuan is able to grow in its use in global trade and the possibility it might one day replace the U.S. dollar as the world's reserve currency. That would be a global game changer.

If China is to continue to grow, however, then it must make reforms, end the corruption in their government, allow the Chinese poor and middle class to engage in business, and build internal demand to drive their economy in the future. This will allow all of the Chinese people to win instead of just those with government connections. China faces several key challenges in the coming years. One is their demographic situation. Like the U.S. (and much of the western world, actually), China has an aging population with a large number of seniors soon to be supported by a declining number of young people. This will put strains on their economy and their people. It will create strains on their pension system. To the country's advantage, however, China does not have the same level of retirement benefits (and liabilities) that most western countries do. Second, as wages continue to rise in China, it will cause companies to begin to manufacture some things elsewhere cheaper, hurting China's exports and jobs. Fortunately, as wages rise, hopefully internal demand will increase and replace some of the lost jobs. Third, largely because of its own real estate bubble, companies and provinces alike are facing major challenges staying afloat. Many inefficient, state owned companies are losing money and need to be reformed...even if it risks jobs. I hope that China's new leader, Xi Jinping, continues to turn China around so that all the Chinese people can prosper. If he can keep the progress going, then one day, China will become the most powerful nation in the world. But this goal can never be realized until they first reform and also invest more in their most important asset: their human capital, their people. I wish the 1.3 billion Chinese people happiness and the best of luck and hope our two countries can maintain peaceful relations in the future.

European Debt Crisis

Although it may seem unrelated to the U.S., in today's global economy, this is very much a story that is related to the U.S. and, indeed, is controversial. Perhaps that is why starting in December of 2011, the U.S. Federal Reserve quietly engaged in unlimited currency swaps with the European Central Bank, taking what could be extremely risky Euros onto its balance sheet in exchange for U.S. dollars. They did so in order to help European banks maintain liquidity and help prevent some of them from collapsing. Although many mainstream media sources would rather talk about simpler and less important domestic stories (some of which very well might be initially more interesting to their target audiences), the European debt crisis is simply far too big of a story to ignore. Especially given the facts that the EU, as a bloc, is one of America's largest trading partners and many large U.S. banks have exposure to European sovereign debt (and associated derivatives).

A reasonable question is how did Europe get into this mess, a mess that poses a threat to the entire global economy. There are several contributing factors. One factor is an issue of spending. Similar to the United States, actually, many western countries (democracies, in particular), have been living outside their means. In an effort to drum up votes, politicians in many European countries have promised benefits to voters that their countries simply could not afford. This is particularly true in countries like Italy, Greece, Portugal, etc. Governments already have begun cutting public sector (government) workers to try and reduce deficits (exacerbating the unemployment problems in these countries). However, as interest rates rise on these countries with excessive debt levels, it creates larger interest payments for the countries and leaves even less money for government jobs and investment. However, there is also an issue of competitiveness. Many of these countries enjoy high salaries, creating high labor costs for businesses that make them uncompetitive with companies or manufacturers in emerging markets, places like China and India (or even EU partners like Germany) where labor costs are much lower or productivity is much higher. Combine all of these things with overregulation and protected classes of workers (laws that prevent new workers from entering a field and competing with existing workers by offering lower prices) and what you get is incredibly high unemployment (over 25% now in Spain and Greece). High unemployment often further increases the costs of social benefits (like unemployment) for the countries and also decreases the amount of tax revenue they collect.

So, if those are some of the causes, what are the actual major global risks that result from the European debt crisis? Well, basically, there are two major risks. One results from the fact that investors loan sovereign nations (like Greece and Spain) money. Nations use this money to run the government, pay for schools, etc. Banks take depositors' money and buy government debt (supposedly the safest debt) with it to earn a return on people's savings. However, private sector investors already took about a 75% loss on much of the Greek debt they owned[31]. When banks in these European countries officially take losses on the sovereign debt they hold, at best they will not be able to loan out as much money to businesses...and at worst some of them will become bankrupt. As it stands now, Spanish banks are already teetering on the edge of bankruptcy, if they aren't actually bankrupt already. In Spain, one of the biggest problems is all of the bad real estate loans and mal-investment that the banks made. So, one threat is that sovereign defaults cause a collapse of major financial institutions who hold that debt and possibly lead to bank runs.

What happened in Cyprus adds another dimension to the situation. In Cyprus, the government (responding to the demands of the Troika), confiscated depositors' money in excess of 100,000 Euros in order to pay for a bailout of the banks...to prevent them from collapsing. Then, the people were prohibited from having complete access to their own money, in order to prevent people from pulling out all of their money and starting a bank run. We were assured that the confiscation of accounts over 100,000 Euros was only done so that Europe wouldn't be bailing out Russian hot money (that was being kept in Cyprus). But don't be surprised if you see savers get wiped out again in the future in other countries. If so, who knows what will happen. The banks in much of Europe are already hanging on by a very thin thread, full of nonperforming loans and increasingly dangerous sovereign debt. Even if the story is not being covered by the mainstream media, the truth is both European banks and governments are on the verge of bankruptcy and the "Lehman moment" could happen in the blink of an eye. If one more country confiscates their citizens' savings, other countries with weak banks might see their citizens running to the bank to take out their money before the government takes it. That could lead to a disaster.

Yet another major threat is the threat of a disorderly exit of a country (particularly Greece) from the Euro. In this scenario, the austerity (cost cutting) measures imposed on the Greek people become so unbearable (as their economy falls deeper and deeper into a depression), that the country decides to leave the Euro and return to their own currency. Currently, Greece (and other economically weak countries) share a common currency with stronger Eurozone members like Germany, Finland, and the Netherlands. On their own, Greece, Spain, Portugal, etc. would have currencies that are much weaker/cheaper. This would make their exports cheaper to foreign buyers and thus more attractive. However, instead, sharing a currency with stronger countries makes their currency more expensive than it would be otherwise and forces them to compete against countries like Germany who also use the same currency. Certainly Greece bears much of the responsibility for being so uncompetitive and for having such excessive levels of benefits. However, handcuffing them to stronger countries through a common currency has made Greece's problems much, much worse (it's also benefited Germany by allowing their currency to be weaker than it would be if it had its own currency). If Greece (or another weak peripheral country) were to leave the Euro and return to their own currency, that currency would depreciate by maybe 40% overnight. One night Greeks might go to sleep with Euros in their bank accounts and the next morning they would wake up with drachmas that might easily be worth 40% less than the Euros they had the night before. Citizens in other vulnerable countries would surely see this and run to the banks to get their money out in Euros before their country was next. This could create a run on banks that hasn't been seen since the 1930's. Right now you have an unholy alliance of sorts. You have sovereign governments bailing out banks (often through more taxpayer money) and then those same banks turning around and essentially bailing out the sovereign governments (through purchasing large quantities of sovereign debt). In fact, banking laws are set up to highly encourage, maybe even essentially force banks to invest in their own government's debt, no matter how risky it may be, in reality. A global bank run would be a disaster and much should be done to try and prevent it, but governments have also not done enough to force banks to actually curb risks and make quality loans.

So, what are the possible solutions? One thing the peripheral countries want to do is to create joint debt. Currently, although Germany and Spain use the same currency, they don't issue the same bonds. Germany issues its own debt and Spain and Greece issue their own. These peripheral countries, including France, want to issue Eurobonds, so that Germany and the other northern Euro countries would be liable for their debt. Obviously Germany and the other stronger, less indebted European countries don't want this. Germany wants to establish a European overseer, who would have some control over countries' budgets and be able to tell debtor countries how they can spend their money. From Germany's perspective, it's like having several irresponsible younger brothers. While Germans have studied, worked hard, lived frugally, and saved responsibly, their younger brothers have been careless and wasteful with their money. And now they all want to continuously ask to borrow more money from their older brother (or have him co-sign for their loans). Germany says, "We'll definitely think about it, but we want to have more control over how you spend your money, including the money we loan you." Obviously the weaker countries do not want to give up this kind of national sovereignty, especially to a country that some of them remember being invaded by and fighting against in their lifetimes. Whether or not these countries will be able to find some level of compromise is certainly hard to say. Of course Germany loves sharing a currency with these weaker countries because it helps their exports. But not if that means they keep needing to spend money to bail these countries out.

Theoretically, central banks could also possibly help reduce a country's debt by taking a haircut on the sovereign debt they hold, similar to the haircut they basically forced on private sector investors in Greece. However, national governments and international bodies like the European Central Bank and the International Monetary Fund have been unwilling to do so. Very strange they aren't willing to take the same medicine they forced on others. However, this would still only temporarily alleviate the problem. In the long term, European countries must reduce their reliance on government spending and become more competitive, by becoming more efficient and reducing their bloated labor costs (through a reduction in wages). It's Europe now. America next.

However, how much will western citizens who have become accustomed to a certain lifestyle be willing to accept? Greeks and Spaniards have marched and even rioted in their streets over proposed austerity measures. The French don't even need a reason to strike. It's practically a national hobby. They don't want to accept lower wages or reduced pensions. Or later working ages (in order to receive government benefits). It's also worth asking how much can many of the people in these countries afford to accept? Central bank money printing has created inflation across the world. Those at the top (certainly many of those in finance) have made hundreds of millions and even billions from low interest rates. But how much of that money has actually "trickled down" to those at the bottom of these countries...especially compared to the effect that easy money has had on prices? It's very possible that the austerity measures being introduced in many Eurozone countries will continue to create massive levels of social unrest until it finally reaches a breaking point. Perhaps if the people are willing to go along with the game, the powerful elite will let the status quo basically continue. However, when people throughout Europe finally decide they don't want to play along anymore, that is when the powers at be might finally pull the plug.

The Eurozone is in a lot of trouble. The debt in Europe is like a powerful river starting to burst holes in a dam. As the European governments plug one hole, the pressure merely creates new holes in the dam. Without a radical and unlikely solution, the dam is eventually going to break and flood the world. Many European politicians speak of wanting "more Europe." To debtor countries, this means joint debt (to which Germany will probably never agree to). To Germany, it means a European budget overseer and a loss of national fiscal sovereignty (to which peripheral countries might never agree). Although they've managed to keep Europe together longer than I expected, I don't expect it to last forever. I don't think those living in the Greek and Spanish depressions can stand it. At some point, I expect Europe to break apart and all hell to break loose. I think world leaders will blame the existence of multiple currencies and the lack of an international budget overseer. The beginning of a major change in world history might begin in Europe. Time will tell how the train wreck might end.

Obama

You know...I liked Obama for a pretty long time. I still think he is **light years** ahead of Bush. I think that he's a very intelligent guy who is very thoughtful. I don't think he just rashly makes decisions like Bush. I think he is much more contemplative. And I think that's likely because there's more of an intellectual force there. I think he's more charismatic, he's a better orator, and a very inspiring figure.

And I agree with him on many major policies. I believe that every American should have access to affordable healthcare. I agreed with him on the auto company bailout. I think that was important even if we didn't get all of our money back, in full. Many, many jobs were saved. Those companies likely couldn't have made it through bankruptcy. They were in really bad shape, for one. But, Obama and the Democrats stepped in, capitalized the firms (under the condition they made changes), the entire supply chain of jobs was saved, and America has re-emerged as a leader in the auto industry. He caught Bin Laden. And he did help slow down the economic hemorrhaging that was going on when he took office.

But, in some ways, Obama hasn't been liberal enough. He's kept Guantanamo Bay open when he said he'd close it. He's kept Bradley Manning, the Wikileaks whistleblower, behind bars in a military prison. He kept our troops in Iraq and Afghanistan and authorized the frequent use of drones which sometimes end up killing innocent civilians by mistake (and he's a coward for that). He'd argue that he's helping keep America safer with his policies in the Middle East. I think that every soldier's life that is lost is not worth whatever little amount of safety we *might* have achieved (and I don't think we've achieved much of it at all). He has continued some of the same policies that curb Americans' rights.

And yet, at other times, he has done things that have been *too* liberal. I think his failure to cut corporate tax rates has been a terrible economic policy. Obama has not done enough to try and make America an attractive place to grow jobs. Obama also hasn't led on balancing the budget. Some Democrats point out that the Republican Party has been very obstructionist...and that is true. People needn't forget that Senator Mitch McConnell said early on that the Republicans' primary goal would be to ensure that Obama would be a one term President. Surely they have intentionally tried to ensure that Obama would not win many policy victories. However, Presidents like Bill Clinton also dealt with extremely partisan Republican oppositions, and yet they figured out a way to score legislative victories and achieve many great domestic accomplishments. That's Obama's job. He's got to figure out how to make the deals required to get things done and he hasn't. Plus, he's done other things that were just wrong. He trusted our economy with many of the people, like Larry Summers and Timothy Geithner, who were behind many of the problems that created the financial crisis in the first place. He has been far from forthright about his administration's role in scandals ranging from the cover up of what happened in Benghazi, to the DOJ's investigation of AP reporters, to the DOJ's failed Fast and Furious program, to the failed investment in Solyndra (despite warning signs of financial troubles). He increased access to healthcare, but did nothing to increase the supply of care or anything else that will *really* bring down prices. Worst of all, and he should NEVER be forgiven for this: he signed a law allowing U.S. citizens to be held indefinitely without a trial. This is unconscionable and unforgivable and no American should ever forget this. And then I believe he has done some crony things, as well. I believe he's looked out for the interests of the Wall Street bankers who heavily financed his campaign. He helps out his buddies and campaign donors (like those at Solyndra) just like the rest of them. And here I thought he was going to change Washington. But in many ways, Obama has been a normal politician and even has simply continued many of the exact same questionable policies as his predecessor George W. Bush. We needed real change. We didn't get it.

W

There is hardly a name that makes me physically ill to my stomach like George W. Bush. If I had to sum up everything that was wrong with America, I think I'd just put up his picture. The arrogance. The ignorance. The aggression. It's all there, fully on display for all the world to see. There are Republican Presidents I admire: Dwight Eisenhower, Teddy Roosevelt, and even some aspects of Richard Nixon. That's right. I respect many of the accomplishments of Richard Nixon. But I freaking hate George W. Bush.

Listening to him debate was like being punished. Did Al Gore come across as arrogant and unlikeable? Absolutely. But can you imagine trying to debate a seemingly retarded 50 year old man? George W. Bush is so dumb that I feel like I don't even need to provide any supporting evidence. The people who point to his Ivy League education (the same freaking people that constantly try and blow off the significance of Ivy League educations) just look ridiculous. If there ever was a poster child for silver spoons and nepotism, it's George W. Bush. The guy partied all the way into the 80's. I'm surprised he still remembers who he is. He was the black sheep of the Bush family.

His policies were the most neo-conservative bunch of garbage. He sent us off to war in Iraq and people knew it was BS. Look at how many of his and Dick Cheney's friends got rich. Everybody knew he wanted to go after Saddam Hussein for trying to kill his father. And we all just watched. A friend of Enron, he also hooked up his business buddies in the energy and defense industries. They all made millions. Other foreign leaders didn't respect him. They didn't like him. A lot of Americans may not care about that, but did you just watch what happens when you can't get enough real support from real allies? We need a leader who will help lead peace in the world and not increase violence. I reject everything Bush claims about making the world safer through pre-emptive war. Iraq was not a threat. The Iraq war represented a huge wealth transfer from the taxpayers to private corporations (corporations that were friends and supporters of the Bush Presidency: the people that make bombs and jets and profit off of war...as well as oil companies). We were warned to be on guard against the influence of the military industrial complex. But we were not on guard.

And not only did Bush screw up foreign policy, he screwed up the economy. He ran on that "compassionate conservative" line, which was a load of crap. He cut various social programs. He cut taxes for the rich. He deregulated and supported policies that pumped the system with money by keeping interest rates low and borrowing trillions of dollars from overseas. He cut taxes for the wealthy, and watched the rich get richer and the poor get poorer under his eight years as President. The national debt grew by nearly $5 trillion during his administration (each of the previous three Presidents had only increased the national debt by about $1.6 trillion[32]). Although the real estate bubble had started growing before he showed up, there is almost no doubt that the SEC's lax regulatory oversight under Bush's watch and Bush's endorsement of what I call "extreme Keynesian economics" helped fuel the real estate bubble and financial crisis. Then, he appointed Goldman Sachs CEO Hank Paulson as his Treasury Secretary who led the Treasury while AIG got bailed out and Goldman Sachs got paid 100 cents on the dollar for their derivative contracts that threatened to bankrupt AIG. There is no doubt in my mind that George W. Bush will go down as one of the worst Presidents in the history of this country. By far. I just hope that he didn't help to bring about its end and that the damage can be repaired.

Clinton

Bill, Bill, Bill. What can you say about Bill Clinton? There are just so many things that come to mind. For people who aren't rightwing hyper-partisans, that was a great eight years. It really was. Relative peace. Relative prosperity. Crime dropped dramatically. And I really believe the man did a lot of good. More good than most human beings. But, firstly, in hindsight, I think he got a lot of extra credit on the economy that might have been a little undeserved. And secondly, there is something so undeniably phony and dirty about the man. He's exactly what you think of when you think of politicians.

The eight years under Clinton were great. There were a few small patches of conflict (Haiti, Somalia, Bosnia). And there were also acts of violence against the U.S. (the bombing of the USS Cole, the Oklahoma City bombing, Waco). But through it all, Clinton always seemed calm and in control. Clinton, I believe, was a natural leader. People like him (although certainly a decent share hate him, too). He's the consummate politician. His foreign policies kept us out of major conflicts. And he helped broker and promote peace in many hot spot areas of the world (Ireland, the Middle East stayed fairly calm, as did the Korean peninsula). But I also think most countries knew he wasn't a pushover, either...which probably only further helped the world remain relatively peaceful and stable during Clinton's eight years in office.

I believe many of his economic policies were excellent. He kept taxes at moderate levels but made the rich pay their fair share. However, the rich were also happy because the economy was growing and they were making more money... so they weren't feeling the pinches of the higher taxes on people in their bracket (or the effects of inflation). He greatly expanded free trade, which I think was an overall good thing (although it was certainly not good for many lower skilled workers). He worked with Republicans to balance the budget. He worked with Republicans on things like welfare reforms. He put gun control measures in place that we really needed. And he helped pass FMLA and the EITC, two more excellent programs that help working families. So many of the laws Clinton signed were aimed at helping working class Americans. It was trickle-up economics. Bill Clinton really is, in many ways, a political hero.

However, I also believe he has gotten *too* much credit on the economy. In order to expedite getting us out of the recession we were in, Alan Greenspan (who led the Fed for nearly 20 years and has a record of supporting what turned out to be reckless policies) supported artificially keeping interest rates low by flooding the system with money. This helped create the dot.com bubble as money was so cheap and available. Furthermore, it was unconscionable for Clinton to sign the Gramm-Leach-Bliley Act and the Commodity Futures Modernization Act. He knowingly or unknowingly helped financial institutions both get too big to fail and be able to take the kinds of gambles that almost ruined our financial system.

But I think, overall, Clinton was ideologically one of the greatest Presidents we've ever had. At the end of the day, we enjoyed eight wonderful years of relative peace and prosperity. It's a shame that his personal weaknesses are so large. He's so afraid of failure. He lies. And he's a womanizer. I think a lot of these things are real "daddy issues." And I think it's sad. Because there will rarely be a man that walks this Earth as smart, talented, and wonderful as Bill Clinton. He's one of the most fabulous people, I believe, in the history of the world. But his pride is his downfall. When pride becomes full-blown hubris, a man can make the mistakes and do the kinds of things Bill Clinton has done. But I still respect him and he'll always be one of my political heroes, even if he is personally flawed.

Bush I

I find Bush I to be an interesting guy. I don't trust that whole family, starting with Prescott Bush, or their business and government connections. Even H.W. Bush seemed to partially make his millions off of his dad's connections with oil companies. So, to that extent, I don't respect him. But Herbert Walker Bush is a brilliant guy. And to the extent that he served his country bravely and admirably, he's a hero. His son may be dumber than a bag of nails, but Herbert Walker is a scholar. He earned his way into and through Yale. He served honorably in the Navy. The guy was a pilot. If there ever was an example of a screw-up desperately trying to live up to his father's legacy, it's George W. Bush: flying onto an aircraft carrier behind a real pilot in that dumb jumpsuit. Herbert Walker was the real thing. Ambassador to the UN. Ambassador to China. Director of the C.I.A., Vice-President, President. He was brilliant and you have to give him that.

His policies weren't particularly great, but he did some good things. He signed the Americans with Disability Act. He agreed to spend money to help improve highways, and schools, and technology. He even signed an Immigration Act which helped increase legal immigration by 40%. He increased unemployment benefits as the economy entered into recession. If there was a compassionate conservative, it wasn't George W. Bush, but George Herbert Walker Bush. He maintained a much more balanced approach to government. Although he ended up regretting it, his willingness to compromise with Democrats and use additional taxes and revenues to help reduce the national deficit was actually a bold act of compromise on his part which I think was good for the country.

Yet, he still racked up a deficit basically as big in four years as Reagan and Clinton racked up in eight. He seemed to be more interested in foreign policy than he was with the economy. He took us to Iraq. But from what I have read, I probably support that. Iraq invaded Kuwait (although some think Saddam at least believed he had received permission from the United States in advance). Either way, the world chose to intervene. Especially given the fact that Kuwait really may be one of the few decent un-democratic monarchies in the Middle East, I think that was a reasonable move. And "41" didn't even push for Saddam to be killed, but instead agreed to merely force (and keep) Saddam out of neighboring Kuwait's sovereign land. I actually don't find a lot of major faults with the way that Bush ran his government, other than he wasn't a strong leader like Americans prefer and he seemed to be weak on economic matters.

My other real objection to him is his actions since leaving the Presidency. He has had such a direct hand in the affairs of a lot of private companies. I really find it hard to believe that he went over to Saudi Arabia and other countries, while his son was President, and met with those leaders as a purely private businessman. Not using any government connections. Even W. admitted in a video that he had benefited in his business life because his dad had been President of the United States. Now, father and son reversed roles and son helped dad get rich...er. Not that H.W. really needed much help.

The way that the Bushes have basically shifted wealth from U.S. taxpayers into the hands of private corporations that build defense weapons (and drill for oil) is just wrong. It's exactly what Eisenhower warned against. And the way they represent private equity funds and advise them on which companies to invest in also disgusts me. I respect some of the things Bush I did, but really abhor others. I believe he is a brilliant guy, but his business dealings disappoint me tremendously.

Reagan

Reagan has been immortalized as a god among conservatives. He is the greatest there ever was and the greatest there ever will be. He could do no wrong and all we need is another Ronald Reagan. The reality, however, is that Reagan was so bad for this country in so many different ways. W merely adopted Reagan's economic model, which should come as no surprise since they used many of the same advisers.

Start with his "trickledown economics" plan. What a bunch of garbage. Yes, let's let the rich keep more and more of their money, and then they will generously give it away to others, out of the kindness of their own hearts. They'll create new jobs, that pay so well, with great benefits...and we'll all get richer together. That's exactly what happened. Not. Shockingly, the rich didn't end up doing all of the great things we were told they would. Meanwhile, although government revenue did grow while Reagan was President, it grew at a lower real rate than before he became President and lower than when Clinton was in office. In other words, revenue grew, but so did inflation. And when you adjust for that, revenues grew at a lower percentage than other times. He cut taxes, real revenue growth slowed, the rich got richer, and...

The really poor got poorer. Their share of total income was lower. More people were living below the poverty line when Reagan left office than when he got in. Unemployment did fall, however, from 7.1% when he took office to 5.5% when he left (for which he deserves credit). But he also dramatically increased defense spending as a result of his anti-Soviet paranoia. We nearly tripled the national debt to a total of $2.85 trillion. All while cutting social programs for the poorest Americans. I guess it should be no surprise, then, that the American public saved less when Reagan was President. His policies helped fuel the Savings and Loan Crisis. S&L's were greatly deregulated under Reagan's administration and S&L institutions gained the ability to invest in riskier and riskier assets, in order to supposedly help them better compete and diversify. Furthermore, tax incentives passed by Reagan caused a real estate bubble which crashed when the incentives were taken away...which exacerbated the S&L crisis[33]. What a surprise it happened again 20 years later under W., a devout supporter of Reagan's policies.

Reagan had just as many problems with his foreign policy. Everybody acts like Ronald Reagan single handedly won the Cold War. Reagan didn't win the Cold War. The Soviets (and their failed economic system) lost it. Reagan just happened to be in office when it happened. He might have outspent them and quickened their collapse, but that's about the best he can say. Nevertheless, conservatives act like Ronald Reagan told Mr. Gorbachev to tear down the wall and then watched as it immediately disintegrated into dust. Reagan also armed Saddam Hussein AND the Afghani mujahidin (and quite possibly Bin Laden himself). I'd say that's not a great foreign policy record, but it does make for high comedy listening to conservatives explain how arming Bin Laden helped end the Cold War. And he claimed to be unaware of illegal arms sales to Iran that helped fund the Contras in Nicaragua. Can you even imagine if Obama's administration sold weapons to the Iranian government?

And what he did with the Air Traffic Controllers was freaking Communist. He froze their strike fund, which was THEIR money, and then seized it and gave it to the airports to hire and train new people. He said they resigned and didn't get fired, so they weren't eligible for benefits. He banned them all from federal service and then blackballed them throughout the world, effectively preventing them from taking their knowledge and skills to other countries to earn a living. And he even arrested some of them. He ruined these people's careers and their lives[34]. In America! That's the conservatives' god and hero.

Jimmy Carter

The four years that Carter was in office were not the best four years in American history. In fact, they were probably four of our worst, in many ways. However, a lot of the things that happened during Carter's administration weren't really his fault. Take for example the oil crisis. America's demand for oil didn't become that high overnight. And the increase in the price of oil was partially a response to the rapid depreciation of the dollar that resulted from Nixon taking the U.S. off of the gold standard. Jimmy Carter simply had to deal with the oil crisis. The oil crisis exacerbated the inflationary problems, which weren't really Carter's fault, either. And Carter dealt with that the way he had to: he appointed a very smart man to chair the Fed and they raised interest rates. That's going to help get inflation under control. And eventually it did. But it can also cause unemployment to go up and can cause GDP to go down. But, that's how inflation has to get under control. And it can be painful. No matter who is President.

Carter, in fact, did several things right. He tried to get Americans to reduce their demand for oil. That was what Americans really needed to hear. But, it's not what they wanted to hear and it's still not what they want to hear. Americans' addiction to oil hurt Carter when he tried to be frank with them about it. Carter led the efforts to deregulate the airline and other industries. He also took on his own party over what he considered to be wasteful spending. In fact, many of Carter's biggest feuds were actually with ultra-liberal Democrats. It goes to show you how nonsensical and biased conservatives' hatred of Carter really is (probably because he was just the first Democratic President many of those people can remember).

However, obviously nobody would say Carter was a perfect President. And he did make some mistakes. I think one of his biggest mistakes was not understanding the way Washington worked. He felt like government was about helping people and doing the right thing. He didn't understand the way politics was played in D.C. He didn't recognize all of the ego that was involved. He took an adversarial relationship towards the Congressional leaders of his own party. It was admirable, because he was probably right, but it was foolish. And Carter ended up being ineffective because he couldn't figure out how to get the system to work with him. He couldn't get his agenda through Congress.

But until recently, after his vocal criticisms of Bush, most conservatives acknowledged something about Carter: he may not have been successful as President, but he was a good man. Unlike many elected officials, he wasn't a crony.

And so although you could argue he failed as an Executive-in-Chief, you should have known he wouldn't stop trying to help people. He's helped calm tensions in Africa, the Middle East, and between Sudan and Uganda. He's also helped ease tensions between North Korea and Cuba and the U.S. Helping bring about peace may be one of the most important things any human being can do...and it's been something Carter has focused on and been successful at for decades.

But, like others, I strongly disagreed with Carter's public criticisms of Bush. I happen to agree with his opinion. However, Carter violated a long tradition that Presidents had regarding criticizing their successors. I understand he truly felt that what was being done was wrong and un-American. And there were people who were saying that, like Dennis Kucinich and Ron Paul, whose job it was to say those things. I loved President Carter and think he is a wonderful person who has done great for the world. But, I think it was not his job to voice those criticisms of Bush and, in fact, I think it was his job not to.

Nixon

This might surprise you: in some respects, I don't think Nixon was a bad President. Seriously. In fact, I think Nixon did many great things. However, hubris was his downfall, like many men before him. He was too desperate for power and too willing to do anything to protect it.

But look at all that he did right. He did what LBJ couldn't or didn't...and that was to end the war in Vietnam. Nixon got the troops home. His visit to China was really incredible. It was a courageous act that opened up relations between the two countries. The Communists took over China in 1949, and it was Nixon, 22 years and 4 Presidents later, who became the first American President to visit. It opened up the doors for the very important and dynamic relationship between the two countries that would follow. He also initiated détente with the Soviet Union and negotiated the ballistic missile treaty. He even did an excellent job of handling the Middle East, which was just as tricky then as it is today. Nixon, in fact, developed pretty peaceful relations with the world and was a master of foreign policy. It was his love. Nixon also helped lead the way on many pieces of legislation aimed at helping to clean and protect the environment. He worked with the Democratic Congress to pass fair budgets that weren't out of control, but still provided for the less fortunate. He also tried to promote the rights of the states.

However, not all of Nixon's policies were good. Firstly, I vehemently disagree with his unilateral decision to take us off the gold standard. Before, if you owed money to a country, you could pay in paper currency or gold. And if countries began to not like the value of your money, they could demand the equivalent debt in gold. This caused you to protect the value of your money. It definitely had some downsides, but it also prevented you from wanting to borrow huge sums of money... or you might lose your nation's gold supply. However, Nixon, fearing that was, in fact, going to happen, decided to get rid of the rule. "Our paper is all you're getting," is what Nixon effectively said. And so now, we feel free to spend and spend and spend. Because now it's really just paper and promise (actually now it's just numbers on a screen). This was ultimately a terrible decision that led to the massive depreciation of the dollar, a rise in oil prices, easily accumulated deficits, and major financial problems. Nixon also interfered with the Fed and pressured them to keep interest rates low[35].

His wage controls were also highly questionable...both in terms of their effectiveness at controlling inflation and their appropriateness. Personally, I probably don't have a problem with it, but I don't know how Republicans so freely call liberals Socialists and Communists when their President, at one point, used his power to prevent people from receiving raises. I also vehemently disagree with his war on drugs and the way he carried it out. There is a whole chapter on this, but I believe that the war on drugs is misguided, unsuccessful, and downright evil, sometimes.

But for all the good that he did at a policy level (and I think, as President, he did a lot more good things than bad), it can't compensate for his lack of ethics. He was desperate for power. He clearly had major daddy issues (like Clinton). And, in fact, although Richard Nixon spoke well of his parents, others did allege that his father was a bitter man who psychologically and physically abused his family. And that would make sense why Nixon was so desperate to achieve. And that desperation caused him to break the law. It caused him to fire government officials in an attempt protect himself. He basically tried to become a dictator. He was so arrogant, and yet insecure...and it ended up causing his disgrace before the world.

LBJ

I have mixed feelings on all of these guys. None of them did **all** good or **all** bad (even W, Reagan, and Carter did at least a couple of things right). And anybody who feels otherwise reveals their partisanship. But, out of all of these recent Presidents, I might be most conflicted about LBJ. He did so many good things to help so many people. But he also did so many things that I think were just so bad. So, so bad.

Whereas the Nixon administration would later declare a war on drugs, the LBJ administration declared a war on poverty. And God bless them for that. If there is one thing I believe, it's that we must find ways to take care of the poor. It is our responsibility to each other as human beings. And LBJ took that responsibility seriously. And he made it a big part of his Presidency. In 1965, Johnson helped pass Medicare and Medicaid. Since Medicare was passed, the poverty rate among the elderly has dropped from above 30% to below 10%. Civil rights was another issue that was important to LBJ. The 1964 Civil Rights Act and the 1965 Voting Rights Act were two of the most important pieces of legislation in the 20th century. Tensions were already flaring, and LBJ knew that by signing that bill, the Democrats might lose the South forever. But it was the right thing to do. He invested money in schools. He passed sweeping gun control legislation.

But as much as I respect his domestic policy, I abhor his foreign policy. He was a conservative, right wing, Commie-phobic hawk who supported Israel no matter what. In the Gulf of Tonkin incident, he lied every bit as much as Bush did about weapons of mass destruction[36]. He was so afraid of the Soviets that he poured our troops and our money into that country, leaving over 50,000 American troops dead. Over 300,000 South Vietnamese. Over 1,000,000 North Vietnamese. And he thinks that was right? To prevent Vietnam from becoming a Communist country (and failing, by the way)? Was it worth it to the 1.4 million Vietnamese that died? In that ridiculous Cold War struggle between the U.S. and Russia? Shameless. Not only did he lie about the Gulf of Tonkin incident, but some believe he lied about the USS Liberty incident. In the incident, Israel bombed a U.S. ship, killing 34 sailors and wounding 171. The administration seemed to feel like they were allergic to the details of exactly how and why Israel attacked our clearly marked Navy research ship[37]. And not for 10 minutes. Try 90 minutes. But for some reason, there seemed to be no real desire from LBJ's administration to figure out how it happened. Some claim he might have set it up as a pretext to start war with the Middle East. It's hard to explain how our ally could attack our clearly marked ship for 90 straight minutes. And with Jacqueline Kennedy Onassis' comments recently being made public, I don't even want to think about how JFK might have really been killed.

As a southern Christian, LBJ had a strong fear of Muslims and Communists. His foreign policy was extremely hawkish and much more like a modern day Republican. And whether you think concern about Communist and Muslim nations is justified or not (I believe they are both partially justified...but mostly unjustified), Lyndon Baines Johnson was a right-winger when it came to foreign policy. And I think a lot of people died because of it. I think it's difficult to try to argue that more than a million people (and more than 50,000 Americans) would have died had we *not* gone to Vietnam. It's possible that "the domino effect" LBJ feared would have materialized and Communism would have begun to spread across the world...one day endangering millions of Americans. However, I seriously doubt it, especially since the Communists eventually took control of Vietnam anyway. And I believe LBJ and other hawks are not heroes, but murderers. LBJ's domestic policy was so honorable, but his foreign policy was disgraceful. And LBJ had almost as dangerous of an ego as Nixon had.

Kennedy

Kennedy is a guy that reminds me of Clinton and Nixon. He probably would have been an extremely effective executive had he been able to serve two full terms. However, there was also something about him that wasn't good. He was part good, part ego. His policies also ranged from excellent to very questionable, at best.

As President, he was fairly hawkish, but not as hawkish as his Vice President, LBJ. Sometimes, his aggressive moves were warranted and brilliant. He did a good job handling the Cuban Missile Crisis (although one could definitely argue that his decision to put nukes in Turkey and Italy is what provoked the Russians in the first place). Nonetheless, Kennedy's strategy was daring, but he showed strength and managed to not get anybody killed. And the Russian missile site was taken down. He took the most dangerous situation and he was able to stabilize it and make it safe. The establishment of the Peace Corps was brilliant and showed incredible vision. The speech he gave in Berlin was historic. And the Nuclear Test Ban Treaty he signed with Russia was at least a great first step to making the world a tiny bit safer.

However, his foreign policy was far from perfect. I believe that he was far too interventionist in his foreign policy. He supported a murderous Baathist regime in Iraq that killed countless suspected leftists. He sent our troops into Cuba during the Bay of Pigs in an attempt to lead a revolt against Castro. That aggressive move ended up costing several Americans (and many more Cubans) their lives. He also was the one who initially sent us to Vietnam. History seems to show that he didn't want to go, but felt like the American people's fear of the spread of Communism was forcing him to send troops. And after he died, with men already in place, LBJ went full speed ahead into that horrible conflict. We never should have been there in the first place. That was nothing more than a Cold War fight between the Soviet backed Communist forces of North Vietnam and the military tyrant the U.S. supported just so Vietnam wouldn't become Communist. I don't believe in that kind of military intervention and I think Vietnam is the kind of thing that intervention gets you. And although his actions in response to the Soviet missile base in Cuba worked out well, I felt like Kennedy was sometimes too quick to flex his muscles and risk war.

He used loose monetary policy to jump start the economy, but just as important, he kept the deficits and inflation relatively under control. There were deficits, but the debt did not come close to rising to dangerous levels and even fell as a percentage of GDP. He was in favor of civil rights, but he seemed reluctant to take on the political challenge of passing civil rights legislation. He even allowed the FBI to wiretap Martin Luther King Jr. He supported the death penalty (a good thing), he tried to help the poor and the immigrants, and he was a visionary for our space program. It is highly questionable, however, whether the accomplishment of landing a man on the moon was truly financially worthwhile to this country. Or whether it was just an expensive pride booster.

Overall, I think Kennedy was a good leader for our country. During his short time in office, we enjoyed relative peace in the world (with a few exceptions) and relative prosperity. And Kennedy was serving during some extremely turbulent times in this country's history. But, I think although Kennedy was a fairly good President, he obviously wasn't a good husband or, therefore, a very good man. Clinton and JFK had a lot in common: both were young and charming (JFK off the charts)...but they were both also big time womanizers. JFK was a cheat and a philanderer. I think as a President he was great, but as a person he had some serious liabilities.

Ron Paul

I believe in Ron Paul. I don't think he is right on everything. And I might even say he's a radical. However, America is in desperate need for radical change. I don't agree with Dr. Paul on all of the changes that need to be made. However, radical change is needed.

Ron Paul is right about two of the most important issues, beginning with the wars. War is the ultimate foreign policy issue. The ultimate goal of foreign policy should be to create peaceful conditions. Some argue that sometimes peace must be achieved through war and claim that the Iraq War, and the continued military presence throughout the Middle East region, were necessary to achieve lasting peace. And Ron Paul disagrees with that and I believe that he is right. I think it is extraordinarily intellectually lazy to simply believe that the terrorists are attacking us because they hate our freedom. I think this narrative about a widespread Islamic movement trying to take over the world is pretty ridiculous. As I explained in a previous chapter, these are often nothing more than organized crime organizations that are partially built around a specific cause: namely hatred of Israel and its allies. I guarantee you that if we did not have bases in the Middle East and such strong support for Israel, they would at least MOSTLY ignore us, like they mostly ignore much of the world. These wars, that are increasing in number, are not making us safer (and they help breed more terrorists) and they are costing us trillions of dollars. That is American money going to private defense companies and foreign countries. If we want to spend a trillion dollars to protect this country from terrorists, we should spend more money here, in our own country, starting with making our borders more secure. Why spend money to secure the Afghan-Pakistan border but not our own?

Ron Paul is right on the most important foreign policy issues, but he is also right on the most important domestic issue: the economy. As Dr. Paul has stated, the Federal Reserve's loose monetary policy has created asset bubbles (dot com and real estate) that eventually pop, forcing the country back into recession. It's also helping drive inflation, which is hurting those at the bottom of our society. Our high corporate tax rates relative to the rest of the world have driven companies to take their capital elsewhere. Our spending is completely out of control. The drug war has not only been a failure, it's really been an abomination. And it's been a huge drain on taxpayers. Paul is also right that the government shouldn't be in the marriage business. He's right on civil liberties as well as on the police state in the U.S. On most of the major issues, I support the positions of Ron Paul.

I don't agree with him on everything, however. He's more libertarian than I am. He opposes any national healthcare plan, obviously, and really is opposed to Social Security and Medicare. However, I believe in those kinds of (limited) government programs. He opposed the bailout for the auto industry and I supported that and think that it has worked out pretty well. I think he's very wrong on the Civil Rights Act and Affirmative Action. I also think he's wrong about eliminating federal spending on education and on gun rights. Ron Paul is a true libertarian. He wants as small of a government as possible. He opposes progressive tax rates, which tax the rich at higher rates. I think Paul's ideology is too rigid and creates too large of a gap between the rich and the poor. But despite these disagreements, I support Ron Paul. I support him because he's right on foreign policy and on monetary policy. I support him because I believe every other candidate is bought and paid for by somebody (often the big banks)... or some special interest group... except Dr. Paul. Dr. Paul has no secret friends...only values that he consistently and publicly stands on.

The Way Washington D.C. Really Works

There are several major systematic problems with our government. This chapter will focus on what I believe to be the biggest four: Congressional districts that have often been severely gerrymandered, the influence of money on the election process, the lack of Congressional term limits, and a two party system that has created two separate entities that look out for their *own* interests and power, rather than the interests of the American people. One of our major problems is that our politicians have gerrymandered the Congressional districts[38]. A free market economy is supposed to foster competition. Monopolies prevent real competition from being possible. State governments often draw districts so that they are increasingly partisan. On one hand, this isn't completely bad. If a district holds solidly conservative beliefs and wants to nominate somebody with shared values to represent them year after year, that is okay. However, many of these politicians quickly become corrupt. They know a member of the opposing party will never be able to win in their heavily partisan district. They then feel safe to do whatever corrupt activities they want. Or refuse to compromise with members of the opposing party.

Our politicians are also (perhaps happily) convinced (and it may very well be true) that they *must* have the big lobbyists' money if they want to ensure that they will win re-election (and be able to further their political career). And politics *is* these people's career. And they learn whose agenda pays the bills. We have corruption in Washington. Everybody knows it. But the only people who can fix it, won't. They bend the rules for their buddies. They fight and make decisions based on winning a game rather than doing what is right. Hyper-partisans in the House of Representatives, especially, usually have no idea what they are even talking about. They don't read the bills they vote for. Somebody tells them how they should vote. Who tells them? Basically, the lobbyists and big time donors whose money they need...

Much (if not most) of the time, the party leadership tells their caucuses how they should vote on a bill (after getting their marching orders from their big time donors and lobbyists). And if a party member goes against the wishes of the party leadership, they'll likely never be appointed chair of any committee and they probably won't get the party's full support during re-election time. None of their bills will make it through Committee. The chairman of any committee can kill any bill at any time (while it's in the committee) for any reason. These people serve as gatekeepers. A bill can not get to the floor unless it goes through the committee and ultimately gets approved by the committee chairman. And the majority party controls the appointment of all committee chairs. So, everybody tries to suck up to their party leadership and tries to be a "team player" so they can one day hold a powerful committee chairmanship. Therefore, it pays for most people elected to Congress to do whatever their party leaders tell them to so that in a future term they can be rewarded with more power, rather than being punished and demoted by their party leader.

We don't have a democracy of legislators trying to do what is best for *us*. We have two evil corporations, Democrat and Republican, fighting for power...and often scratching the back of the powerful and rich to give them the funds they need to stay in office. The politicians need the money to win re-election and these big donors need political favors. The cozy and corrupt relationship between our politicians in D.C. and Corporate America and various lobbying groups, in addition to the hyper-partisanship and dangerous games the two parties play, threaten the U.S.' future. *We need term limits.*

Campaign Finance and 21st Century Elections

In 2012, Obama raised (and spent) over $700 million on his Presidential campaign. Mitt Romney spent over $450 million[39]. People gave these two men over $1 billion. And that was just what these two men spent to run for President. That doesn't even include all of the money that was raised and spent by the party committees. Or the Senate candidates. Or Congressional candidates. Or PAC groups. Or anybody else. We are a country whose government is bought and paid for.

It's hard to even really try to rationalize it. It's one of those things that I think most people secretly know in their heart of hearts is really messed up. This country used to be about ideas and making the country better. There was partisanship (don't let anybody try to tell you there wasn't partisanship). Politicians have long fought some of the same federal rights vs. states' rights arguments that we're still fighting today. However, the end goal of both sides was usually to make the country a better place. That was the ultimate goal. I'm not convinced that's still the case. Who was donating millions of dollars to our Founding Fathers' campaigns? Yes, the country was much smaller then. The modern day media didn't exist at that time. (Good thing? Bad thing?) But, my point is a valid one still: what corporations and special interest groups donated large sums of money to our early national campaigns? And is that influence in modern day politics a good thing?

The 2010 Supreme Court ruling that the McCain-Feingold Act of 2002 was unconstitutional...because the Constitution gives corporations the same right to freedom of speech as individuals...may be one of the worst Supreme Court rulings ever. This is a liberal Roe v. Wade. Conservatives complain that they see no right to privacy in the Constitution that would protect a woman's right to terminate her pregnancy. Likewise, I see no indication that the Founding Fathers envisioned granting corporations ("a collection of human beings") the same rights it gives to individual people. It's ridiculous frankly. The fact that the Supreme Court has stated that this country has no legal authority under the Constitution to limit the ability of corporations to use money to influence our elections...is insane.

These people: lobbyists, special interest groups, etc. spend BILLIONS of dollars every year on lobbying and then donate even more money to the two parties and their campaign funds[40]. This shit is robbery. This is almost no different than the Chinese way, where companies constantly bribe Communist party officials for sweetheart deals. When it happens in China, we call it bribery. In America, we make one or two restrictions, and then call it "lobbying." Over and over again, we see our elected officials taking money from these groups and then voting on legislation that favors them. And we let it continue.

These guys end up spending tons of precious time (that they could be using to study policy and the effects of policy) fundraising. They have to basically curry favors. If they vote on legislation that a particular industry might suffer from, those lobbyists threaten to shut off the funds. And he/she needs the funds. Private financing of campaigns comes with so many dangers. If the goal of elections is to ensure that the best candidate with the best ideas gets elected, wouldn't we want to minimize the potential influence of money? Why wouldn't we want public financing of elections: where each side gets equal funds and then must use those funds most effectively in order to get their message out? Then, it becomes more about the message and the strategy...and less about who was able to most effectively raise money and cut deals with special interest groups. It might even teach some of these politicians how to budget.

The Constitution

The U.S. Constitution is an incredible document. It established the formal, most basic rules of our republic, the vast majority of which are still in effect to this day. The document wasn't perfect, which is one of the reasons why it's been amended (plus, the world simply changes). But the Constitution has held up all this time and given us the basic framework of our society. It's part of the foundation on which this country was built and part of how it became the most powerful nation in a world of many nations.

There are many things one could marvel at when thinking about the Constitution. One of the most brilliant aspects is its system of checks and balances. The Founding Fathers, seeing the consequences of too much power leading to corruption and tyranny, wanted to develop a government that had separated powers that provided mechanisms for holding another branch of government accountable. For example, if a President violates the law or the Constitution, he should be impeached by the House and then convicted by the Senate. This helps serve as a check to the President's power. If a small majority in Congress passes a bad bill, the President is able to veto it and force a larger majority of Congressmen and women to agree. This is a very large power and allows the President to make it very difficult to pass certain types of legislation, especially in today's political party system. Supreme Court justices can also be impeached. Legislation must begin by being passed by Congress. This makes them very powerful. The role of Commander-in-Chief and the ability to appoint Supreme Court justices who will interpret the law also make the President powerful (along with a few other hats). The ability to strike down any law and being the final voice on what is legal makes the Supreme Court extraordinarily powerful. The only way to get around a Supreme Court ruling is a Constitutional amendment. And that's only happened 27 times.

Which is a great lead-in to the next point: the Constitution is great and all, but can we really pretend like it's perfect? Isn't that weird that we've only felt that the world had changed enough that we needed to alter our Constitution 27 times in over 235 years? Really? Some partisans are thinking, "Absolutely. Everything America does is perfect." Got it. But, I think the debate about whether the Constitution is (or should be) a fluid, evolving document is a fair question. Our Constitution is the oldest in the world. Perhaps it's really that perfect. Or maybe we're almost foolish to think that virtually everything that was good 235 years ago is definitely still good today.

Look at the second amendment. Do you really think that the framers could have imagined handguns and automatic weapons? When they guaranteed the right to bear arms, what was our military like then? And should we even care what the framers (would have) thought about all modern day issues? We don't listen to what they thought about slavery. Times change. So, one could argue, that is why they allowed amendments. But they've made passing amendments so difficult, that one could easily argue that *that* is one weakness of the Constitution. Others also argue that the Electoral College is basically undemocratic.

I believe America would be smart to sit down and think about *possibly* drafting a new set of rules. Every system has weaknesses. And ours is no different. I'd say we should just sit down and try to patch the existing system that worked so well in the past, but I think politicians and the big money interests have become entrenched. And unless we start all over, it might never get any better. The politicians have figured out how to beat this system for their benefit. *Maybe* it's time for a newer, better system.

Forms of Government

Each of the four major forms of governance: anarchy, autocracy, direct democracy, and republicanism (or indirect democracy) has inherent strengths and weaknesses. I think the downsides that come along with anarchy, most notably nearly certain chaos and lawlessness, simply make it not an option. In some ways, this is a form of government that represents ultimate freedom. But, is total freedom a good thing? Or do people need laws in order to help curtail self-serving behavior that can ultimately destroy a society? In order for a society to flourish, private property rights must be protected and the rule of law instilled. A quick look at societies who have basically operated, effectively, as anarchies (like Somalia) gives us a pretty good idea that it doesn't work.

What about autocracies? Instead of having no order, order is imposed by one individual (or possibly a very few). People don't vote on things. Some person has the ability to make the final decisions on their own and ultimately has final authority. This system, unlike anarchy, can establish the rule of law. Furthermore, it's very nimble and prevents the paralysis that can occur in multi-party democracies. Socialism and Communism are usually implemented under autocratic governments: such as totalitarian dictatorships and oligarchies. But autocracies put a tremendous amount of power in the hands of just one person or a few people. Power corrupts and absolute power corrupts absolutely. There are many autocratic nations in this world…and corruption and a lack of rights wreak havoc on most of these countries. Benevolent dictatorships have existed before, but they've never stayed benevolent forever.

What about direct democracies, where the people vote directly on the laws that will govern the people? The Founding Fathers in America were extremely distrusting of direct democracy. They feared that factions would form in a direct democracy and that the self interests of groups, rather than the good of the society as a whole, would determine the laws. There is always the possibility, in a direct democracy, that a majority could easily impose its beliefs on (and restrict the rights of) a minority.

This is why the Founding Fathers really advocated representative (or indirect) democracy, where people elect representatives who create the laws. It's also why they preferred the Electoral College rather than choosing the President by popular vote: they had a distrust of common people. They felt like this would help protect the minority from the majority as more reasonable representatives would help protect minority rights (in theory this should also hopefully prevent people from directly voting for excessive benefits that are a long-term detriment to the country). They also felt like in a big enough group of people, levelheaded reasonable representatives could be elected by the people to ensure that reasonable laws and governance were achieved. How has that worked out lately? Has representative democracy protected us from factions? Has it ensured that levelheaded representatives, who reasonably vote to do what is in the best interest of society as a whole, are elected? Have you ever listened to the House of Representatives? Also, representative democracies can both cause policy paralysis (when parties refuse to compromise) as well as create inconsistent shifts in policies, that are also often late in responding to economic problems.

Winston Churchill famously stated that, "Democracy is the worst form of government, except for all those other forms that have been tried from time to time." Is democracy at the top of the evolution of governments? And is it even right (or possible) for every country? Throughout history, human beings have changed the way they organize and govern themselves. Democracy, in much of the world, is fairly young. Is there a future form of government, yet nonexistent, which will replace democracy as the most preferred and most effective in the world?

One World Government

Many people have made the accusation that people are conspiring to create a one world government. Like most people, I used to hear those people and think they were kooky. Some groups point to the UN, but the UN has virtually no real teeth. If somebody defies the UN, most of the time, the UN just barks. It has little bite, little real authority...especially when the U.S., Russia, and China exercise their veto powers. It's not the UN that concerns me as much as the various groups that meet secretly...as well as the things that have been happening in the world recently.

What exactly are some of the conspiracy theories? There are several prominent groups of people who meet very secretly. Groups like the Bilderberg Group, the Council on Foreign Relations, and the Trilateral Commission. All three of these are real groups of some of the richest, most powerful, and the most influential people in the world...who meet ultra-secretly. Is it possible they are really just innocuously meeting in secret to discuss ideas? With no other, underlying agenda? I guess. Is it likely? I'm not sure.

It certainly seems like we're headed towards global bankruptcy. It feels like this idea of what I call "Extreme Keynesian Economics" has been used to pump the entire world economy full of growingly worthless paper. If much of the world economy is a deck of cards and collapses, what do you suppose world leaders might propose as a solution? A world government? "To ensure that the same thing never happens again," will they suggest more centralization? Does that sound like something governments might suggest? Some world leaders have actually been vocal about such suggestions. U.S. Treasury Secretary Timothy Geithner stated that the U.S. was open to an international currency by the IMF.

Let's pretend that is the goal: to create a one world government. Would that be a bad thing? Look at the way many of the leaders in Africa, Eastern Europe, Southeast Asia, and in much of Latin America treat their people. These governments are full of corruption, leading millions of people into poverty. Would a world government help prevent this kind of rampant corruption which leads to rampant poverty? Could a world government end the days of oppressive, tyrannical leaders who exploit their people?

Or would it help exacerbate it? I can't help but always go back to the old phrase "power corrupts and absolute power corrupts absolutely." A benevolent leader over a one world government might be incredibly effective and efficient.

However, think of the power that would exist. Who would have control over all that power? How would it be used? What kinds of checks would be in place to protect the people of the world from a global tyrant? What about the size of such an endeavor? It seems as though the larger the number of people, the harder it is to manage. It's like a ship or a car. A big ship or a big car is less maneuverable than a small one. An economy and a government are no different. How could a world government possibly be the most nimble and efficient? Not to mention the potential for power abuse...

And surely the talk of a one world government would send Christians into a fever pitch. The Bible predicts a one world government before, or during, the final days before Jesus supposedly will return. Such an event would only ensure them that they are right. No mind that during the time the Bible was written, Rome was trying to establish a one world government. The fact that it was being attempted again would somehow assure them of the Bible's validity...even if it proves nothing. It's unlikely that the Romans would be the last group of people to try to achieve a one world government.

Religion and Government

The first amendment states, "Congress shall make no law respecting an establishment of religion, or prohibiting the free exercise thereof..." This part of the first amendment, addressing religion, obviously makes two separate mandates regarding religion. One, that Christians frequently like to point out, is referred to as "the Free Exercise Clause." It gives people the freedom to practice their religion. However, some conservative evangelical Christians conveniently forget the first part of the first amendment, called "the Establishment Clause." This part of the amendment prohibits any law "respecting an establishment of religion." This part is equally important. Not only is the government forbidden from preventing people from practicing their religion, it is also prohibited from creating laws that establish a religion.

People have different opinions on exactly how these clauses should be interpreted, as well as what limitations should apply to them. However, the Supreme Court has given us some insight. Firstly, with regards to laws that prohibit the free exercise of religion, the Supreme Court has ruled that the government can pass laws that, although are not targeting a religion, may affect their practices. For example, the government can pass laws that prevent murder...which interferes with the religion of a person who believes in human sacrifice. The same would be true of somebody whose religion endorses child brides. The Supreme Court has also ruled that laws that restrict religion should usually be "generally applicable" meaning applicable to most religions and not just one. And, just as important, the Supreme Court has generally held that the government must show a compelling interest in regulating a particular religious practice. However, if the government can do so, although people are free to practice their religion, the government can pass laws that interfere with a religion's practices.

The Establishment Clause has also been carefully interpreted by the Supreme Court. It's hard to discuss the Establishment Clause without discussing the idea of the separation of church and state. This term, coined in a Thomas Jefferson letter, is never used in the Constitution. I don't think, based on many of the words and writings of our Founding Fathers, that they wanted to ban religion in public life. As Christians point out, the Founding Fathers definitely wanted *government* out of *religion*. But did they want *religion* out of *government*? I think in some ways yes and in some ways no. I don't think they minded people voting their conscience and letting their religious values guide their decisions. But, I do think they wanted to protect the religious rights of all people. And Christians must understand that some things that they take for granted are "right or wrong" are not that way to everybody. Laws should be based on whether an action harms another person. Not based on what a particular book says. By not allowing gay marriage, for example, the government has basically selected one religion over another...as not all religions say homosexuality is wrong. The government has basically established a religion. Should we also have laws against lying? Or jealousy? America should not and can not become a theocracy.

Religious people, and those who oppose religion, should respect both the Free Exercise and Establishment Clauses. Whether an unborn fetus is a human being or not is a religious belief and everybody should have the ability to make that decision for themselves. People should have the right to decide for themselves if homosexuality is okay and the government should not establish a law that restricts gays from enjoying the same rights as heterosexual couples. But some atheists are also known for trying to suppress Christians' abilities to express their beliefs. Everybody should oppose this with the same tenacity that they oppose Christians trying to have the government establish religious based laws.

Society is the Byproduct of a Union Between Culture and Politics

Societies are like human beings, which makes sense considering societies are merely a big group of human beings. But societies are like human beings in the sense that they are the byproduct of a union between two things. A human being is a byproduct of the union of two people. The two people come together in some kind of (Random? Chaotic? Organized? Pre-destined?) way to create one singular person that is some combination of the two of them. Societies, likewise. Culture is the mother and politics is the father of a society.

Societies are a byproduct of culture. Religion, history, customs, and all other aspects of culture affect societies at both macro and micro levels. How much does religion affect the society in the South? How about in the Middle East? What about in Russia (atheist)? Religion has a major impact on society. So does history. Where have we been and what have we been through? Where did we come from? What has happened to us? How have we interacted with others? All of these things affect our society today. As do our customs. I'll tell you, people in Korea and China (and all over the world) are, in many ways, just like you and me: they get happy and sad, live and die, etc. But many of their customs are very, very different. In China, for example, the entire country (including most restaurants) basically shut down for one to two weeks to celebrate the Lunar New Year. (All of the MBA's are thinking, "But what about all of that lost revenue???" And all of the Chinese are thinking, "I just love spending time and celebrating with my entire family every year.") How we as a society tend to feel about sex and divorce and relationships affects how our society lives. Culture absolutely shapes our societies.

But societies are also the byproduct of politics. People often say, "I hate politics." I think we should probably all hate politics. It always seems to get dirty. And that's probably because you have to deal with some very, very dirty people. But if there ever was a necessary evil, it's politics. Politics is what determines if we have an open and free society. Or if we have a society like Iran and North Korea. Or if we have a society like Somalia...where the problem isn't as much that the government is authoritarian as it is that the government is nonexistent. Politics shapes societies. A large part of politics is like the collective bargaining agreement in the NFL: it determines who gets how much. That also helps to shape our societies...at both a macro and micro level. It helps determine the distribution of wealth and income in a society as well as the incentives to build, work, and grow. Politics also determines how we interact with other societies...which also, to some degree, shapes our own society.

When there are neighborhoods in the United States that are basically law-less, with shootings in the streets, that is a result of both culture and politics. And you have one side in this country that basically wants to throw money at it. They want to do a little more than that. But not much more. Not enough more. They want to try to fix it politically without addressing the cultural issues. The other side, however, says, "You can't throw money at it! It's a culture problem." And it IS a culture problem...but it's also a political problem. Societies, even at the micro level, are a byproduct of both culture and politics. People who commit acts of violence are often people who feel like they don't have a real opportunity and they don't have anything to lose. Our political decisions can help cause those kinds of feelings. If we truly want to fix our country, on both macro and micro levels, we must be willing to address these problems both politically and culturally.

Religion

Some people today passionately feel like religion is the answer to all of the world's problems. Others, interestingly, feel like religion is the *cause* of the majority of the world's problems. As usual, both are probably partially correct. Gun owners are well known for saying that guns are not capable of good or bad, but that they're tools that can be used by people for either good or bad. Religions, including both Christianity and Islam, are the same in this way: they can be used for either good or bad.

Islam certainly has been used for both good and evil. For starters, Muslims made many very important contributions to math and science which, in turn, made major contributions to the world as a whole. Some Islamic charities have gone to great lengths to try and help improve the conditions of people in many parts of the world. Muslims, especially in much of the Middle East, have struggled under bad and corrupt leaders. But when Muslim people have had the opportunity to live under benevolent leaders, like in Turkey, Muslims have often lived mostly peacefully and prosperously with those around them.

However, obviously Islam has not only been responsible for good. One doesn't have to look far to see people using Islam to commit horrible acts. 9-11 is just the most famous example. But, there is a whole laundry list full of attacks on innocent civilians committed in the name of Islam. The radicals often cite atrocities that are committed against Muslims to justify their murders. Although some of their claims of injustice committed against them may be valid, some Muslims ignore the failures of their own leaders...and instead conveniently point the finger out at foreign influences (like U.S. presence) so they can use retaliatory tactics that are completely evil and murderous. There's also the complete mistreatment of women in some fundamentalist Islamic sects. They use Islam to justify their actions and encourage others to follow. Here, religion is being used in harmful ways.

However, Islam is not alone in this regard. Christianity has also been used to justify much evil. People always like to point out the Crusades, but we don't have to look back nearly that far. The KKK claims to be Christian. The radical in Norway who went on a shooting spree claimed he was a Christian (although not in the way American evangelicals consider to be truly Christian). I could go on and on. However, Christians simply say, "Those people aren't real Christians"... but then insist that Muslims who commit acts of violence are "real Muslims." The truth is that all religions are used by some for good and for bad.

Mormons are some of the nicest people you'll ever meet. And I think much of their religion is built around getting their believers to love and help other people. And that part of their religion is great. However, I also believe they use major peer pressure and groupthink to force people to conform to many unnecessary religious beliefs. And I think when they do that, they are using religion for bad. People should be very careful whenever somebody tells them what God thinks about things.

And that should be the ultimate test for any religion: when a religion promotes things like love, peace, forgiveness, compassion, justice, and other worthwhile behaviors and values, then religion is good. Just like Jesus supposedly said, a good tree produces good fruit. If a religion produces good behaviors, then it is good. However, when it's used to control people, judge people, or hurt people, then religion is bad. There is no reason people can't take advantage of the good parts of religion, without also implementing some of the bad things that some people sometimes bring with it.

Christianity

Christianity, ultimately, is the belief in Jesus as the Savior of the world. That is a very broad definition and incorporates many different denominations of Christianity, which have some fairly different beliefs. The degree to which Christians interpret the Bible literally varies tremendously. The things they believe about who will go to Heaven and Hell (and why) can also vary pretty dramatically. But in virtually all Christian sects, Jesus is the Savior.

I used to be a Christian for a long time. I was very devoted. I wanted to be an evangelist and then later decided I wanted to become a missionary instead. The two jobs I wanted were to either get paid for going around speaking about Christianity or to get paid for doing mission work and trying to spread Christianity. And I believed in evangelical Christianity with all of my heart. More specifically, I believed that all human beings were sinners. The standard to get into Heaven was perfection, but we're all short of it. And so we needed to believe in Jesus as the only way to Heaven so that God would forgive us of our sins. That is what modern day Evangelicals believe and that is what I believed. I knew many of the verses. I still do. I saw the (supposed) prophecies that were made long before Jesus existed. It all made sense to me (it didn't really occur to me that the people who wrote the New Testament knew the Old Testament and could make their story about the life of Jesus fit with the prophecies in the Old Testament).

Christian belief, the belief in Jesus, is entirely based on the Bible. Evangelical Christians believe it to be the Word of God. They pour over every word and even analyze the text down to the word order. To them, it is God's Word and that's how they know if something is true or not. There are some very, very good lessons in the Bible. A lot of the things that Christians believe in (such as love and forgiveness and charity) are things that *do* make for a happier life. I would argue that they even draw you closer to God. But Christianity takes a big leap when it jumps from, "Some of this guy's teachings, as presented in the Bible, are very good" to "This guy really died and came back to life, like this book says, and you have to worship him if you want to go to Heaven." Claims that we should worship a guy who died, and then supposedly rose from the dead, need to be supported by some good evidence.

But Christianity and the Bible don't really pass any sort of reasonable standard of plausibility. It's possible that the Bible, exactly like it is written, is completely true. But it's not very likely. And the next chapter will talk more about why.

But Christianity, like Islam, has really been a force for good or bad...depending on how people have used it. Even within a single denomination, faith may have both good and bad manifestations. I know for a fact that Southern Baptists have done such an amazing amount of good in the world, providing food for the hungry and shelter for the homeless. They've shown a lot of love, at times, to the outside world. However, Southern Baptists have also led the march of hatred towards gays and other groups. They believe that their Bible and their beliefs are the only way. They can't accept any other beliefs. They believe Jesus said that he is the <u>only</u> way.

This kind of extremist belief can often manifest itself in horrible ways. It has been used by so many people to judge others. Some Christians believe that they are better because they believe in Jesus and that their lifestyle is correct, while nonChristians' lifestyles are evil. But regardless of how Christians may behave at times, the Bible and the story of Christianity simply are almost certainly untrue.

The Bible

Although I once fell into this category wholeheartedly, I now find it quite amazing that some people take the Bible literally. It's really phenomenal.

The first major issue is the issue of timing. Most scholars believe, even most Christian scholars, that the gospels were written *at least* two decades AFTER Jesus died. That's a really big deal. You're having guys, we don't even know for sure who some of them are, writing two decades or more after the events in question. And we want to take the Bible, and every single word in it, literally? You could argue that at least a few of the gospel writers likely took notes that they used to write the gospels. But, have you ever tried to transcribe something somebody is saying before? Even with a computer or typewriter, it's hard. "Hey. Can you say that one more time? Did you say it like 'this' or like 'that'?" Did the writers transcribe what Jesus said during the Sermon on the Mount word-for-word, like some people try and interpret it? In addition, the writers weren't even firsthand witnesses of at least SOME of what they wrote about. Certainly it is almost impossible that the gospel writers were at the birth of Jesus (which might be why it's completely left out of two gospels). We don't know for sure what parts were witnessed firsthand and what parts were second-hand accounts. In fact, we don't even know who wrote the gospels to begin with. Let me repeat that. There is absolutely no evidence of who wrote the books we call "Matthew, Mark, Luke, and John." The writers never identify themselves and we don't even really know why anybody thought they were written by Matthew, Mark, Luke, and John. Sheer tradition. So, really, anybody could have written them. And we're going to take what they wrote so literally? Who believes in a book that they don't even know who wrote it?

Furthermore, you have the issue of how they chose which books go in the Bible. Basically, a group of people got together with many different books. The Bible, as we read it now, is composed of 66 books written by a variety of authors (maybe 30...we don't even know). It didn't come as just one big book, perfectly organized like it is now. A group of men gathered together and decided which books should go in the Bible and which ones should not. How did they make that decision of what went in and what didn't? Well, one major way was whether or not they agreed with what the books said...if the books fit Christian traditions. And many of these decisions were made over a thousand years AFTER Jesus died.

Furthermore, much of the New Testament was written by a man who never heard Jesus teach. Paul supposedly encountered Jesus on the road to Damascus...

but never met him while Jesus was alive (the "first time"). Many of the Christian teachings are not things that are recorded in the gospels. They are simply things that Paul has mentioned. So, much of the Christian faith is not trusting in Jesus' teachings (as recorded by the mystery gospel writers whose books were selected by men 1,000 later to be included in the Bible), but trusting Paul, his story, his teachings, and his letters to various churches (some of which might not *actually* have even been written by Paul).

Finally, you've got multiple copies of the same book. Basically, we have no originals and only copies...many of which are slightly different. And they use many different methods to determine which copy to use: including which one seems older, as well as which one fits better with traditional Christian doctrine. Yet again, decisions are being made based on what people believe. And then finally, the books have to be translated out of the original language and into English (or other languages)...with many things being difficult to translate, or people translating them differently. And people want to take the Bible literally???

Jesus

I'll just jump right into what I think happened with Jesus. I think Jesus was a Jew. And I think, more than a Jew, he was a guy who had really strong ideas about who God was and the way we should live our lives. He was a great teacher who had many followers. He likely created a lot of enemies, as he continuously preached against the powerful religious interests at that time. He also preached against the rich. There were a lot of people who felt threatened by Jesus' teaching. They probably set him up and had him killed. Jesus likely died because he preached against the powerful religious and money interests of his day. He preached a message of generosity, of love, and of equality. And that message was a threat.

Then, years after he had been killed, some people made up some stories. Even Biblical scholars agree that the Gospels were written decades after Jesus died. After so many years, it would be easy to claim that there were "witnesses." Much of the Bible's, and Christianity's, credibility rests on the claim Paul made in 1 Corinthians 15:6, "After that, he appeared to more than five hundred of the brothers and sisters at the same time, most of whom are still living, though some have fallen asleep." Bottom line: either Jesus rose from the dead and there really were more than 500 people who saw him....or Paul is lying, Jesus never rose from the dead, and he was likely just a very special guy who was preaching a powerful message.

There are stories almost identical to the stories that Paul and the gospel writers (very smart, and obviously well-read people) tell about a person rising from the dead, that long predate the life of Jesus. For example, there is the Hindu epic, the Bhagavad-Gita, a story of the second person of the Hindu Trinity, who took human form as Krishna. He claimed to be "the beginning, the middle, and the end." His coming was heralded similar to the way Jesus' supposedly was. He was supposedly born of a virgin. Many of the stories about Krishna are nearly IDENTICAL to some of those told about Jesus. Such strong similarities also exist between the story of Jesus and the story of the Egyptian god Osiris, which also predates the Jesus story. Since Jesus wasn't even the first to have that story, I'm going to bet that Jesus was just a great prophet who was executed by the Romans for causing uprisings. Those interests threatened by him had him executed and then somebody brilliantly interwove the story of the real Jesus with the story of Osiris. And a religion was born.

So, am I still a follower of Jesus in that I believe he is the Savior of the world and the only way to Heaven? No. But am I still a follower of Jesus in that I believe he might have been a special guy with a special message and who was truly seeking the will of God...and that I want to try and live my life a lot like he supposedly did? Yeah. I am. But it's not that I need to be more like Jesus as much as I need to be more like God...and in the ways that Jesus was like that, then, I too, should emulate them. I know that this will undoubtedly cause some fundamentalist Christians to publicly call me the anti-Christ. What I am is a seeker of truth, peace, love, forgiveness, kindness, and compassion for the poor and lowly in this world. What could be less "anti-Christ" than that? If you ask me, THEY are anti-Christ...they are worshipping the wrong person/thing...and not God, love, humanity, and peace. They worship division, superiority, power, and many other things. In the Old Testament, the Israelites were always begging for a king or wanting some physical thing that they could worship. Jesus is exactly that: the greatest idol of all time. The people wanted to be able to have a God that they could picture and imagine. And that is exactly what the Jesus myth gives them: an easy to understand, human image of God that the people can worship.

Islam

I've heard many people say that Islam is a problem. There is absolutely no doubt in my mind that this is incorrect. As previously mentioned, many conservatives try to say that a gun is simply a tool: not good or evil, but merely used to carry out good or evil. This is a compelling philosophical argument (but one that still leaves me passionately opposed to gun ownership). However, I take that same argument and apply it to religion. Religion is a tool. It can be used to promote good (civil rights, charity, and countless other things) and it can be used to promote evil (killing abortion doctors, bigotry/hatefulness, the KKK, and terrorism).

Good is done in the name of Islam. And so is bad. Islam is not the problem. We see in countries like Turkey, the United Arab Emirates, and even in America, huge Muslim populations can enjoy relative peace and prosperity. But, it's also foolish to deny that there is a problem with a noteworthy percentage of Muslims. There are problems in Kashmir. There are problems in Chechnya. There are large problems in much of northern Africa. There is a war going on right now within Islam. On one side are those that preach an Islamic message of peace. And on the other are those that preach a much more violent message. The truth is that Muhammad's legacy is very complicated. Islam means peace. And Muhammad at times taught his followers to live in peace with those around them. However, his army also led raids on people and they captured rival groups. And then after his death, some of his followers focused on the messages of peace while others have focused on more violent teachings and imagery. Those that focus on peace have accused extremist groups of hijacking Islam's message.

But these hijackers of Islam are, ironically, just that: hijackers.19 of them flew planes right into the heart of America (and there are more in the world who think just like them). But I do not believe that these extremists' actions are in line with the core message of the Q'uran. Yes, I've read large parts of the Q'uran. How much have you read? How many suras (chapters) have you read in their entirety... compared with how many passages have you seen, but you're not really sure of the context? What kinds of crazy quotes do you think I could find in the Old Testament...the same Old Testament that many Christians strongly believe in?

Although I do not believe Muhammad was at all perfect, I also do not believe that the religion of Muhammad is the problem. But, I do believe that a noteworthy minority who claim to be his followers are really evil people. They are evil people with evil hearts. And they wish to control women and control others. They don't respect life and they have purposefully used Muhammad to propagate their hate and evil. And I hope that real Muslims will unite and defend their religion of peace from these liars and thugs.

Has America treated many Muslim nations unfairly? Yes. We have our military bases on their lands. We have supported, and even armed, the corrupt dictators that have oppressed them and suppressed them. We have supported Israel even as they oppress the Palestinian people. But many Muslims' own leaders have harmed them far more than we have. We should take responsibility for what we have done and continue to do. But Muslim nations need to clean their own houses first. They need to unite for peace. And let God protect them from those who wish to do them harm. They must trust in God and not in themselves. When you take the law into your own hands, you blasphemy God just like your enemies. Muslims, and Christians, should not follow, allow, or defend evil under any name.

Mormonism

You know, I feel really bad about this. I really, really do. Because most Mormons that I've met, and virtually 100% of the sincere Mormons that I have met, are the nicest freaking people in the world. I will never be as nice as they are. I want to be like them, in many ways.

But what they believe is f'ing crazy. Seriously. I actually get a little joy out of pissing jerks off. I really do. But I feel bad about being so harsh towards Mormons and their faith because you don't want to unnecessarily anger good people. But Mormonism is just crazy. The idea that God was once a man with flesh and bones who worked his way up to being God...that we can become gods and populate our own heavenly planets...that Jesus came to North America and appeared to the Native Americans...that Joseph Smith encountered an angel. And that he found the Book of Mormon and translated parts of it. There are secret ceremonies that Mormons can't share the details of with non-Mormons. And special religious undergarments. It's crazy. Not to mention Joseph Smith shot people that were in a mob that attacked him while he was in jail. Seriously. Sounds like a winner. Sign me up for that guy's religion.

Evangelical Christians, and just about every other religious group, have some pretty ridiculous beliefs, as well. But Mormonism and Scientology are really two of the *most* ridiculous (and that's really saying something). And a great example of exactly why Mormonism is so crazy is The Book of Abraham. Joseph Smith found this spiritual text written in Egyptian on papyri. He translated the papyri into English and it was canonized in one of Mormonism's most holy of books: The Pearl of Great Price. This was the word of God, as translated by Joseph Smith. The one and only. Well, guess what. Later on, they thought the original papyri had been destroyed in a fire...but actually they hadn't...and one day they were found. And just for fun, they gave it to some real experts who could read Egyptian hieroglyphics. You guessed it: absolutely <u>nothing</u> like Joseph Smith had translated. Completely different. They were things like pagan burial documents. He's a total fraud. And I have no idea why people would believe what this nut said. Just like I don't understand now why people don't think Paul was a nut for claiming to have seen Jesus.

But here is the one part of Mormonism that makes me the most nervous. It's the secrecy and the ostracizing that goes on. I don't think secrecy in religion is healthy. I just don't. And when you have secret ceremonies and rituals that you can't tell other people about...that makes me not trust you. And furthermore, when a Mormon's own parent can't attend the Temple wedding ceremony because only Mormons can go in? That's wrong, in my opinion. And it scares me a little. And if a child is Mormon and they stray away from Mormonism, many Mormon families will disown their own kids. Their friends will disown them, as well. Are all Mormons like that? Absolutely not. Just like not ALL Southern Baptists are judgmental, right wing bigots. But, a lot of very devout Mormons behave in this manner and it causes me to really be very untrusting of Mormonism. It's really crazy and manipulative.

The strangest thing is that their secrecy and willingness to ostracize former followers who turn away from Mormonism just doesn't seem to jive with what incredibly nice people they are. But I think it's just brainwashing. There are far worse things you could brainwash somebody into believing and doing. Mormons are extremely nice people. But, I think they just believe in some things and do a few things that I don't agree with. But some of the nicest people I've ever met are Mormons and they deserve a lot of credit for the way they treat other people outside their religion.

Atheism

Atheism is really pretty stupid. At least "die hard" atheism. That's the weird thing about it: there are some people that are super adamant about the fact that there is no God. They mock religious people for believing in something that can't be proven. How can you criticize somebody for believing in something that can't be proven (that God exists) while you, yourself, believe in something that can't be proven (that God doesn't exist). It's like this irony has passed atheists by. I can totally understand how somebody could be agnostic. I think agnosticism should almost be the default position of human beings, since it's so hard for us to be able to answer a question like whether or not God exists with any degree of certainty. And yet many people seem to take these very strong positions about whether God does, or even doesn't, exist.

Hardcore atheists always like to point out the evil and murderous acts that have been carried out by people professing to be religious. True enough, but what about all of the murderous and evil acts that have been carried out by people proclaiming to be atheists? By people like Stalin and Mao. Some people don't believe in God for very understandable reasons. But some people clearly don't want to believe in God because they think that means they can do whatever they want. If there is no God to judge you after this life, then you can do almost anything you want. There is no moral authority to judge you. We are all animals and life is not sacred. That is not the feeling of all atheists, but that is the goal of quite a few.

This world can be confusing, painful, and sometimes just horrible. I think that feeling like there is no God and that this is all there is…that's perfectly understandable. Just like it's perfectly understandable to see the order that exists in the universe and acts of love and peace and forgiveness and feel that there *is* a God. But they can only be feelings. We can't know for sure. And that's what I don't understand about people who are hardcore atheists. It's really a religion to them and they believe it (that God does not exist) with all of their hearts. And I wonder how they can feel SO strongly about it that they believe it to be fact.

How do they explain the starting point? If scientists agree that the universe is constantly expanding, then at some point there was a starting point at which the universe came into existence. Atheists believe that something came from nothing. If you look around at the beauty of the Earth…and how this is the only planet that we really know of in the *entire* universe that is perfect for sustaining human life (not that another one might not be out there…but we haven't found one yet).

The universe, in a big bang, exploded into a perfect solar system with a perfect planet and then the primordial ooze turned the rock into a fish and then the ape became a human. It's crazy that people believe this garbage! It's just like the Garden of Eden and Creationism...but they just call it science. *That* story is your proof that God doesn't exist?

Albert Einstein, perhaps the smartest man in the world, probably said it best. "I'm not an atheist and I don't think I can call myself a pantheist. We are in the position of a little child entering a huge library filled with books in many languages. The child knows someone must have written those books. It does not know how. It does not understand the languages in which they are written. The child dimly suspects a mysterious order in the arrangements of the books, but doesn't know what it is. That, it seems to me, is the attitude of even the most intelligent human being toward God."

Sex

First of all, sex is obviously a very complicated issue and there are many, many different opinions on the subject. But, it's one of the favorite subjects for many people to talk about. I believe that most Americans' general attitude towards sex falls into one of five general categories. The first category is people who view sex as absolutely nothing more than a physical act...and might even be willing to have sex for money. For these people, there is absolutely nothing sacred about sex. Some certainly believe that human beings are animals and they see sex completely as something for procreating and feeling pleasure.

The second group of people sees a lot in common with the first group, but doesn't believe that sex is something that should be bought or sold. They do, however, believe that sex is something that should be enjoyed with as many people as you can and want. This group is actually divided up into two groups. One of the groups always wants to be very honest with their partners. Either they want to be in a relationship with that partner, or at least have an understanding with that person that they aren't looking for a relationship, so that no feelings are hurt. Everybody is on the same page. That begs the question, "Is 'friends with benefits' actually possible?" It's very hard to say. Sex is a very special thing. It is very difficult for most people *not* to develop feelings. And then there is the other group of promiscuous people out there who basically believe that the ends justify the means. They are willing to say and do whatever it takes in order for them to get what they want. Many times "friends with benefits" is actually "some girl ends up falling in love with a guy who has no intention of ever being in a committed relationship." I believe it's wrong when you *know* sex is eventually going to result in somebody getting hurt.

There's a fourth group of people who believe that sex should really only be between two people who care about each other...and likely are in a committed relationship (but not necessarily marriage). The people in the previous groups are typically satisfied to appreciate the physical aspect of sex, which is great. However, what some people never learn (and what likely produces the truly best experience) is sex with somebody you genuinely love and trust. Most people are unwilling to make the kinds of sacrifices that are necessary, and to make themselves vulnerable enough, to really love another person. They enjoy the obvious part of sex, but usually never experience when love and passion collide.

The final group of people believes that sex is of the highest degree of sacredness and is only to be shared between a husband and wife. If a person believes they should never have sex outside of marriage, then that is their choice. Some people would actually object to that. "What if you get married and things don't work well in the bedroom? What if you don't connect sexually?" That might happen to the person asking such a question, because sex is obviously one of the most important parts of the relationship...to *that* person. For them, a relationship can't be satisfying if it's not also satisfying sexually. Other things, to this person, are probably negotiable. They can tolerate some things, but not unsatisfying sex. However, people's priorities are different. The things one person can tolerate, another person might have a really big pet peeve about that. Sex is not the most important thing in a relationship to everybody. However, some people get married young, partially or even primarily because of sexual tension in their dating relationships, which they don't believe can be relieved (morally) outside of marriage. It causes some people to get married younger than they should and then sometimes inevitably get divorced (probably for other reasons) later down the road. People should never get married or even be in relationships just for the sake of being married or in a relationship...or just so they can take care of their physical needs.

Relationships

Relationships are incredibly complicated. People approach relationships differently. People are looking for different things. Some of them are not right or wrong. Just preference. But, like with sex, there are some actually bad ways to conduct relationships and wrong behaviors that should be avoided.

In America, we are as diverse in the way that we approach relationships as we are diverse ethnically and demographically. Some people are looking for a partner they can lead. Maybe this person is a control freak (not always in a bad way). They might just feel the need to lead and be in charge. But they don't necessarily abuse it. There are also people out there, women AND men, that are looking to be led. I have more than one friend who always gets in relationships with very strong women who guide him. Other people are looking for more of an equal partnership. The one major problem with that is that most people want a partnership, but don't actually know how to be a good partner (or don't exhibit the behaviors).

Similarly, some people want (need?) to feel head over heels in love...even if the other person isn't head over heels in love with them back. I've known so many people that were completely in love with somebody that treated them badly and didn't really love them back. But they craved that feeling of passionate love. Other people prefer that the other person be in love with them. This person sometimes is a control freak and wants to stay emotionally guarded by having the other person love them more than they love the other person back. These people are also probably more likely to feel like they can separate sex (even with people other than their spouse) and love. Obviously many people, maybe most people (maybe?) are hoping for passionate love that is equal, rather than one-sided.

But that brings us to more differences in the way people look at relationships. Some people, especially many Asians, believe that love and family can be separate sometimes. Marriage is more of a pragmatic decision than a decision based on love. Either you consider the families, or the backgrounds, or the career, or the way a woman would raise children. It's less about passionate love or finding that soul mate who you are in love with and who is in love with you back (but then again, I'm not so sure these marriages actually have a lower rate of divorce than any other approach anyway). But for these people, they often get married when they feel like they've found the best person that they're going to find. They add up the person's strengths (looks, job, etc.) subtract their weaknesses, and then when they think they've found the highest scoring person they have a chance with, they marry them. Often without considering chemistry.

Many often think, "This person is pretty good looking. They meet the looks standard." (And this, by the way, is a major mistake with the way people choose their mate...they start by weeding people out based on looks and *then* start considering the personalities of the remaining people who first met the looks standard. People should start with personality...and then consider looks last. You might be surprised with the diamonds in the rough out there).

Some people approach relationships by expecting their partner to change to fit *their* preferences. In other words, "If he really loves me, then he'll _____." Rather than, "I love my partner, so I am going to love them just the way they are." One distortion of this, however, is the philosophy really underlying, "If he doesn't love me at my worst then he doesn't deserve me at my best." This is true...except when you use that as an excuse to be an asshole all the time and not try to improve yourself. For a relationship to work, each person needs to always try to become a better partner, while also accepting their partner just like they are. Is it easy? Hell no. But the key is mutual love, sacrifice, and hard work...by *both* partners.

Divorce

There is a stigma that comes along with divorce that is either real or perceived...and I think it's fairly real. And there probably should be. Personally, I never thought I would end up divorced. Although I don't have the same beliefs I used to, I still believe divorce is not a positive thing or something that should be taken lightly...ESPECIALLY if you have kids. I don't think, even as miserable as my ex-wife and I were, that we would have gotten divorced if we had had kids. Divorce with children is a major factor, I believe, in America's precipitous cultural downward spiral. However, we didn't have kids and we did get divorced. And I have no regrets about that decision. I made the best decision, in the long run, for both people. Yeah, it was a decision that wouldn't have had to have been made if we had made better decisions earlier on. But is a lifetime of misery for two people (who deserve to be happy) really a better choice? I say no.

Most states have waiting periods for divorces. In Texas, you must wait 60 days from when you file. In Virginia, I think you have to be separated for an entire year. That's so stupid. I know that it's religious nonsense that causes it, but I don't think people who get divorced take it lightly and just need to think about it a little harder. If you're going to possibly lose half your crap and possibly spend thousands of dollars on attorneys, trust me...you've thought about it long and hard. What they need to do is create a longer waiting period before you can get married. I know that it's terrifying for the religious people to think that we might make it more likely that people will have sex outside of marriage (gasp!), but maybe it just might lower the divorce rate in this country. The lesser of two evils.

The divorce rate in the U.S. among all couples is about 50%. Part of that could be because they make it so easy and quick to get married. But, among second marriages, the divorce rate jumps to 67%[41]. Some people clearly just shouldn't be getting married. And here's why: even long after the divorce, most people focus on what their spouse did wrong. My ex wasn't perfect. But I believe that the vast majority of our problems were the result of bad luck, bad timing, and my actions... not hers. That's the key. Are you the kind of person who never can admit that you did wrong (and will take that attitude into every relationship you ever have) or can you look back and learn from your mistakes? As badly as I hope to find love and believe that I have so much to offer somebody, I think she deserves it more than I do. Believe you me, we both have some very unique personality traits that probably make it difficult for many people to be with us. But, actually, she was probably one of the most flawless people I have ever met.

So, then why the divorce? I don't still believe what she believes...and we will always be like oil and water as long as that's true. There's nothing wrong with oil. And there's nothing wrong with water. They just don't mix real well. That often happens in relationships. You have two people who are perfectly good people. But they aren't right for each other. People in this country often choose who they will marry based on an analysis of their assets and their liabilities. We worry about whether the person is rich or good looking or smart. We often fail to think about chemistry and finding somebody that complements our strengths and weaknesses. In chemistry, some elements are perfectly stable on their own, but react violently when they are joined with certain other chemicals. Two people in a relationship can be like that. And occasionally, two already dangerous chemicals or substances combine to create an even more dangerous substance. And divorce happens for both of these reasons (and surely others): sometimes two perfectly good people just don't mix well and sometimes both people are just bad chemicals. Truthfully, most divorces happen because *both* people weren't really ready. Sometimes, it's just one person who ruins a marriage...but usually it's both.

However, we also should definitely not forget that sometimes two elements (like Hydrogen and Oxygen) can combine together to create something magical and vital. This is the kind of special relationship that we should all be looking for, so that hopefully we don't experience the pain of divorce. When I used to go to church, they would say that divorce is like ripping apart two pieces of paper that are glued together. It hurts, frankly, and little pieces of one paper will always be stuck to the other. It's true.

Spanking

Spanking has become a very controversial practice in America. Some people are big proponents. "Spare the rod, spoil the child." Other folks think it's cruel and practically barbaric, not to mention unproductive. The truth, as usual, is likely somewhere in between.

I think extremes are typically never good and spanking is definitely a good example of that. Very few people would advocate the merits of child abuse. Clearly, there is some point at which it is no longer punishment and it becomes abuse. Part of that has to do with the extent of the physical punishment. Was it a spank on the bottom? A slap to the face? A closed fist? How much damage was done? Was the skin briefly red but it went away? Or did you leave a bruise? Or even worse? These things are all very different. Furthermore, intent likely comes into play. Were you, as a parent, trying to teach your child a lesson? Or did you get caught up in your anger while you were punishing...and it became more about you than them? All of these things are hard to measure (and prove). And so some people try to create blanket statements like "spanking your child is just always wrong" because they think it's too hard, sometimes, to pinpoint where the line between punishment and abuse is.

But I would argue that the effects of <u>not</u> spanking can be tragic, as well. Perhaps great parenting skills could, theoretically, eliminate the need for parents to spank their children. Perhaps, if parents setup a good enough foundation with their kids and taught them to be good decision makers, parents could rationally workout most of their problems with their children more diplomatically. But most parents aren't that good. And neither are a lot of kids. I have seen kids whose parents have tried *everything*. They've tried every tactic. And none of it works. And I think a lot of people, at their core, are very animalistic. They need somebody to smack them occasionally and say, "No!" Especially when they are kids. How many children can really reason and understand why their parents tell them to do all of the things they want them to do? Yes, you can punish them in other ways, but many kids nowadays just walk right through any discipline their parents try to impose. Sometimes, spanking is the only thing that works.

I think the drastic stance that many have taken against spanking is a combination of two factors. One is more historical. Some of our parents grew up under parents who survived the Great Depression. Many of these parents really suffered at the hands of angry parents, some of whom were alcoholics, struggling with difficult times. Some of our parents were on the receiving end of more than just punishment. They were often the recipients of abuse. And some of them have continued that cycle and have gone on to abuse their children. But, I believe others have decided to take it to the other extreme and, therefore, don't believe in spanking children at all. I think that's where some of the anti-spanking sentiment comes from. And I think some of it just comes from the general wussification of our country.

My parents spanked me growing up. Not only did I survive, looking back, their only mistake was probably not spanking me more. I don't think all parents have to spank their kids. I think some can probably do a great job parenting without it. But many can not. And I don't think anybody should judge parents for choosing to spank their children. No parent has the right to abuse their kid, but every parent should have the right to decide that spanking is an appropriate way to discipline their children.

Parenting ("Raising" Kids)

It's not a bad place to start by pointing out that people who correct other people for saying "raising kids" (instead of the more formal...and technically correct "rearing kids") are extremely annoying. It's 2013. Not 1713. We raise kids now. Not sheep. In fact, I know some sheep that have been raised better, and are better behaved, than many American kids in 2013. But, these days (like in all times throughout history) there are both good parents and bad parents. And generally good parents can occasionally make some bad mistakes...and generally bad parents can occasionally do good things for their kids. It also seems worth noting that in some aspects of parenting, there is no right or wrong, but just a difference in styles. However, some parenting behaviors are clearly good and some are clearly quite bad and harmful.

Being a parent is one of the most important responsibilities of your life: you are teaching another person how to act. You are raising the future. You are helping to determine what kind of person will end up going out into the world. Many people don't take this responsibility nearly seriously enough. And many people are just simply not fit for this responsibility. They are not good people, themselves, and they end up hurting their child and sending them out to wreak havoc on the world around them. Frankly, many people should not be allowed to reproduce. We should try and help them not to. Many parents in America (and throughout the world) have raised monsters. Sometimes, the parent was a monster themselves. Other times, their mistakes helped to create a monster. And still other times, they had nothing to do with it at all. Sometimes, a kid is just bad. You try everything you can, but sometimes nothing works. It might be biological or chemical. Who knows? However, sometimes, it's simply not a parent's fault. Unless there is some subconscious thing going on, all of the mistakes I've ever made in life have been because of my own choosing. Because I am an idiot. My parents have nothing to do with my mistakes. And that, in itself, is a sign of my parents' good parenting. They taught me to take responsibility (although I often ignore this lesson). Many parents, themselves, never take responsibility for their actions...and their children learn this behavior from them and replicate it in their lives...often even taking it to new levels.

Which leads back to the point that although some parts of parenting are a matter of style, there ARE both good and bad parenting behaviors. One of the most important parts of parenting is to make sure that your child feels loved. If your child feels loved by you, then you have achieved the most important success.

If you haven't, *then all of your other successes as a parent are for nothing.* However, after that most important aspect of being a parent (making your child feel loved), there are other very important good parenting behaviors. You must teach your child right and wrong. So many American parents want to be their child's friend. In the previous chapter (on spanking), we discussed how sparing the rod can, indeed, spoil the child. Right behind love, instilling kids with discipline and a sense of right and wrong are great parenting behaviors. However, you can also be TOO strict and focus TOO much on discipline...causing your children to resent you and turning them into cold individuals.

And that is one of the keys to being a great parent: finding the correct balance. Kids need to be able to have fun and enjoy life. But they also need to learn to appreciate learning and how to work hard. You want to give your child some autonomy, but still protect them, guide them, and even monitor them. How you do these things also changes as your children get older (and even as technology and society changes). Being a parent...in America...in 2013...is almost unthinkable. Parenting was already hard enough. But to have the job in *today's* world and in *today's* culture...what a monumental (and vital) task.

Stereotypes

One of the biggest problems with racism is that it makes conclusions about an entire group of people (blacks, for example). That's preposterous. It is extraordinarily unlikely that in any group of people that large, everybody will be either good or bad or exhibit almost any trait. When people prejudge somebody based on stereotypes, they are showing their ignorance. Instead, we must realize that there are good and bad people in all groups: good and bad men, good and bad blacks, good and bad whites, good and bad Chinese. You must judge each person as an individual. Furthermore, some stereotypes are baseless attacks based on nothing but racism. However, some stereotypes do exist for a reason...

Virtually no large group is so homogenous that you could say 100% (of that large group of people) are like ___. But maybe 70% are. Or maybe even only 25% are...but that can still be a pretty huge number of people. Why should we deny these things exist? In fact, it's this kind of refusal to accept the reality of some stereotypes that help fuel the behaviors. Rather than fixing problems, we prefer to deny they exist. Look no further than the black community. Blacks have suffered...and continue to sometimes suffer...from vicious stereotypes. Blacks have been accused of so many things, which have caused whites to fear and/or hate them. Most of these things are completely baseless and untrue. However, in today's black community, some people do fit a certain modern day stereotype. This stereotype is that of a thug. They listen to rap, don't care about education, and glorify violence. They impregnate women, they speak barely comprehensible English, and they wear their pants down to their ankles. Are all black people like that? That is preposterous. But that stereotype exists because there's a large subculture of people who do fit those characteristics. And rather than deny that exists, we should simultaneously fight that subculture...as well as the belief that all blacks are part of it.

Blacks aren't the only people that there are stereotypes about. Everybody knows about rednecks. Are all southern whites beer guzzlin', gut totin', racist rednecks? Absolutely not. In fact, some southern whites are the most polite, sophisticated, well-mannered people you'll ever meet. But many southerners ARE rednecks. They love to listen to shitty country music and get drunk with their racist buddies after shooting some deer. And it doesn't do society any good denying that culture exists. Instead, we should acknowledge that sometimes these problems are common in certain communities and address it.

Each gender is associated with certain stereotypes. Men are stereotyped as being uncaring, crass, and aggressive. And many men are exactly that way. However, not *all* men are like that. Women are stereotyped as being airheaded, overly emotional, and materialistic. And jealous. Religious groups can be stereotyped. Not all Christians in the South are judgmental and dogmatic. But many are. Not all Jews love a good argument. But, I used to go to a temple many Friday nights and many Jews *do* love a good argument. (I fit right in). Even professions can be stereotyped. Not *all* lawyers and politicians are vicious, life sucking leeches. There's got to be at least one good lawyer and politician out there. Somewhere.

Some stereotypes exist for a reason. The important thing is not to deny that certain groups of people usually, or often, act or look in certain ways...but to treat every new person as if they were "one of the exceptions." It's when you decide everybody of a group is a certain way, and then treat them differently based on that, that stereotypes become a problem.

Judging a Book By Its Cover

"Don't judge a book by its cover." In America, we have heard this so many times. We have been warned much of our young lives to not judge people based on their outward appearance. And yet that's exactly what most people do. Why? And is this a good thing or bad thing?

"Judging a book by its cover" could really mean a number of different things. Some people might say that to "judge a book by its cover" means to believe a person is a good person or a bad person based on their physical appearance. The emphasis, in this interpretation, is on the word "judge." People shouldn't look at somebody and think they are a worse person or a bad person because of what they look like. Maybe it's because of their race or their weight or their physical attractiveness. Regardless as to exactly what the prejudice is, one shouldn't judge a book by its cover...in this way.

One could take it a step further and say that to "judge" here means not only a person's goodness or badness and their overall quality, but also what their personality is like. Don't assume because I dress a certain way that I believe or do certain things. Just because somebody likes to wear hip hop clothes doesn't mean that he's a gangster. Just because somebody wears plain clothes and doesn't shave all the time doesn't mean he's stupid or bad with people. Those are superficial things.

However, does that mean we should completely ignore physical appearance? Or are at least some people trying to tell a story about themselves by the way they dress and how they look? When a young teen dresses goth, are they trying to send a message about who they are and how they want you to perceive them? Same for teens who dress preppy or any other way.

Every human being's life is a story. Companies who publish books spend some time thinking about what should go on the cover. This book has a cover and I created it to look the way it does for a reason. I'm sending a message about my book's content and message. People, too, make decisions about what to put on their cover. Some people, through the basic disregard of their physical appearance, send a message about their priorities. Most people, through the way they consciously and subconsciously choose to look, are trying to tell a story.

And so we can use those visual clues to *help* us guess another person's story. But the cover is just the beginning. Sometimes, publishers choose to make the covers of books misleading. So, too, people can purposefully mislead others with their physical appearance. Other people are just unaware of the messages they are sending off. There are many reasons why the book might not perfectly match up with the cover. Many geniuses have appeared very ordinary. Many heroes have looked like ordinary Joes.

At the end of the day, it can really be summed up like this: there are parts of a person's cover they can control and there are parts they can't. If somebody can't control the way they look (perhaps they are ugly, perhaps they are handicapped, etc.), then it's not fair to judge a person by that, at all. They can't control it. And even the things that people *can* choose (the way they wear their hair, the clothes they wear, any piercings or tattoos) are just clues that should help us learn more about a person and who they really are on the inside. Look at the cover. Consider the cover. But read the pages, too.

Race in America

The truth is there are still racial problems in the U.S. Many people realize it, but virtually nobody really wants to talk about it. If nothing else comes from Barack Obama's historic presidency, I believe the slight increase in the amount of discourse over race in America will be a positive takeaway. And speaking of Barack Obama, nothing I could say in this chapter could better cover the issue of race in America than his speech in Philadelphia, as his candidacy for the Democratic nominee faced a defining crisis due to the words of his pastor, Jeremiah Wright.

The truth is, as Obama noted that day, the racial problems in this country are due to both sides. I believe with all of my heart that "institutional racism" is very much alive in America. Less than 50 years ago, blacks couldn't even drink from the same water fountains as whites in certain parts of the country. They couldn't eat at some of the same restaurants. 50 years is a long time, but does anybody really think it's enough time to make up for more than 300 years of racism (blacks were enslaved long before America declared its independence)? Do you think that when Jim Crow and segregation were abolished, that blacks magically all of a sudden found themselves as attorneys, doctors, and engineers...much less Senators, Governors, and CEO's? Does anybody think that when segregation ended, the ghettos were magically turned into suburbia? No. It is true those things will take time and can't be forced to change overnight. However, blacks were held down by the rules and the laws for so long...why is it so crazy to think that now they deserve to be helped up by those laws?

And having gone to a school that was more than 50% black in one of the worst sections of town, I can tell you that institutional racism *does* still exist. My middle school was officially built in the 1930's. But my sister and I swear we remember a sign that said the school was built in the 1890's. Either way, it was a middle school in Georgia that lacked air conditioning. Our textbooks were always at least 10 years old. Gang violence was always on the back of your mind. We knew people who were victims of it. Try to tell me that somebody in that environment can learn as effectively as a student at a school in an upper-middle class, predominantly white suburban area with a new building and new textbooks. And try and tell me that the same quality of teachers want to teach in both schools. No. Institutional racism is alive and well and it's one reason that race is still a problem in the U.S.

This doesn't even factor in some of the overt racism that still exists. You can easily look online to find evidence that racism is alive and well. Following President Obama's reelection, both Facebook and Twitter were full of just blatantly racist comments. Comments that aren't worth repeating. And then finally, there are stories like that of the three teenagers in Jackson, Mississippi who ran over a black man with their truck. That night the white teens decided to go "fuck with some niggers" and drove around until they found a black man, whom they beat and then ran over multiple times with their truck, killing him[42]. Those who say racism doesn't exist in America have no idea what they are talking about and would be better off keeping their mouth shut.

However, blacks (and Hispanics) are not completely innocent either. Whites have not forced many minorities to embrace a hideous, violent rap subculture...a subculture that embraces violence, drugs, and sex. Whites have not forced black men to leave women as single mothers at unbelievably high rates. Whites have not forced black women to have children out of wedlock at truly shocking rates. And although I think blacks have real disadvantages in the court system, I don't believe that most of the blacks in U.S. Correctional facilities are innocent. They may be trapped in a cycle of poverty that is not their fault, but the vast majority of blacks in prison absolutely made the choice to commit the crimes they were convicted of. Nobody else is to blame for that. There is a culture problem that exists in parts of the black community. And while some like Bill Cosby and Oprah Winfrey and Barack Obama have tried to address it, their cries seem to be falling on deaf ears. The black community gets defensive. They point to problems in the white or Mexican communities or try to justify the problems in their community. How does that help? So what if whites or Mexicans have problems? Does that mean you shouldn't try to fix the problems in your own community?

Ultimately the biggest problem with race in America is this: nobody wants to take any responsibility. Whites want to blame black culture. Blacks want to blame institutional racism. The problem will never be solved like that. Everybody must admit the truth about how THEY are at fault...and focus on how to correct the things that they are able to control. As long as people choose to ignore their own faults and only blame the other group, race will continue to be a problem in the United States.

Rednecks, Cowboys, and Good Ol' White Trash

One of the things that I find interesting is how basically similar whites in rural parts of America are to each other. (Urban blacks, as well. Many blacks in Atlanta, D.C., New York, L.A...and big cities all over the country share a very similar culture). The same is true for rural whites. Many of them are the same, all over the country. A redneck in Georgia is pretty similar to a redneck in Pennsylvania and a redneck in Northern California. For some reason, rednecks are basically the same everywhere.

Rednecks are a special group of people. Jeff Foxworthy has made a rich career out of this. A redneck is a good ol' boy. They love drinking. And shootin' guns. And wearin' camouflage. And fishin'. And doin' things they feel are masculine. They usually talk with an accent. They don't like minorities or foreigners. They often don't really respect women. And they prefer being out in the country.

Cowboys are similar but different. Rednecks don't mind traveling around and taking their wonderful culture and sharing it with other places, sometimes. But cowboys like to stay home. They've got to stay close to their animals and their land. So, they stay around their town, mostly. Drink a lot. Fight a lot. If there is one thing that cowboys LOVE, it's to fight. (And drink). They would do anything to be able to fight. It's their favorite hobby. Everything is about being manly, fitting a certain image, and doing what other cowboys do. In some ways, at least, there is even less diversity in cowboys.

White trash is different than either of these previous two groups. They don't really have anything that is unique about them. They don't necessarily wear special clothing (they might barely wear any clothing, in fact) or necessarily speak with an accent. They might not like the outdoors. But these people are dumb, uneducated, poor, and just dirty people. Many of them also engage in criminal behavior. They don't teach their kids right from wrong. They are just plain old white trash you might find in almost any trailer park (going back to the stereotypes chapter, there are some very nice people that live in trailer parks. And there are also some child molesters).

These three groups are not completely the same. However, they do share some similarities with one another. The first is that they are typically all white

(I've seen a few Mexican cowboys, but it's just a little odd and a very small percentage of cowboys). All three groups typically like alcohol...usually too much. Some whites, especially these three groups of whites, really look down on black people. Which is ironic since these groups have some very, very unfavorable characteristics...and some of the same characteristics they like to criticize others for. You see, there are a few characteristics that really tie these three groups of whites (rednecks, cowboys, and white trash) together...that also apply to many of the other groups that we use pejoratives to discuss: they all tend to be lazy (except for cowboys), poor, and uneducated. The next chapter is about "the N word." There is a much darker history behind "the N word", but in 2013, the words "redneck" and "nigger" are often in some ways effectively equivalent in their ultimate meaning. (Yet because of the difference in history, we don't need to say "the R word"). These similar qualities actually tie rednecks and niggers together. It's really rich listening to some stupid, lazy redneck complain about a dumb, lazy "n word." It's almost ironic. The two groups hate each other, but they are actually more similar to one another than they realize.

"The N word"

I find it interesting that we call it "the N word." Many Americans, myself included, are foul mouthed. Not all of us. But a lot of us. And we take pride in it. The American white collar professional cusses in anger. The American blue collar worker cusses. All the time. Almost no word is off limits. But "the N word" really is. And in some ways, I think it's a good thing. The word definitely has a bad history. But it has a present, too. And a future. And it's as ignorant, in my humble opinion, to refuse to accept the evolution of language as it is to ignore its history.

I've been around "the N word" a lot. I grew up in Macon, GA...a town still seething from the days of segregation several decades ago. People there remember how they were treated. They were alive. You don't forget. My best friend growing up was a black girl that I went to church with and lived in my neighborhood. However, that was more the exception than the rule. Growing up in the South, you know that whites and blacks are different. You have different cultures. Different ways of speaking. And you usually go to different churches. But this friend of mine's family was different. They just wanted to be like everybody else. They recognized the struggle of being black, but they felt perfectly comfortable around whites. And that family loved that church. But typically, blacks and whites, in the South, are just different...and still live separate (but not usually equal) lives. And neither race in Macon (and in many other towns in America) particularly likes one another. It wasn't often, but it wasn't unheard of for whites to mutter "the N word" under their breaths or in exclusive company. One time, I remember my friend's racist dad coming home and just yelling, "Hey, nigger, nigger, nigger, nigger. It's Nigger Doug. And Nigger Christopher." He was just a racist old redneck who loved using the word. This word has been used by some whites to belittle black people simply for being black. That's one usage of the word. And I think it's despicable. I think to try and put somebody down simply because of the color of their skin is evil.

The word has actually evolved in its usage over time. For one, it's not just whites using the word. Many young, urban blacks have adopted the word and embraced it. In fact, it's very common to hear it spoken by young blacks. Here, the word might not be used negatively. "Look at this nigger right here!" It may make some older blacks (and some younger blacks) cringe, but the word for some just doesn't have the same meaning anymore. Like "gay" used to mean happy. Words and their meanings change. They just do. And you may not want them to change that way, but they change nonetheless. But it's also used by blacks negatively. "Who you think you are, nigger?"

Another meaning of "the N word" these days is that particular kind of un-educated, and really criminal, African American. Are all black people like that? Of course not. That's offensive. But even Chris Rock said there's a civil war going on right now between "black people and niggers." Are there white trash in this country? Tons. Are there niggers? Yeah, there are. I don't think you should ever call somebody that to their face because of the historical stain of that word. But in 2013, the reality is that there are black people and niggers. And there are educated whites and there are rednecks. That's what they're called. We may not be able to admit it. We may not say it out loud or put it in print (except for me). But, that's the truth.

America's Inner Cities

Some Americans are perplexed as to how and why the inner city operates the way it does. It's so different from the upper middle class world of suburbia. Many inner cities are, in some ways, closer to third world countries than they are to the wealthier parts of America. Violence. Drugs. Organized crime. Bad education. Right in the heart of American cities. What are the incentives that created it? Why does it operate the way it does?

The two most important things to understand about America's inner cities are organized crime groups and cycles of poverty. Organized crime is obviously about money and power. Organized crime funds itself by engaging in the activities that our governments have outlawed (drugs, prostitution, and gambling). It makes one wonder if these things were legal, how would these organized crime groups fund themselves? Organized crime groups fight over territories. They increase their membership by wreaking havoc on communities...creating unsafe neighborhoods, whose members often feel like they have no choice but to turn to a gang to ensure their own personal safety (from the gangs). This is how the gang increases its membership, its strength, and its power.

In much of the inner city, people don't have much. They're caught in a cycle of poverty. How they got in poverty (most blacks ultimately came from poor backgrounds, since most free blacks very early on were not wealthy or educated) makes little difference. At some point, the cycle must be broken. Many children born in inner city America do not have a parent or a grandparent who has been to college. Not a brother or a sister. Not an aunt or an uncle. Nobody in their family has ever been taught the importance of an education. Somebody must become the first.

But, in many parts of the inner city, education is looked down upon. You're made fun of for being smart. The cycle reinforces itself. Most people in the inner city simply lack marketable skills. What can they do if they don't have a strong education? People without strong minds can really only do something that doesn't require thinking (something that a machine can usually do now). And as mentioned in other chapters, low value-add labor (labor that really doesn't think or add anything...something anybody can do) has become commoditized...and it's often cheaper to rent uneducated labor overseas.

The inner city's only hope is to embrace education. However, getting a good education in the inner city is made even more challenging by the bad schools, the gangs, and the culture problems. How does organized crime grow into such a problem? Criminals know of the dangers they take when they turn to a life of crime. Why do they do it? Gangs recruit members with ease when people feel like they are being kept down. When people feel like they aren't able to get their fair share through legal means, some of them will always turn to trying to get their "fair share" illegally. It's why organized crime is such a problem in places like Eastern Europe, Latin America, and in much of Africa. Corrupt governments limit the opportunities for people to get ahead through hard work. If you want to get rich, you must either have political connections or turn to a life of crime. Some people, in America's inner cities, have never known somebody who was rich...other than gang leaders. People make rational decisions. If the only rich people a person knows are gang leaders, rappers, or athletes, then that's what kids from there will want to be. We must teach inner city kids that the gang life leads to short-term gain, but that education leads to safer, long-term gains that can never be taken away by police or rival gangs.

Police

There are quite often controversies with police in most places in the world. It comes with the territory of giving certain individuals huge amounts of power. Some places have more reputable police than others...and a country's police force will likely change and evolve over time. For example, police forces in America suffered from major corruption in many places, including New York City, even up until recent times. Relative to much of the developing world, America's modern day police force tends to be fairly effective and relatively honest. And police in the U.S. have one of the most terrible, dangerous jobs where they are forced to basically deal with the scum of the country for much of their day.

However, that's not to say there aren't still major problems with many police in the U.S. In fact, being a policeman is such a bad job many places in America, that there are really only two types of people who want to do the job: the noblest of citizens who want to protect and serve their communities...and people who are desperate for power. Almost everybody, at this point, has run into that officer who is on a power trip. I've run into numerous examples. These officers are so desperate to show you that they can do whatever they want to do. They are bullies.

Furthermore, police are trained (and it is constantly ingrained in them) that they need to be out there catching criminals. Everybody has a job and different metrics you can use to determine if you are doing your job well: how much you sell, how many complaints you get, whatever. Some of these guys feel like the only way they are doing a good job is if they are catching people do things they aren't supposed to. The more people they arrest, the more successful they feel. Some places, cops have enough *real* bad guys, that they don't have to bust people for bull shit to feel like they are doing a good job. Some places, however, there's nothing else to do, and they are constantly feeling like they need to be doing something. Plus, they are just bored. Not to mention the possibility of quotas for citations and arrests.

One of the arguments that police constantly make is that they should be given a lot of latitude because of the types of people (criminals) that they encounter all day long. And part of me is sympathetic to that. Police in America, especially due to the rapid social decay, never know when somebody might pull a gun on them and put their life in jeopardy. It's been said, though, that people who are frequently exposed to counterfeit bills become especially adept at spotting fake bills. Likewise, if police really do deal with criminals all day long (and some of them do), then they should be able to tell the difference between a little old lady going six miles over the speed limit and a real criminal. Yet that doesn't stop police from being complete assholes and/or abusing their power with even the most innocuous of people. I've personally seen police in Austin, TX arrest somebody for walking into an unlocked school, buying a drink from the vending machine, and then leaving. And I've seen the Tempe Police arrest somebody for trying to catch a cab and then steal his phone. The Tempe Police were later alerted and refused to investigate further. How can trained professionals, who are around criminals all day, be so stupid? Or evil? Police in the U.S. have committed police brutality and even killed people...and then either gotten away with it completely or simply have lost their jobs. If you beat a police officer, you go to jail...probably for a long time. If the police unfairly beat you, they might lose their job. Probably nothing worse. If you kill a cop, then you'll probably get the death penalty. If they kill you, even if you were unarmed, they might get a reprimand (or lose their job). They've got their unions and their buddies on the discipline boards who will usually protect them. Especially in places like Tempe, Arizona.

A huge part of the problem is that you are trusting people, many of whom were lucky to complete a high school education, with almost unlimited power. Have you ever been to the DMV? Or almost any other municipal government agency? Municipal workers, quite honestly, are often the bottom of the bottom, in terms of quality workers. Does anybody really think that most police are the exception to this rule? When they often have even less education, a bigger ego, and bosses and unions who protect them?

Men in the U.S.

Most men are pretty disgusting, actually. All over the world. Same. Men in some places are more disgusting than others. Some aren't horribly, horribly bad. But most are fairly bad. And, although I think some women know this, I don't think most women really have any idea to what extent. You see, when you are the member of a particular gender, you are privy to conversations that the members of the other gender will never hear. It's like a secret society. I would give the women readers an example of things they talk about that they KNOW they would never talk about in front of a man, but since I am a man, I don't know what they are. I just know they exist. They do. And men are no different. But the things that they talk about, especially about women (when women aren't around), are quite disgusting.

There are two major reasons why men are disgusting. And neither of them is what you're probably thinking (hormones). I have decided that hormones and biology actually play a much smaller role than we give them credit for. I am NOT saying biology doesn't play a role. That's just stupid. I am a man and hormones are very real. But, without being graphic, there are multiple ways to satisfy those hormonal urges. And although some are more enjoyable than others...not so much so as to explain the way that men act...or their *obsession* with sex. And some men are able to take the same hormones and then choose to satisfy them in ways that aren't completely selfish and don't require using or manipulating women. All of us have occasionally met very large, strong guys with lots of testosterone who are complete gentlemen.

The real two reasons men are disgusting are a male created culture and fear. Most men tell other men that the way they "prove their manhood" and that the way they "fit in" is by acting a certain way. One of the biggest parts of "being a real man" and gaining social acceptance is to have sex with as many (preferably beautiful) women as possible and then bragging about it with other men. They've convinced themselves that this is normal, natural, and even ideal. So, in order to fit in and do what "normal" men do, men act this way. And it's very competitive. Most men constantly try to "one up" each other with what they've done and with whom. But this issue of masculinity and machissimo doesn't end with sex. You're usually expected to drink a lot (and this is very competitive, too). Men in America can be quick to try and live by a "might makes right" philosophy. Many men in America almost instantly resort to fighting to solve any disagreement. And to be a real man, you can't be open about your feelings. Men have convinced themselves that love and compassion and empathy make you less of a man. Some of these behaviors may make men feel good physically, but it's as much about following the crowd and fitting in as it is about the pleasure that they get.

But other than this culture that men have created to define what is acceptable male behavior (and what isn't), I think fear is a huge reason men behave the way they do. Men are deathly afraid of making themselves vulnerable and getting hurt. So, it's easier to be the one that does the hurting. So, like an animal seeking its prey, men try to find women they can sleep with. They rarely allow themselves to get attached because then they might get hurt. It's just a game. Can they make the kill? If not, move on to the next prey. If so, add another mark on the chalk board. This is what most men are really like and they just don't want you to know.

And amazingly, men in America actually treat women much better than most men in the developing world. Man has a thirst for power and for domination. It seems to be in many men's DNA. And it's men who have ultimately been behind almost every war in the history of mankind. As bad and dysfunctional as many women in America have become, they still have a long way to go to catch up to men. And frankly, I doubt they ever do. Or we'll be in even bigger trouble. But many women are certainly trying their hardest.

Women in the U.S.

In the previous chapter, I talked about how dirty and conniving and downright awful many men are. And that is true. But this is also true: a lot of women are insane. Whereas most men are more sane, but are deceitful and dishonest and often cheat, many women are just nuts. I think a man almost always knows what he's doing. It may be incredibly simple (like sleep with some girl and then never call her again...or only call her for sex). But he knows what he's trying to do. All women, at various points, seem to have no idea what they are doing. They are confused. They overanalyze everything. One minute they feel one way. The next minute they feel another. For no reason. Total random chaos.

But, the other problem, more specifically with attractive women (like attractive men), is that they know how to use their attractiveness to their advantage. Many attractive women are incredibly, incredibly manipulative and incredibly, incredibly selfish. The other problem with a lot of women, during college and their mid-20's, is that they think they are hotter than they are. They don't realize that the average man will sleep with any girl. Any. Girl. He might not enjoy it as much. He might claim he was drunk later. Or even deny it altogether. But most men will sleep with any girl he has the opportunity to. And so many insecure ugly girls THINK that because they can get a guy to sleep with them, that they're hot. Or maybe they're trying to fake it until they make it. But they're simply not as hot as they pretend they are. Many young women try to please men by being extra promiscuous. Or by pretending to be attracted to women. (There's nothing wrong with ACTUALLY liking women. But be who you really are. Don't pretend).

Women also gossip, love drama, and ask questions just to hear you say the answer they want to hear. Women are jealous. They're often incredibly needy. They tend to be extremely insecure. And overly sensitive. And bitchy when it's that time of the month (and it always seems to be that time of the month). Most women can't drive worth crap. Some women nag you about *everything*. And women are notorious for trying to make their partners change to make them happy. They domesticate the man and control him.

In our society, women have learned how to effectively leverage men's insatiable thirst for sex and, in many ways, have gained an upper hand. Take divorce for example. Dead beat dads are terrible. Typical dirt bag men. But some women, married to men with high incomes, will take him to the cleaners. Child support...I think that's important. And alimony. I think if the woman needs to raise two kids or is really unable to start a career, I think it's fair to force the man to share his income. But if a woman files for divorce because she's not in love anymore or even because she cheated on her husband, she shouldn't get huge alimony payments. At any time, simply because she wants to spend more of their money than the husband thinks they can afford (or for any reason at all), women in many states can divorce their husbands and get half their money plus alimony. It's terrible.

There was a day in this country when women really were treated unfairly. They were discriminated against in the work place (they still are, sometimes). And for many years, they couldn't even vote. But, in the 21st century, women have made lots of progress. I would argue that although they still suffer from some inequalities (like unequal pay), women also enjoy some advantages over men. They can get free dinners and drinks. Attractive women can get almost anything they want. They've decided to fight back against men's evilness and bad treatment by being evil themselves and treating men badly back.

Old People

Old people are quite interesting. Human beings go through stages in life... and old age is just one of them. Many old people share some similarities, but there is also some diversity. I really believe that most old people tend to either be fabulous, kind people...or are completely grumpy and rude. Why does this happen?

Old people are interesting because they've seen so much. People have a tendency of always thinking they know everything. When you're 16, you think you know everything (and that the older folks have forgotten what it's like to be young). And you think the same thing at 18. And 21. And 24. And 30. If you're a fairly intellectual person, your perspective usually changes over time, as you've learned and been exposed to more things. Therefore, many old people are extremely wise, because they've seen most of the same things you have...and so much more.

But old people have less endearing qualities, as well. They often really struggle to adjust to a lot of the new technologies. *Some* old people are very quick, as they have kept their mind agile. Others, however, have allowed technology to pass them by and have not put forth the mental effort to stay current. Old people are often extremely slow, in general. They often walk slow. They talk slow. They think slow. A lot of old people are frankly in no hurry to get anywhere (except for when they are cranky). They become confused more easily. And some of them *love* to talk. They will talk your ear off. Yet other old people don't seem to want to talk at all. They don't want you to say one word to them.

I think once you reach a certain age, you just start dropping all of the pretenses. Either you're a nice person or you're not. No more pretending. I have met some of the kindest, sweetest old people. For whatever reason, their lives have turned them into cheerful and generous people. Other old people's lives have caused them to turn completely bitter and untrusting. These old people are often very impolite and rude. They're done trying to pretend that they are nice and happy people. They're not.

And it's interesting how old people are treated now in America. In Korea, for example, old people are respected. You must listen to what they say, even if you don't agree. You almost never argue with somebody who is older than you. You just bite your tongue. Old people are really at the top of society. However, here in America, old people are nearly at the bottom of society. People (like me, I guess) complain about how slow and annoying they are. We feel like we have better things to do than to talk to them. They are old school and not with the times. Old people are often even targeted as the victims of crimes. In Austin, TX, one of the safer cities in America, an old lady was killed while being mugged by a middle school student trying to get into a gang. And that was in one of the safest cities in America. Old people are not respected in American culture anymore.

We, as Americans, must find a healthy balance. Some societies, like Korea, probably give old people *too* much power. There, some old people often abuse their special status. They cut in front of lines and try to force their ways on other people. That is too extreme. However, contrast that with America, where old people are almost looked at with disdain, and it's obvious to see why some kind of balance between these two extremes is needed. Old people should be respected, listened to, and taken care of...but not allowed to be rude, control others, and throw around their weight...just because they're older.

Young People

It seems like every generation looks at the younger generation and just shakes their head. For decades, and probably much longer, Americans have looked at the younger generation and felt like that generation was less responsible, had looser moral principles, and even put the future trajectory of the nation at risk. But then again...over the last several decades...has that not, at least kind of, been the case? Have things not gone downhill, in at least some important ways? How many can remember a time when the streets were mostly safe and you could trust a stranger? When people could hitchhike with little fear of danger? Haven't the recent generations, as of late, been every bit as bad as many have worried?

Occasionally, you meet a young person and think, "Wow. That is a really impressive young man/woman." But these days, it seems like that is becoming more and more rare. Instead, we see more and more young people engaging in crazy and almost unthinkable behavior. That seems to be one difference between today's young generation and previous generations: many in today's young generation have basically no sense of moderation whatsoever. Basically, for the last 50 years, kids have begun doing crazier and crazier things and making worse and worse decisions. Turn on the news. Read the headlines. And ask yourself, "Could I have ever dreamed of reading about a kid doing that 50 years ago?" Of course many times the answer will be yes, but many other times the answer will be, "No way."

In addition to being less moderate in their behavior, today's young generation is also a lot less disciplined and hard working. In past generations, many Americans basically adopted a philosophy of, "Work hard. Play hard." Now, young Americans just want to play hard. All play and no work. And this laziness of today's young generation manifests itself in other ways. They are intellectually lazy. Past generations were curious. Ambitious. They had been taught hard work during the Great Depression. The young generation today doesn't care about learning. Some even make fun of smart people. They aren't curious about gaining knowledge. They're content and complacent. They don't appreciate money and they are entitled. They think they just deserve to have things without working for them.

One final problem with today's younger generation (although there are many, many more), is that they often lack respect and a moral and ethical code. I don't believe schools should teach a particular religion. However, I do believe that students need to have schools teach them basic values and ethics. We have become such moral relativists that we have convinced ourselves that we cannot teach right and wrong. And I think the impact of that kind of thinking is being seen all across America. The young generation seems to have completely lost their grip on right and wrong. And I'm not talking about harmless things religious people criticize like drinking, smoking marijuana, or having premarital sex. When I say that young people have no moral or ethical code, I mean they cheat. They lie. They steal. Recently there was a story about a young teen in Florida who killed his parents and then threw a party at their house while their dead bodies (that he had bludgeoned to death) lay bloody on the floor of their bedroom. It's hideous. Many young people now have absolutely no sense of right or wrong.

Looking into America's future, you have to think about this younger generation. What does America's future look like based on today's young people: a little bleak?

Rich People

One of the most important things I think we can remember, as I mentioned earlier, is that there are good people and bad people of all kinds. Rich people are no different. Some rich people are some of the world's biggest philanthropists, giving to many great causes and helping people all over the world fight poverty and disease. However, there's another large group of rich people. It's so ironic that these rich people complain about poor people feeling "entitled"...because a lot of rich people are the most entitled people I've ever met. They think they deserve to make 100 times more than an average person makes per year and to be treated like they are some kind of king...just because they have more skills and more money. They think they are superior.

Although these people exist all over the country and even all over the world, in the United States, there seems to be a heavy concentration of them up North. They are all chasing the same money and the same material things. But the interesting thing is that they don't seem happy at all. They seem miserable. They are bitter. Rude. Selfish. And stingy. They are like real life Scrooges.

What I want to know is why they think they deserve such ridiculous salaries. These people believe in completely free markets, but they typically believe in them because it rewards them and punishes others who don't have the same background or ability. They attribute everything to hard work and nothing to upbringing, connections, and biological factors like intelligence. It's a common fallacy to over-attribute our successes to our abilities and to frequently dismiss our failures as being caused by others. However, rich people truly believe that they deserve to make (and keep) millions of dollars per year and that others deserve to earn practically pennies. Many rich people have an arrogance that is really almost unparallel.

What's really amazing to me is how selfish some rich people are. They see people suffering. They see people who have fallen on hard times. And many usually look the other way. Many rich people don't want to share what they've been blessed with. They'll talk about teaching a man to fish versus giving him a fish, but they don't spend any of their time teaching men how to fish. In fact, I think many of them don't want to teach others how to fish because they think it will only make the market more competitive and threaten their advantage and their wealth.

Warren Buffet once said, "There's class warfare alright...only it's my class, the rich class, that's making war...and we're winning." The top 1% of Americans earn over 20% of the nation's income (and own over 35% of the wealth). The top 20% of Americans own 85% of the nation's wealth, leaving 15% to be divided among the remaining 80% of Americans. That is incredible, unnecessary, and really inexplicable. Profit potential is necessary to drive innovation and entre-preneurship. People need to be able to profit to give them the incentives to take risks, try new ideas, and ultimately put people to work. However, how much do we have to let these people keep? How much financial inventive do they think they need? At some point, economics really becomes a zero sum game. We can create new wealth, but slowly over time. There is a limited amount of money right now. There are people in this world who are starving and people in this country who have trouble making ends meet. Those rich in this country who do not actively give back to their communities, through their money and through their time, are incredibly selfish. Certainly a small percentage do, but many do not.

And that is the problem with a lot of rich people. They are greedy, arrogant, selfish, self-absorbed, and entitled. And many just like to spend money and talk about the ways they spend their money. No thanks.

Poor People

For all of rich people's problems, poor people aren't all perfect, either. I've met some great poor people in my life who are very kind, good-hearted people who love their family. And I've met poor people who weren't so good-hearted and family-oriented. Poor people sometimes have a culture of their own. And it's not always pretty.

It doesn't matter whether you're a poor white, a poor black, a poor Mexican, or a poor anything else. A lack of a good education is one of the most common characteristics of poor people of any race. A lack of education leads to poverty. And it's usually a cycle. You don't teach your kids the importance of an education...because you didn't get an education. You probably don't value it. And in fact, there are some subcultures in America where people make fun of people who are smart and educated. And this is one of the most destructive cultures imaginable.

Although the rich can also feel very entitled, the rich are right that some poor people are extremely lazy and entitled. Some poor people do seem to think they deserve things without working for them. They want to impregnate girls (or get impregnated) at young ages. They want assistance from the government when they have to drop out of school and take low paying jobs. I think people deserve a fair wage if they are willing to work hard, but some poor people are the laziest people you'll ever meet. They want to blow their money on booze and cigarettes because they make them feel good, but then ask for money from others. They make very bad decisions with their money.

Their bad decisions are not only financial. In addition to ignoring education and often having children at very young ages, poor people also commit violent crimes at a disproportionate rate. Poor people often feel like they don't have the ability to become rich or earn an honest living (even if it's because they, themselves, have made a choice not to study and learn marketable skills). So instead, some turn to crime in order to make the kind of money they seek. And it's a violent and dangerous path. This is why the poorest neighborhoods are usually the most dangerous neighborhoods. Plus, as Chris Rock once joked, "If you live in an old project, a new jail ain't that bad." Outside of jail, these people often have a hard time finding work and ways to support themselves. And they go back to crime and back to prison because of this strong connection between poor people, a lack of education, and crime. It's a vicious, vicious cycle.

And I think, as a country, we have to take a balanced approach. We have to recognize that a child born into a stable, two-parent, middle class home has a ton of advantages over a child born into a poor, single-parent household with a poorly educated parent. And although we must demand people take responsibility for their lives, we must realize that as a society we have a strong interest in helping poor people make good decisions, get an education, break the cycle of poverty, and become productive members of society. The alternative to not just helping, but even pushing poor kids to get an education and skills, is to build more prisons and more security systems later down the road. Because we know from experience, all over the world, that when people are uneducated and poor (especially when they also have a weak family structure like here in the U.S.), they often turn to crime.

The Homeless and Beggars

Homelessness is obviously a big problem. The good news is that it affects a relatively small percentage of America's 300 million people. But for that relatively small percent, which is still a pretty large number, the issue couldn't be much bigger. Let's look at the numbers. According to a report titled "The State of Homelessness in America in 2012" published by the National Alliance to End Homelessness, there were over 636,000 homeless people in 2011. Homelessness among veterans decreased from the previous couple of years, but still was over 67,000 people (representing over 10% of the homeless population). Furthermore, the general population experienced a rate of homelessness of 21 homeless people per 10,000 people. Veterans, however, had a rate of 31 homeless veterans per 10,000 veterans. Therefore, veterans are experiencing higher rates of homelessness (by nearly 50%) in comparison with the general population. Two other statistics: the number of chronically homeless (often those homeless for more than one year) was over 266,000 people and the number of unsheltered homeless (like those sleeping on the streets) was over 243,000 people[43]. Although a small percentage of Americans, these are still pretty big numbers.

Now what are the causes of homelessness? According to the Substance Abuse and Mental Health Services Administration, between 20 and 25 percent of the homeless population in the U.S. suffer from serious mental health problems (maybe an equal number have more moderate mental health issues)[44]. Most people who have been to major cities (New York, New Orleans, San Francisco...or any major city) have encountered severely mentally ill homeless people. They're a little scary, frankly, because some of them are so mentally disturbed, you can't know for sure what they are going to do. They're not all there. There is no way these people, in their current states, could ever hold down a job to support themselves. As discussed in more detail in the next chapter, these people are often more like zombies or human bodies walking around on auto-pilot. These people must have access to and receive help and treatment if they're ever going to have anything close to resembling a life of dignity. And one must not forget that some, if not many, of these mentally ill experience their problems after returning from the horrors of war (that our country seems to experience more than many other western democracies). I once saw a cartoon of somebody in a $50,000 SUV with a "Support Our Troops" bumper sticker and a U.S. flag driving past a homeless veteran and yelling out the window, "Get a life you worthless bum." That cartoon captured the irony quite well. To support our troops should mean to help make sure that those who come back can end up on their feet. But many times when we ignore the homeless, we're also ignoring those troops.

Of course alcohol and drug addiction is also a cause of homelessness. And some people are simply lazy. And others have had back luck. And a few have never been able to learn how to fish for themselves and need people who will teach them, motivate them, and push them. The problem is that while we are busy working and enjoying our lives, or walking by people begging for money (some of whom aren't homeless or poor at all...but most of whom probably are), we don't know how to tell the difference. It's not easy and it takes time, hard work, and commitment. But there's little that the Bible talks about more than looking out for the poor, the homeless, the fatherless, and the widows. People who criticize religion need to remember this...but so do those who believe in it. To NOT dedicate yourself to donating time and/or money to helping out "the least of these" is to completely ignore a major theme of a religion that so many claim to believe in. I know it sucks to think you might be giving a dollar or two to a lazy person who is just going to use it to buy drugs or alcohol. Because some will. But for those who will spend it on having something to fill their bellies and keep them alive, isn't it worth it? Or just buy them a sandwich...

Crazy People

People who are psychotic can plan. They are not completely incapable of any rational behavior. Sometimes, maybe not often, but sometimes they can appear normal. But their brain is like on auto-pilot. They're kind of like a ticking time bomb. They have inputs going in just like you or I, but they process some of the inputs extremely differently, often in a completely irrational way. For example, let's say you're watching the evening news. And at the end of the news, the broadcaster signs off good night. "Goodnight everyone." Totally normal to you. But to the psychotic mind, they might genuinely believe that the newscaster is speaking to them. And they may hear voices that instruct them to do certain things.

I really believe there may be some overlap between things like paranoid schizophrenia, long-term psychosis, and what religions call evil spirits. I'm not sure if what we call psychosis is really an evil demon...or if what religious folks call evil demons is really a mental illness...of if maybe sometimes it's one and sometimes it's the other. But some people are effed...up. Completely cookoo. If you talk to them, nobody's home.

I'll tell you how I think it happens. Look at the crazy guy that shot the Congresswoman in Tucson. I had read somewhere that he was always shy and awkward, but kids in high school thought he was otherwise nice. At one point, he even had a girlfriend. I'll tell you this kid's likely story: the kid had mental problems. They never got diagnosed. He went to school. He couldn't really interact with the other kids because he was a little crazy. So, he mostly kept to himself. He probably knew he was crazy, but was embarrassed to say something. Maybe his parents didn't know what to do. Who knows? He gets this girl in high school to date him. She says he would get overly jealous and angry, common traits among people with mental illness. So she broke up with him. The kid goes nuts. Have you ever been around a kind of crazy chick (or guy) after a break up? Imagine that... times a thousand...because this guy is ACTUALLY crazy. He drops out of school. Starts with drugs.

I believe that the more people who are going crazy interact with normal people...the more exposure that they have to reality...it kind of keeps them on the fence sometimes. Countervailing forces. But when crazy people eventually retreat and isolate themselves from the rest of society (like after a bad break up), they have no sane forces pulling them. They are only exposed to their mind's crazy, messed up thoughts. And they lose their grip on reality. They hear things that aren't real. Believe things that are just crazy. But to them...*they* understand. Other people are all crazy. Other people don't see the truth. Only they do.

And I really do think that there is likely a point of psychosis when it's just over. It's like your motherboard is fried. Your brain is effed. And then you're not even a person anymore. You're like a thing, walking around, completely not in control of yourself. There's a virus in your brain, or something that is controlling you...based on whatever the heck it's doing with the inputs it's receiving...

Crazy people's brains are probably processing the inputs partially randomly and partially with some kind of crazy psychotic system. It's freaking scary. Who knows why people become like that or are born that way? A person definitely has a responsibility, though, to tell somebody when they think they might be having mental problems. And people have a responsibility to try and get other people help if they start sensing a person might be experiencing mental health issues... for everybody's safety.

Stupid People

Dealing with stupid people is one of the most frustrating things in the world. And let me start by clarifying that I believe there's a difference between a person not being smart and a person being stupid. People who are simply not smart realize that they're not smart. The horrible thing about most stupid people is that they often don't realize that they're stupid. That makes them even more frustrating and even more dangerous.

One big problem when dealing with stupid people (or even people just significantly less intelligent than you) is that you can understand *them* pretty well, but they can't understand you. It's like when a teenager talks to an elementary school student. The teenager knows what it's like to be an elementary school student and to think like an elementary school student. But the elementary school student really has no idea what it's like to be a high school student. Smart people can understand stupid people's overly simple worlds. But stupid people aren't able to understand all of a smarter person's world. And when somebody can't understand, it's basically pointless to argue with them. It's like arguing with most second graders about physics. It's just not realistic at all and you usually shouldn't even waste your time trying.

I don't think that all stupid people are bad people with bad intentions. I've known some stupid people (who had no idea they were stupid) who were otherwise nice people. You wouldn't want them running a company. Or doing surgery on you. Or almost anything, really. But, they are friendly and never really cause any problems. But they can still be incredibly hard to work with sometimes. Almost everybody has worked with that person in their career, or at some point in their life, who was really, truly incompetent. And you really wondered not just how they kept their job, but almost how they even functioned on a daily basis. You really wonder how somebody could possibly be so dumb and survive. And yet many of these stupid people will still argue with you...even when they are completely and totally wrong...and even if they have absolutely no facts.

Some stupid people often seem to almost delight in being stupid. They think that being intelligent or knowledgeable makes you less cool. These people often only care about the most basic animalistic desires. Their whole lives revolve around eating, sleeping, getting drunk, having sex, and watching TV. They don't care about improving their skills and abilities. They don't care about helping other people. And if they actually do care about anything, it's usually only improving their bodies and not their minds.

Is there a relationship between stupid people and crime? Obviously not all (or even most) stupid people are criminals. However, there is a very strong correlation between low educational attainment and incarceration rates. High school dropouts are strongly overrepresented in the prison population. Certainly some of these prisoners could be very bright people who just never applied themselves. But how many of them are stupid people, who could never cut it in school, and eventually just turned to a life of crime?

Truth be told, every society probably needs at least *some* stupid people. There will probably always be some jobs out there that no intelligent human being would ever want to do. And, as terrible as it sounds, stupid people serve this purpose. They can do the jobs that no one else wants to do. Now, remember. There's nothing wrong with not being smart. You don't need to be smart to be a good person or even to be successful. But if you're stupid, and you don't realize you're stupid, then really you deserve your fate.

Fat People

America is the fattest nation in the world. (There are a handful of countries, although only a few, with a higher percentage of obese people than the U.S. However, those countries have **a lot** fewer people, and so the U.S. has more obese people than anywhere else in the world). Obviously America is the richest country in the world. Many Americans choose to lead lives of excess: excessive eating, excessive drinking, etc. So, it should come as no surprise to anybody that our country is so fat.

There are really at least three levels of overweight. The first level is a person who is slightly overweight. You wouldn't really call them "fat", but you definitely wouldn't call them skinny, either. The next level of fat is somebody who is obviously fat. Most people would call these people fat. They are inarguably overweight from a medical standpoint. There are tons of people like this in America (just like the slightly overweight category) and even my parents fit into this category (personally, I'm the skinniest guy you've probably ever met). However, there's still another level of overweight. There's what is basically morbidly obese. These are the people who can't fit into one chair. The people who have a hard time walking up even a few flights of stairs. These are people whose health really is in jeopardy because of their extreme obesity.

Having lived in Asia for more than a year, I can tell you that there are obese people in Asia, as well. However, the difference in number is quite noticeable. In Asia, you might walk around every day, and once or twice a month you would see somebody who was incredibly obese. It is so rare, that extremely fat people in Asia REALLY stick out like a sore thumb.

One of the reasons Americans are so fat is because of the types of foods that they eat. American foods often taste delicious (as do many of the Italian, Mexican, and other ethnic foods Americans like to eat). However, many of these foods are loaded with high calorie and high fat ingredients. (That's why they taste so good!). But it's not just what Americans choose to eat that is making them fat, it's also how much they choose to eat. Americans love to super-size their meals and some restaurants have responded to rising costs by providing larger portions to justify the higher prices. All of this has led to a perfect storm that has created the fattest nation in the world.

Regardless as to whether you're in the second level or the third level of obesity (as described earlier), the health consequences can be quite severe. Perhaps the most common and well known adverse effect of obesity on people's health is heart disease. Virtually everybody has known somebody who has died of a heart attack. Obesity, along with cigarette smoking, is a leading cause of heart attacks. Obesity can also lead to diabetes and problems with joints (which were not made to support huge amounts of weight).

I know that a lot of people have a genetic predisposition to being fat. However, as I've said for years, "I've never met a fat person that didn't eat a lot." Genetic conditions might make it easier for a person to struggle with their weight, but 99% of fat Americans' lifestyles are at least as big of a cause. We live in a country that glorifies being overweight. Some men say that fat women provide "more meat to love." We have a restaurant called "The Heart Attack Grill" that serves morbidly obese people for free. We've become a sick, sick society that delights in being overindulgent and disgusting.

Bullies and Jerks

Having lived and traveled in other countries, I can tell you that there are bullies and jerks everywhere. They are certainly not unique to America. Americans, however, (on average) tend to be more aggressive than people from many other parts of the world. Americans have really adopted somewhat of a "might makes right" kind of culture. We teach our kids that you have to stand up to bullies. And I think this is because bullies are such a big part of American culture, that you almost HAVE TO learn to stand up to them. Or they will just run right over you.

And that is exactly what most bullies do: they simply ignore people in their way and run over anything that tries to get in their paths. That is why they are bullies. However, one of the biggest problems with bullies is that they are always willing to fight (and go to war). It often seems like the best move for the entire group is to just stay out of the bully's way rather than to confront them. However, you can quickly see the problem. This is *exactly* the bully's strategy: to make confronting them (and preventing them from getting what they want) as unpalatable to other people as possible. I think the biggest difference between somebody who is a bully and somebody who is simply "a jerk" is that bullies are usually jerks for a reason... they are ultimately trying to get something they want. A jerk doesn't necessarily want anything whatsoever. They are just rude to people, often for seemingly no reason. They literally seem to get pleasure, sometimes consciously...sometimes subconsciously, out of pissing other people off.

But one of the commonalities between jerks and bullies is that average people usually choose to just stay out of their way. Rarely does somebody stand up to the bully or tell the jerk that they are a jerk. Some people would argue that there is no point. It's a waste of time. Telling a jerk that they are a jerk, or standing up to a bully, will only make matters worse. Everybody will suffer because of the resulting fallout. But yet that is exactly the problem: then the jerks and the bullies win. They ultimately get what they want. They are like terrorists. And the kind of "might makes right" culture that they want (and is so destructive) is ultimately reinforced.

But somebody has to be the one to break the cycle. Somebody has to stand up to the bully. And somebody has to tell the jerk that they're a jerk. Even if it will do no good. Even if they won't listen. Somebody needs to tell them. "I'm sure somebody has told them before." Well, apparently they didn't get the message. "Maybe nobody has told them yet, but they'll eventually get what's coming to them." But that is what everybody ends up saying. And those people continue to be jerks and bullies because they almost always ultimately get what they want because nobody wants to make waves.

Somebody has to be willing to stand up for everybody. The sad thing is that in our society, this is the person that often ends up getting blamed for causing the problems. "If they had just kept their mouth closed like the rest of us this never would have happened." Why people would just rather accept the "natural order", where bullies ultimately get their way and everybody else just deals with it, rather than stand up for yourself and deal with the fallout, is beyond me. Perhaps I am just a fighter. Perhaps I just have Napoleon complex. But if you don't stand up to a bully or a jerk, then you can look in the mirror and realize that you're a partner in crime for not fighting the jerk for everybody else.

Northeast, South, Midwest, and West Coast

The different regions in the U.S. typically have very different cultures. Perhaps four of the regions with the most differences in culture are the Northeast, the South, the Midwest, and the West Coast. One could also mention the Southwest region, but that region differs so much by state. Colorado is so different from Utah and both are different from Arizona and Nevada. Each southwestern state has a culture that is pretty unique from the others. However, many of the states in the four regions mentioned previously share a little more in common.

The South is the region that I know the most about. And I love the South. The South definitely is the most religious region in the U.S., especially with regards to evangelical Christianity. It's also a lot more conservative politically than I am. And at times a lot more racist than I am. There is a certain element of southern culture than can be a little backwards and a little redneck-y. But most people in the South (aside from the poor and uneducated) are some of the nicest, friendliest, most wonderful people you'll ever meet. In many places in the South, to make eye contact with somebody and not say, "Hi. How are you today?" is quite rude. Add in the sweet tea and fried foods and there's a lot to like about the South.

The Northeast seems quite different. Not only is the weather much colder, I have found people in big cities there to be much colder, too. I don't know if it's the weather, the population density, or the money, but for some reason people in the Northeast often don't seem too friendly. It does seem worth noting that when I say "the Northeast" I am referring to a lot of the big cities on the coast and not places like Maine, New Hampshire, upstate New York, and western Pennsylvania. I have found these people to be much friendlier and more laid back than those on the coast in places like New York City, Philadelphia, and much of New Jersey. The Northeast is expensive, crowded, and cold. After a summer in New Jersey, I can't imagine a place I'd rather be less. Somalia, maybe?

The Midwest seems to be a very quiet place. I've had limited trips to the Midwest, but outside of the big cities, people seem to be very kind. The Midwest is easily the second most religious region in the U.S. I think perhaps the Midwest is the closest thing left to traditional America. There's still a lot of farming and people tend to be very politically conservative there, as well.

Finally is the West Coast. The West Coast seems to have a very hippy, liberal feel to it. And to an extent, I like that about the West Coast. Think San Francisco and Seattle. However, like anything, extremes are not good. Just like the folks in the South are probably quite a bit too conservative in their thinking, people on the West Coast often seem to be far too liberal in their thinking. There are simply some weird people (in California, for example), and I'm sure that although real estate (and all other) prices have been pushed up by people wanting to live in their beautiful weather, prices have certainly also been pushed up by some of their weird overly liberal values. Just like the Northeast.

One of the neat things about America is its size and diversity. In some ways, Americans all over the country are basically the same. But in other ways, we're very different. We don't always understand each other, agree, or even like each other. But that variety and diversity of choice are a couple of the things that help make the U.S. special.

New York City

I can understand why many people like New York City. You can find almost anything and anybody in New York City. It is as diverse as I think any place could possibly be. There is something like 170 different languages spoken in the city. You can go to Chinatown which is right next to Little Italy. When you walk up and down the streets, you will see all kinds of different people. There is always some kind of street festival or special little thing going on somewhere in the city. The city is also very much a party city. The great public transportation makes it fairly easy to go out and have a great time and still be able to make it home. New York City is the city that never sleeps. It's home to movie stars. There are hot men and women everywhere. And tons of famous landmarks to see and bars and clubs to visit. It can be fun.

But, there's a lot of bad in the city and I hate it there. First of all, it's a great lesson in the winners and losers of capitalism. Some neighborhoods are riddled with old, crumbling buildings. Meanwhile, other parts boast beautiful, billion dollar skyscrapers. On one part of Manhattan, a billionaire executive runs up a thousand dollar tab at a restaurant. At the same time, some children in Midtown go to bed hungry.

There are a lot of hurting people in New York City. You've got the drug addicts. And the homeless, many of whom are suffering from mental illness: basically doomed to walking around like a zombie until their body finally dies. New York has so many of these people, that you either have to turn off that part of your humanity and ignore them, or get bummed out by it. And there are tons of people that are all trying to get other people's attention by being even weirder than everybody else. And some people enjoy this battle for being the weirdest...but I don't. I also remember pulling up to Penn Station and thinking, "This doesn't *smell* like the greatest city on Earth." Places reek of urine because the homeless have nowhere else to piss. Store owners (understandably) don't want homeless people peeing all over their floors and so instead the whole city just smells like piss. And it's polluted.

The crime, as a whole, has gotten a LOT better. They helped get rid of a lot of the corruption in the police department. Murders have come down. But there are still some places in New York City where you don't want to go. It's almost lawless. It may be down to small swaths of a few neighborhoods here and there, but there are still some places where the law is severely limited.

The winters are brutal. The summers can get quite hot. Ridiculously humid some days. Traffic is awful. It's crowded. People are often extremely rude. Because it is just so densely populated, owning and renting property is just insanely expensive. There's just so much money in the City (especially in the finance industry) that pushes prices up. And the impact on many poorer New York City natives (who have tried to stay in the city) has been quite harsh. Somebody once told me that in order to enjoy New York City, you have to ignore New York City. I think it's true. You have to make sure to stare at all of the pretty women and big buildings. And you have to look past all of the homelessness. The people who partied themselves right into the ground. The people plagued by mental illness. The people who have turned out very tough from having been raised in tough neighborhoods in tough conditions.

I can understand why people love the City. But it's because they just look past all of the bad that's there.

Jon Stewart

Jon Stewart is truly brilliant. I've talked to a few people who don't like him. And I can *kind of* understand it (mainly if you were a conservative). But, I think Jon Stewart is truly brilliant and hilarious. Furthermore, I think that although I don't agree with him on everything, he's trying to use his show to make a positive difference in this country. His show is actually one of the most important shows on television. Not because everything Jon Stewart says is right (although most things he says *are*, in fact, right), but because Stewart is getting people talking about the issues...people who wouldn't ordinarily pay attention to what was going on in their country.

I am naturally predisposed to like Jon Stewart. I'm somewhat liberal and I love sarcasm. But one of the great things about Jon Stewart is that although he has an ideological bent, he's not a hyper-partisan. He busts Obama's (and the Democratic Party's) balls, at times. After some criticism, he even went after his own good friend who was involved in a sex pic scandal. Jon Stewart calls it like he sees it. He doesn't really have a "team." And I *really* respect that. Right is right and wrong is wrong. That's how it should be.

I also really like his sense of humor. I love sarcasm. My favorite standup comedian is David Cross. Cross and Stewart both have extremely sarcastic styles. Both are quite political and quite liberal. (In fact, they are both more liberal than I am). I think Jon Stewart probably has a much better grasp of economic issues than David Cross probably does (just a guess), but I also think Stewart's full economic understanding is flawed. And I think this causes me to really disagree with some of his economic leanings. But Jon Stewart is actually easily one of the media personalities that I most closely align myself with politically.

The thing that I probably like most about Stewart is that I truly believe he wants to save this country. I think he has no real personal agenda. The fact that he can be rich and enjoy a wonderful life and make people laugh are certainly added bonuses. However, I really believe that for Stewart, it predominantly goes back to trying to make a difference and save his country.

But there's one thing that I don't like about Jon Stewart. Jon Stewart is brilliant, no doubt. But sometimes he can come across as kind of a d***. And I hate to say that, because I respect the guy so much, but I think when he acts that way, it really undermines his great arguments. I've known people that are just completely turned off by him because they perceive him as being so smug. Which sucks, because one: I think his arguments are brilliant and it's unfortunate they get dismissed just because of his demeanor and two: I really do believe Stewart is a great person with a great heart. But he sees these people doing things that he thinks are destroying the country. He sees them as incredibly dishonest. And he sees how much smarter he is than they are. And I think it pisses him off, frankly. And like Steve Jobs (in one of the next chapters), I think Stewart is brilliant and a visionary in his own right...and sometimes it's hard to argue with people in a civil manner when you're usually smarter and/or more honest than they are. I do hope Stewart can try and be a little nicer sometimes. But otherwise, he's another one of my heroes and I am so thankful that he's on the air. I try to never miss his show and I really think people should watch it, even if they don't agree with it. It's funny and very informative. Best show on TV.

George Carlin

I have really recently developed a strong appreciation for George Carlin. Carlin is obviously a controversial comedian. For the longest time I did not like Carlin or listen to his acts. The reason was because all of the comedy that I had heard of Carlin's was anti-religion. At that time, I was very religious and so I decided to tune Carlin out. That's probably a shame. Although my religious views have changed since those times, I still often find myself uncomfortable with some of his jabs at religion. Furthermore, it's one thing to take jabs at organized religion. I don't have a huge problem with that, assuming it's not completely distasteful. But Carlin really seemed to want people to know that the evil and hurt in the world made him doubt God's existence. And that's okay. That's his right. But even though I don't begrudge his strong doubts one bit (doubt is quite understandable, actually), I still don't share them and certainly wouldn't vocalize such doubts.

I don't know why I stumbled across some of Carlin's other stuff recently, but I'm sure glad I did. Carlin is a brilliant thinker, comedian, performer, and story. It was amazing for me to listen to Carlin's routines on America and Americans...after I wrote the rest of this book (this chapter was actually the last chapter written). Some of this book covers the same things he discussed in his routines (which were much more humorous, obviously, than this book). It's obvious that Carlin spent a lot of time thinking about things: thinking about the kinds of funny things that people do and why they do them. He was great at mimicking people. His content was brilliant and his style was hilarious.

I've watched a couple of interviews with George Carlin recently and what really blows you away is his deep self-reflection and openness. He obviously had spent a lot of time thinking about his childhood and why his life played out the way it had. His father was an abusive alcoholic whom he and his mother ran away from. He grew up in New York City in an extremely diverse neighborhood, filled with Irish, Puerto Ricans, blacks, and all kinds of people. His mother was a very strict Catholic and he grew up going to Catholic schools, which helps explain some of his real animosity towards religion.

Certainly Carlin wasn't a perfect guy. He obviously had anger built up inside of him. He had an attitude towards people that I can really relate to. In one interview, he talked about how he hated groups of people, but he loved individuals. And that in his interaction with individuals, he felt acceptance and like part of a family of humanity that substituted for the family he never had growing up (he once said that his mom tried to control him and obviously didn't completely approve of his lifestyle and beliefs). Here's a guy who talks about feeling like part of the family of humanity. But at the same time talks about really having a hatred for most of humanity. Carlin had a real love/hate relationship with people and I can completely understand and relate to that.

I think the greatest thing about what Carlin did was to challenge people to think for themselves. If people actually listen to his routines, they might not always come to the same conclusions that he did. I bet you that although in a perfect world Carlin and I might desire reasonably similar economic aims, I have a feeling that we'd have a pretty different idea about how to achieve it. Carlin was just such an enigma and I love that about him. You're talking about a guy who, despite fame...and drug addiction (and tax problems), was married to his first wife for 35 years...until *she* died. And then was married to his second wife for nearly ten years...until *he* died. So, he must have been at least a decent partner (even though he was always on the road and so I wonder how often he was even home). Fascinating, brilliant individual that knew from a young age exactly what he wanted to do...and he did it. And what a crazy journey he had along the way.

Steve Jobs

Steve Jobs was obviously a visionary. He was one of those people whose products literally touched the hearts of many Americans. Many of his products made our lives simpler, more efficient, more enjoyable, and just better. Steve Jobs was a very complicated man, however. Americans have a tendency to deify famous people, as well as deceased people. When people die, we often choose to ignore their weaknesses. Or even just the things we didn't like or agree with. And we choose to only remember the good. With Steve Jobs, there was a lot of good to remember. However, he wasn't perfect, and I think it's equally important to remember that.

There are several things about Steve Jobs that really impress me. The man was obviously a genius. If you haven't read Walter Isaacson's biography of Steve Jobs yet, I would highly recommend you do so. Steve Jobs was a fascinating man. I find it interesting that he was born to two unwed graduate students. Although I believe educational standards have come down, a graduate degree is still impressive to this day. It was even more impressive back then. His biological father apparently got his PhD and became a corporate executive. His biological mother was a speech pathologist. He also had a biological sister he never knew about growing up who ended up becoming an author, a professor, and an Ivy League graduate... even though they were raised by completely different parents...with Jobs being raised by a simple machinist and payroll clerk. It really makes you wonder about how much of a person's intelligence is nature (biological) and how much is nurture.

Another thing that I find interesting about Jobs is that he was a big proponent of trying acid, and yet that's something that most people seem to want to ignore. It's been said for years that LSD can have powerful effects on a person's creative ability. It can change your perspective. In fact, Steve Jobs said that doing acid was one of the two or three most important things he had done in his lifetime. And yet our government has actually outlawed this thing that one of the richest, most successful, and admired people believed was instrumental in his life's trajectory. Apple might not be the company it is today if it wasn't for Steve Jobs' experimentations with LSD, at least if you listen to him.

Yet for all that I admire about Steve Jobs (his intelligence, his boldness and willingness to take risks and be different, etc.), he was far from a perfect person. Firstly, like many men, pride was a huge problem for him. It'd be hard not to be arrogant if you were Steve Jobs. He really was *that* much smarter than most people around him. He was a visionary. He could see things that they couldn't see and understand things that they couldn't understand. It's hard when you're usually right. However, Steve Jobs and his pride, at times seemed to almost resemble Icharus.

And the way that he treated other people, at times, was simply completely unacceptable. Many people said he had a foul, foul temper. He would scream and belittle people. I think for a variety of reasons (being adopted, being so much smarter than everybody else, etc.), Steve Jobs was a very emotionally closed-off person. I'm sure he could be emotional at times, but it seems like he often intellectualized things so much that he struggled to identify with people's feelings and emotions. Or he just didn't care. I hope that one day I can be half as smart and inspirational as Steve Jobs was (maybe even just 10%), but I also hope that I treat people a lot better than he did sometimes during his life.

Oprah

I really think Oprah is one of the most fabulous people to ever live. I really find it shocking that there is even any debate over this. I think some of it is jealousy. Some people never like to see a person be *so* successful. However, I know that some of her views are controversial. Some believe she isn't Christian enough, essentially. I completely understand why they feel that way, but their opinion represents a problem with religion today: it is too fundamentalist. Jesus supposedly once said that you judge a tree by its fruit: a good tree produces good fruit and a bad tree produces bad fruit. Look at Oprah's life. Look how many people she has helped. Look how much money Rupert Murdoch has. Who has helped more people with their wealth and done more good to help people's lives? How can Oprah be bad, essentially, when her fruit is so good? She has changed so many people's lives and promoted so much good.

Oprah grew up under very difficult circumstances. Unfortunately like far too many children, she was born to a single teenage mother. There seems to be some confusion about who her father even is. Oprah's mother was very poor and not supportive of Oprah and her academics. Oprah says she was molested by a cousin, an uncle, and a family friend. She had a half-sister, a sibling that her mother didn't even tell her about (that she gave up for adoption), who later died in her early 40's... partially as a result of her cocaine addiction. And her half-brother (another one of her mother's children) died due to complication from AIDS. Tired of abuse, she ran away from home. She got pregnant, but her baby died shortly before birth. And she made even more mistakes.

However, Oprah managed to turn her life around at a young age, despite all of the obstacles that were in her way, and despite coming from a background that almost always produces a person who makes bad decisions that destroy their life. Everything was perfect for her to fail. But she didn't. She was blessed to be brilliant. She got into some good activities that allowed her to show off her talents. She worked hard. She got lucky. And she tried to make the world better along the way...no matter how successful she became. She's an amazing success story.

If I were to make a criticism of Oprah it would be in her personal life and not her professional life. I don't know Oprah, obviously. And I have no right to judge her. It does seem, however, that she's never been able to achieve a consistent and permanent loving relationship (or at least not one that resulted in marital commitment). I don't know why she's been unable (or maybe unwilling) to do so. I just know that she's dealt with more adversity in life than I might ever know (and usually with such dignity and grace).

I will also say that I don't believe that she's a Christian (at least in one of the main senses of the word). I don't think she believes that Jesus is the only way to Heaven. And there will be people that never fully accept her because of that. But I believe she loves God so much. And she wants to answer God's call on her life to make the world a better place and talk to people about God. I believe she respects many of the teachings attributed to Jesus. But unfortunately, there will always be people who criticize her for not being Christian enough...and others that criticize her for talking about God and faith at all. She really can't win, but she just keeps going out there and tries to do the right thing: trying to spread peace, and love, and give a better life to so many people. She has invested her life into others, touched their hearts, and helped changed lives. What a force for good and an example to us all. Thank God for Oprah.

Mike Vick

I really feel terrible for Michael Vick. What Michael Vick did was wrong. I don't dispute that at all. I have had a dog for much of my life. My dog is my family member and I love her with all of my heart. However, that's me. There's no MORAL law that says *these* animals are okay to kill, but *these* aren't. There may be a national law. But you can't convince me that it's morally okay to kill a deer or a bird for fun, but morally wrong to kill a dog. Now sure, there are some ways that are more cruel than others to kill an animal. And I oppose dog fighting. It's excessively cruel, I've never done it, and I never would. But these are still animals they are abusing...not people. And we should remember that.

Therein lies my biggest problem with the treatment of Michael Vick. Did he deserve to be punished for what he did? Absolutely. He abused and tortured those dogs...and that shouldn't be allowed. But they're *dogs*. And was punished more harshly than players who have (allegedly) raped women, killed another human being (DUI), and many other horrible things. He went to jail. He lost his career and $100 million salary. And people *still* hate him...almost like he killed their mom or something. Meanwhile, you've got another NFL player who was driving drunk and hit and killed another human being. I don't care if the guy was walking in the crosswalk or not. The player was speeding and drunk (after a long night of partying) and killed a human being. And he got 23 days in jail...while Vick served a year and a half.

I understand that we love animals. And I understand that most of us believe that animals are innocent and that they shouldn't be harmed (and certainly not tortured). But, I think the hatred of Michael Vick is, in some ways, a sign of just how sick we are as a country now. Many of these people turn their nose up at homeless people walking down the street but want to nail a guy to a cross because he hurt and killed a dog. A dog. This kind of mentality is just not human. As a society, we seem to care more about animals than people.

And highlighting this bizarre sense of values is PETA. It should be no surprise that they took the lead in this sanctimonious public display of hatred of Vick. It's a shame that PETA doesn't always care if humans are treated as ethically as they seem to want people to treat animals. The leaders of PETA have, in the past, compared the movement for better treatment of animals to the cause of slavery...and have justified criminal acts, if they are deemed necessary to protect animals. They've given money to people who have advocated (or even committed) crimes in the name of protecting animals (such as arsonists)[45].

Who here hasn't made a mistake? Certainly some mistakes are bigger than others. But in a day and age when we have athletes who have killed somebody or been associated with the killing of someone. When we have athletes who sexually assault women (or "allegedly" sexually assault women). Look at all of the conduct that we see that doesn't seem to get half the outrage that the killing and torturing of these dogs got. We have our priorities wrong as a society.

I think Mike Vick knows, in retrospect, that he wasn't a good person. And I think he knows that he did some bad things...and I believe he is truly sorry for what he did. But the federal government made an example out of him. They used him as an example to the rest of the country about how serious they were about hurting animals. If only they were as serious about people who hurt people. And Mike Vick paid the price. But he's really turned his life around. I believe he's at least trying to be more aware of who he hangs out with. Many fans hate Michael Vick. But some still adore him. And I still pull for him.

Football vs. Basketball vs. Baseball

First of all, let's agree that football, baseball, and basketball are the big three American sports. Soccer is the world's game, but it's not America's game. Hockey is terrible...and is better suited for Canadians and Russians...where it's too cold to do anything else. Golf isn't a sport; it's a great game. There certainly are physical aspects to the game (ask Tiger Wood's knee). But as interesting as golf can be, it doesn't require nearly the athletic ability that the other sports do. If one of the best in the game can be in his 40's, then it's not a sport. Or is **barely** a sport. All three major U.S. sports, in their modern form, were really begun and popularized in America. And, for the most part, we're the best in the world at them (although a few Latin American and Asian countries have become very good at baseball and a few international countries are really good at basketball).

Baseball is America's pastime. I mean that in both a good way and a bad way. It's become a thing of the past. The game is slow and a little boring, frankly. It's also barely a team game. But its past is amazing. Babe Ruth. Hank Aaron. Mickey Mantle. These guys were the stars of the old days. There were famous football and basketball players. But, I don't know if any of them became the icons that baseball players once were. However, baseball has taken a major turn for the worse. The strike in the mid-90's was a very bad time for the game. Then came the steroids era, which really ruined the best thing about baseball: statistics. The game is okay. But it's really not *that* interesting. But baseball is the perfect game for statisticians. It's interesting to compare the game's greatest players across different eras and see how the game has evolved. That was partially ruined when we knew that the record holder of the mother of all records, the all-time home runs record, used steroids. Some baseball players, in the quest for those million dollar contracts, turned to cheating. They disgraced the game and themselves. The game has been further ruined by the lack of a salary cap, which leads to teams with payrolls three times those of small market teams.

Basketball is different. Basketball is a little more exciting, with dunks and long three point shots. Hard fouls. The NBA relies too much on isolation plays, but the games are interesting. Financially, it's in rough shape. Whereas some professional sports leagues and other businesses show accounting losses (while they are actually profitable), some NBA teams are *actually* losing money[46]. And quite a bit. It makes, by far, the least amount of revenue of the three major sports. Hell, they make almost as little as hockey. On one hand, they play half as many games as baseball (and make at least a third less revenue). But football only plays 16 games a year. And yet they generate BY FAR the most revenue[47]. I wonder if basketball, which has taken a marketing approach that is much more urban and international in nature, has chosen wisely.

Football has become America's greatest sport. Football is an exciting game. And it's quite violent, which plays to the American culture. But it's also quite strategic and intellectual. It's this combination of brains, brawns, and exciting moments that makes us love football. But the NFL is also run extremely well, which is a large reason why they are able to generate $9 billion in annual revenues. A hard cap makes it easier for all teams to potentially become successful. Contrast that with the luxury taxes in both baseball and basketball...and the huge advantages that big market teams like the Lakers, the Celtics, the Yankees, the Red Sox, and the Phillies have on the other teams. Sure, some small market teams have won in baseball. But not really consistently. Not with the consistency of some of the aforementioned big market teams (once they committed to spending). Football, as Bill Maher recently pointed out, is run more like socialism...and it's more competitive and more interesting because of it.

Alcohol vs. Cigarettes vs. Marijuana

When you compare marijuana to alcohol and to cigarettes, it really is baffling why marijuana is illegal. Look at alcohol. Alcohol is an extremely dangerous substance. First of all, virtually everybody has done stupid things when they were drunk. It's why Mike Tyson's iconic line in *The Hangover*: "Like you said – we all do DUMB SHIT when we're fucked up," is so funny. Also look at how many people die every year as a result of drunk driving. Many, many people smoke marijuana in this country. But how often do you hear about somebody being killed by a high driver? I'm not saying it has **never** happened. But it happens SO, SO much less often. Alcohol causes aggressive, even violent behavior in men (and women) sometimes. It causes liver cancer. Think how many people struggle with alcoholism to the point that they are forced to get treatment. Compare that with the number of people who need to get treated for marijuana addiction. And yet alcohol is legal and marijuana isn't.

And look at cigarettes. Cigarettes are one of the more addictive substances on the planet. Virtually everybody knows somebody who has tried to give up smoking but has had such a hard time following through, because nicotine is just *that* addictive. And then combine that with all of the heart diseases, lung diseases, cancers, and other serious medical problems that it causes. Comparatively, the largest meta-analysis ever done (by researchers at UCLA's David Geffen School of Medicine) showed no major correlation between marijuana usage, even heavy usage, and increased occurrences of cancer[48]. You'll be able to find studies that show some negative side effects of marijuana usage. I have no doubt that marijuana use has some adverse effects on your memory, cognitive functioning, and possibly your mood. But those side effects usually pale in comparison to the negative side effects associated with alcohol and cigarettes. And yet because our government has told us that one of them is illegal (and wrong) and the other two are legal (and therefore not so bad), many of us blindly believe them.

Another allegation people make about marijuana is that it's a gateway drug. People make that claim and point out that a large percentage of hard drug users smoked marijuana first. Correlation simply does not show causality. First of all, a large percentage of hard drug users drank coffee before ever using hard drugs. Is coffee a gateway drug? Or more reasonably: what percentage of hard drug users drank alcohol or smoked cigarettes before ever using hard drugs? I bet a very, very, very high percentage. And yet we have decided to blindly trust our governments to tell us what is okay and what is not okay...what is a gateway drug and what isn't. We don't look at the actual facts and use our own minds.

One day people will realize that their governments are not always right. Not only do the side effects associated with marijuana use pale in comparison to the negative side effects associated with alcohol and cigarettes, marijuana also has some purported positive effects. One thing I firmly believe is that we can't truly understand other people's bodies. Some people have problems with their body that just don't make sense to me. I wish everybody could sleep soundly at night or build up an appetite. But that's not reality. Reality is that some people have a very hard time sleeping at night. Or eating (like those with cancer). Or dealing with anxiety. And maybe marijuana can help people with some of these issues... while still having far fewer negatives than alcohol and cigarettes. If we're going to commit so much time, money, and resources to lock up millions of Americans, we should have a lot better excuse than because somebody uses marijuana. Especially if we're going to allow people to consume alcohol and tobacco. It's hypocritical and illogical.

Good Management/Leadership vs. Bad Management/Leadership

Almost everybody has had a terrible manager. There are a lot of them out there. And as you work more and have the opportunity to be exposed to different managers, you begin to figure out two things very quickly: virtually no manager is perfect (although some are a lot better than others)...and there are good management techniques, bad management techniques, and personal preferences. In addition, the qualities of a good manager will also differ somewhat based on the specifics of the job. The qualities that make a great leader, or manager, in a war zone are not all the same qualities needed to make a great leader, or manager, in a nursing home. But, I believe we can make some reasonable generalities about some of the qualities that are usually found in good leaders, as well as qualities usually found in bad leaders.

Bad managers, in many lines of work, micromanage their employees. Micromanagement often stifles creativity and destroys an employee's sense of freedom. However, at the same time, a good manager also gives *some* direction about what he or she ultimately wants. Too often, some managers give very vague descriptions of what they want...and then are shocked when things don't turn out exactly like they had imagined in their mind. Another common trait in bad managers is being quick to delegate but slow to actually do anything themselves. Managers *do* attend a lot of meetings and have a lot of responsibilities. However, many managers seem to consider chatting and playing office politics "working." Another common bad managerial trait is an inability to accept and respond to criticism. Some managers believe that negative feedback should really only come from above and not from below. They don't listen to their subordinates. They assume they know more and are smarter...and that they understand the bigger picture. And they might. But the dynamics on the ground are just as important as the big picture...and many managers have been burned because they didn't listen to their employees who were on the front lines. Bad managers are quick to criticize, slow to give credit, and slow to apologize and accept responsibility.

Great managers, no matter in what field, care about their employees and the people they are leading. Have effective managers existed who did not care about their employees? Yes...but I believe they were deficient in that part of being a good manager. Nobody is perfect. But a perfect manager cares about the people he manages. A good manager genuinely thanks his employees for their hard work and tries to reward them for doing a good job. Good managers don't have meetings for the sake of having meetings. Good managers think about what their goals are for each meeting, how to achieve them, and then try their best to achieve them in every single meeting. This is one of the most common and annoying inefficiencies in bad managers. They waste so much time talking and spend so very little time doing. Yes, it's important to make sure that everybody has a chance to voice their opinion and lend their knowledge and expertise. Yes, it's important to make people feel like they've had their say. But how many meetings have been held by managers where you walk out thinking, "We accomplished absolutely nothing in that meeting"? Too often it seems like managers just show up to meetings with no coherent strategy and waste everybody's time. And then their employees lose their faith that their leaders are truly in touch with reality. Good managers build a short-term and long-term vision that employees can understand and be excited about.

Perhaps the biggest difference between a good manager or leader...and a great manager or leader...is passion (and energy). You can't teach passion. Either you have it or you don't. And passion spreads from a great leader to the rest of the organization. It makes employees excited about coming to work and makes them want to give their very best. It can't be fake (that's even worse). But genuine passion is powerful.

Profanity

What the fuck is people's problem with profanity? Seriously. I think really it's primarily the result of religious whackos. As I've mentioned several times, I used to be extremely religious myself. I went to church three times a week, I used to preach, and I wanted to be a missionary. But I never understood Christians' problem with profanity. I think it comes from a combination of things. The first is a total misunderstanding of what I think the Bible means when it talks about cursing. Today, we use the word "curse" to describe using words like the "f word", the "s word", and others. However, I don't think that's what the Bible means by cursing. I think it means actually wishing ill will on somebody or calling them a name. I think the other reason, besides sheer misunderstanding, is the desire to be overzealous. I think Christians long to make additional easy rules to make themselves feel like they are being a good Christian. It's much easier for them to follow a laundry list of things they shouldn't do than it is to go out and give to the poor and sacrifice themselves for others. But this isn't about that...

I think that it's probably bad to call somebody else an idiot...regardless of how true it may be. And it is certainly bad to call somebody one of the "b" words. The purpose of calling somebody one of those words is usually to offend them. That is why you're doing it. You're cursing them. However, let's say I am using a hammer and I accidentally hit my finger. If I yell the "f word", what the hell is offensive about that? Absolutely nothing. And who got to decide that "shoot" and "shucks" are socially acceptable, but "shit" isn't? What, in terms of their meaning, is different? Why is one bad and one okay?

See, there are two types of profanity. There are words that are inherently offensive and words that are artificially "offensive." When I say inherently offensive, I mean that the very nature and purpose of those words is to offend. However, other words are artificially "offensive." In other words, they aren't *actually* offensive at all. People just choose to be offended by them. When I say "shit" I am not actually saying something that is negative about anybody else.

The response I get is, "Well, why are you choosing to use <u>that</u> word? You're doing it to offend. You know that word is offensive." It is absolutely amazing what people are offended at. In Korea, I once went out with a girl who was offended that I wore shorts and sandals the first time we met (it wasn't a date). Personally, I don't think that's offensive. But she was offended. Should I stop wearing shorts because one person is simply choosing...wanting to be offended? And frankly, I don't understand why some people want to be offended. It doesn't make sense to me. And I might take people who claim to be offended by cursing more seriously, except 80% of these same people watch at least some TV shows or movies with these same words in them. If they are willing to choose to listen to bad words for entertainment then they can choose to listen to me, too. Or don't listen. That's their choice.

But that is why I believe cussing in the work place should be limited to people that know you well or you feel comfortable around. Because people *should* have that choice. And if somebody in a social situation politely asks you not to use those kinds of words, I think you should politely oblige. And if there are kids around, I think you should voluntarily pay this courtesy to children and parents. So, there *is* a time and a place that should be socially acceptable. But if I'm in a public setting of adults or in a social situation, I should be able to use whatever fucking words I want. These words show great emphasis and truly add "color" to a discussion. People shouldn't choose to be offended so easily.

TV and Modern Culture

I know most Americans absolutely love TV. Americans watch TV all the time. My parents, for a long time, had two TV's sitting side by side. TV has changed our society. However, I don't think, overall, that TV has changed our society for the better. Mass media is such a powerful force. A single advertisement or television show or movie or song can now reach tens or hundreds of millions of people almost instantly. Mass media is possibly the single most influential force in the world today. People are easily influenced and manipulated...and are prone to believe what they see and hear. It reminds me of when Orson Wells' "War of the Worlds" was first read on the radio and people who tuned in late believed that it was really happening and panicked.

Fast forwarding to 2013, what does mass media in the U.S. tell us? What kinds of messages is it sending out? Are they positive messages about being good people and shaping our world? Or are they negative messages that tell us to do whatever makes us feel good and to think of ourselves first? Is TV helping us to become better people...or showing us how and encouraging us to become worse? The level of sexuality and violence on TV these days is extremely disturbing. I don't believe I can really be pegged as an extremely conservative and old fashioned guy. The first sentence of the previous chapter was, "What the fuck is people's problem with profanity?" I am pro gay marriage. And yet at some point, I think we must open our eyes and face reality. Do I oppose sex before marriage? No. But do I think that we should live in some sort of Hedonistic society where sex is nothing more than a physical act to be done with anybody you can? Absolutely not. And yet that is the message that TV (not to mention movies and music) is delivering to our children and to our society. Combine that with religious conservatives objecting to safe sex education in schools and it's no wonder why STD's and abortions are so high.

We also watch realistic portrayals of horrible violence every day when we turn on a variety of programs. Even our news inundates us with stories of crime and murder. It's all we ever seem to see any more. At what point do we stop and think, "Maybe all of the graphic (and realistic) violent images we see on TV (and hear in music) are making our society more jaded to violence?" When do we look at the levels of STD's and unwanted pregnancies we see in our society and ask, "Maybe we need to change our attitudes about both sex and safe sex awareness?" And when will we see how the media in our country pits one American against another on the political shows we watch?

But I think one of the worst things about TV is how we waste our lives watching it. Rather than reading a book...or going out with friends...or studying the most important political and economic issues facing the country...or volunteering, we instead just sit on our couches, get fat, and watch Jersey Shore and other shit like that. Because it entertains us. And that's all we want in life now. To sit in front of a box, waste our time, and hope we can be entertained a little bit before we go back to our boring lives. Instead of doing stuff ourselves, we watch other people do stuff.

TV ultimately leads to the age old debate of whether life imitates art or whether art merely imitates life. The real answer is: both. Most of the things we see on TV are real. Sexuality and violence are part of the real world. But people see the sexuality, the violence, and the total disregard for other people on television and decide that those behaviors are normal...that they are acceptable. Mass media intentionally or unintentionally endorses the behaviors and affirms them as ok. And it's ruining our society.

Celebrity Worship

One of the things that really blows my mind, and it's a worldwide phenomenon, is celebrity worship. I love music and I love movies. And I love sports. I listen to my iPod all of the time. I love how music takes us to another place and reminds us of ideals and the way the world can be. And I love movies, as well. I have over 250 DVDs. Movies make us feel emotions: happiness, sadness, love, etc. They capture the real world and reflect it in their art. It's amazing.

But they're just freaking people. I don't know why we can't appreciate somebody's talent without being so obsessed with them. My parents love to watch that TMZ crap: where people follow stars around, harass them, and videotape them. On one hand, I don't feel that bad for them. They're rich and famous and everybody cares so much about everything they do. I bet it's a little annoying, but there are far worse lives out there. My parents also watch Entertainment Tonight. And I don't get it. At all. These are just people. Who cares where they went? Or who they went with? Or who they are sleeping with? Who cares what they are wearing? It's so stupid. People want to get lost in the fantasy and live vicariously through these famous celebrities.

Then, these famous people often give their opinions on various controversial issues...and people care what they think. I support every famous person's right to use their fame to speak out for causes they believe in. In fact, I admire it...usually even when I don't agree with the cause. However, why anybody would actually care what they think is beyond me. I might listen to what they have to say, but I would never give an argument *more* weight...just because it was coming from a celebrity...even one that I respected. And yet there are people in this world who actually care what some of these famous people think about the issues. Who cares what they think...just because they're famous?

People all over the world are fascinated by celebrities. I think most people want to have something or somebody they can worship. And some people just choose to worship celebrities. James Houran, a psychologist with the Southern Illinois University School of Medicine, led a team of researchers from universities in the United States and Britain that surveyed more than 600 people. They identified a psychiatric condition they have dubbed "celebrity worship syndrome." It's an unhealthy interest in the lives of the rich and famous. According to the researchers, about a third of people have it to some degree[49].

And all of this attention just leads to even more crazy behavior from the celebrities. Some of it is because "there is no such thing as bad PR." It keeps their names in the news, keeps people interested in them, and keeps the demand for movies with them high. Furthermore, celebrities have seen that they tend to get preferential treatment in our judicial system, if for no other reason than they can afford to lawyer up. They think they can get away with anything. And sometimes it seems like they can. (Think of the initials L.L.).

It is absolutely astounding what sheep a lot of people are. Tons of people emulate what these famous people do. They'll try to dress like them. Or make their hair like them. A famous person will have some legal trouble and then you'll see youth in this country copy their behavior. Celebrities have such a powerful influence over our culture. And I just have no idea why. These people pretend. They act. (Or they sing songs. Or play a sport). Why does that mean our country should care *so* much about what these people do, try to be like them, and let them have such an influence on our culture?

Superficiality

I thought America was one of the most superficial places on the face of the Earth...until I went to Korea. Apparently, the humongous emphasis on people's appearance is a universal phenomenon. I thought America was probably the worst... but let me assure you: it's not. I think out of all of the cruel ironies of life (and I think there are many), maybe one of the biggest is how easy it is to see what's on the outside and how difficult it is to see what's on the inside. It's so much easier to tell if somebody is good looking than if they are a good person. I think this relatively simple truth is the cause of so much pain in the world.

I will admit that many people just aren't good judges of character. I think being able to quickly judge somebody's character is really a talent...and one that most people don't seem to have. Sure, sometimes I am wrong, but far more often than not, I can quickly ascertain what kind of person somebody is...and whether or not they are a person of good character. A lot of people aren't able to do that.

However, that being said, I had a major breakthrough recently. For so many years, I always felt bad for girls who dated these good looking guys, only to get their heart broken after finding out the hard way that they were not good people. However, I eventually realized that that usually happens because the girls weren't good people either. They only dated that guy in the first place because he was good looking. That's not the quality of a good person.

I'll tell you what I think is one of the biggest problems in dating. The first thing we do is give people a looks test. We eliminate all of the people who don't meet our looks standards. Then, with the leftover people, we apply a personality test. Shouldn't it be the opposite? Shouldn't we get to know people, find out if they are the kind of person we are looking for, and *then* maybe consider if they are "good looking enough"? So often, great people, who we might love (and might love us), get passed by because of their outward appearance.

Why do you think divorce rates are so high? Many Americans marry based on looks. Then, they realize, "I have to wake up next to this person every morning and I can't stand them. They are not a good person." Isn't that what <u>really</u> matters? Shouldn't we long for somebody who is a good person? The problem is that not only is it much harder to tell whether somebody is a good person...truth be told, there are a lot fewer good people than there are good looking people.

One of my favorite movies is V for Vendetta. In the movie, there is a man that wears a mask. He wears the mask all of the time partially because of a horrible fire he was in that badly burned his body. At one point, somebody tries to take off his mask and he says, "There is a face beneath this mask but it's not me. I'm no more that face than I am the muscles beneath it or the bones beneath them." I love this quote. You are not your body. You are your mind, your heart, and your soul. Although we can't see these things, they are who we really are. Not our bodies. There's another movie..."Liar, Liar." It's about a lawyer whose young son made a birthday wish that his father couldn't tell a lie. When the boy realizes what has happened, he starts to ask his dad. "My teacher tells me beauty is on the inside..." and his father interrupts him and says, "That's just something ugly people say." I might only feel the way I do about superficiality because I am ugly, but even if so, then I am lucky that I am ugly because the reality is that superficiality is dumb and can lead to an unhappy life surrounded by shitty people.

Greed and Selfishness

One of the defining things about religion to me should be the hatred of greed and selfishness. One famous verse says, "The love of money is the root of all evil." Many a Christian I encountered in churches (likely out of a love of money) would proudly remind people that it doesn't say that *money* is the root of all evil, but *the love of money* is the root of all evil. Well, what is the love of money? It's greed. And so we can also read the verse as saying that "greed is the root of all evil."

And it is greed that dominates many of our lives in America. Most people are greedy...but most people also think that it's *other* people who are actually the greedy ones. Those that "have" accuse those that "have not" of being greedy. "You just want what I earned." Forget the fact that 1% of Americans earn over 20% of the total income earned in this country. And forget the fact that the top 1% own over 35% of the nation's total wealth while the bottom 80% own about 15% combined. In the minds of the rich, they've earned it. All of it. And the other folks are just lazy and want what they earned. Ironically, it's greed and selfishness by *both* of them.

Greed and selfishness destroy companies and the economy. Enron. Worldcom. Lehman Brothers. All major, major U.S. corporations now bankrupt and defunct. Thousands of people out of jobs. Investments worthless. Why? Largely because of greed and selfishness. Enron and Worldcom both lied about income and assets in order to inflate their firms' performance and earn big bonuses and raises. Lehman Brothers lied about their finances as well, but they were also greedy in another way. Lehman Brothers took incredible risks (including overleveraging themselves and overexposing themselves to risky real estate assets...both in the name of big profits). As long as housing prices soared, Lehman's risky strategy would pay huge (short-term) dividends for the company and its executives. But, if the bubble were to burst (and it did), Lehman would come crashing down. And it did. And it was greed that caused the real estate bubble and financial crisis that has put our economy in such tumultuous times.

Greed and selfishness also destroy governments. The U.S. government, for example, has become little more than crony capitalism. There are powerful business interests, billions and billions of dollars on the line. And this money flows into our political system so that elections must be bought more than won now, and the power ultimately lies with those who write the checks. It's all greed and selfishness. Furthermore, greed causes people to demand more and more social benefits while wanting other people to pay for them. And causes rich people to want to pay less and less of their greater share of wealth to help pay for those benefits and services for those that have less. It causes doctors, pharmaceuticals, and insurance companies to drive up the costs of healthcare. And sometimes even causes some nations to invade others.

And greed and selfishness destroy our relationships and our society. Most people choose a partner based on what they think they can get from that person... not what they can give. We think, "If I don't look out for myself, then nobody will." If every single person said that, our society would devolve into chaos. Chaos caused by selfishness. If instead, everybody said, "I need to look out for my neighbor and my neighbor needs to look out for me." How would our society be then? Some people call this idealistic. As mentioned elsewhere in this book, "I know what you're trying to say, but you're damn right I'm idealistic. Isn't that what we should all be wanting? The ideal?"

Caring About What Other People Think

One of the most important decisions people make is how much they are going to care about what other people think. How much people care about what other people think varies by country and culture, by gender, and by individual. In certain countries, like in Korea and many other Asian societies, there is a near obsession with what other people think. You constantly worry about what your parents think, your friends think, your coworkers think...even strangers that you've never met. That's not unique to Korea and Asian societies, but it's a huge part of their culture. Contrast that with America, where as a whole, we tend to be on the other end of the spectrum and believe that you can't please everybody and you can only worry about yourself. However, I've known some people in America that have a similar obsession about what other people think about them (they are typically women, but occasionally men, as well).

I think it's fair to ask how much *should* people care about what other people think...if at all. I obviously believe that obsessing about what other people think too much is wrong and unhealthy. You should be "the master of your fate and the captain of your soul." It is YOUR life. Yes, you have family. Yes, you interact with other people. However, we only have one life and we should be happy. We deserve to be happy. Many people give up on their dreams because they are too worried about what other people think. The *really* amazing thing is when people obsess over what complete strangers think. They worry about their clothes. And their style. They choose their words carefully. *Who cares?* You're probably never going to see most strangers you meet again. And even if you do, then so what? What really matters?

There's also the opposite approach to caring *too* much about what other people think and that is, "Who cares? It's my life. And NOBODY else's opinion matters but mine." And I believe that like most extremes, this extreme is also very prone to error. I think it's *at least* equally as unhealthy to live your life like, "I'm going to do whatever the f*** makes me happy and I don't give a s*** about anybody else." This is the opposite extreme (from a near-OCD obsession with what other people think). And it produces selfish people who only care about themselves. We can't make all of our decisions based on what other people will think about us, but we should go through life considering other people's feelings and comfort. If "not caring about what other people think" means you think you should have a free pass to be an asshole, it doesn't. Perhaps we *shouldn't* worry about what people *think*, but we *should* worry about how they *feel*.

And that brings us to another group of people. These people listen to what other people say and then think about it. They consider it. But they don't worry about it. They don't let it consume them. But when they make decisions, they might briefly consider what other people's thoughts and responses will be. "How will people feel about this and how will they be affected?" Sometimes, a person will need to do (or even just want to do) things that others might not approve of or might judge. Or might think is silly. One of my favorite images of John Lennon is him walking and dancing down the streets of New York. He didn't care if other people were going to think he was weird. He just wanted to dance. And he wasn't hurting anybody. He was just happy and enjoying life...not worried about what anybody else thought. We must find this balance of considering how others will feel but not worrying about what they will think about us.

Depression

Depression is very, very common in America. Major depression affects about 15% of Americans at some point in their lives. That represents tens of millions of people. And sometimes, it's hard to know whether that number represents *over* diagnosis or *under* diagnosis. Or maybe even some of both. Most "normal people" have a very hard time understanding the mind of a truly depressed person. I think that is because although many people may be insecure, they have no idea how negative the depressed person's self-image really is. The depressed person often hates themselves. Deep down, they don't understand why anybody likes them. Most depressed people feel like the world would be perfectly fine without them...and may be even better off. I've often said that two main kinds of people kill themselves: those who think nobody will care, and those that know somebody will care but either doesn't care or is even glad (they believe that hurting the survivors is an act of revenge). These kinds of attitudes seem so extreme and irrational to normal people. But they make perfect sense to a person who is struggling with depression.

Depression is a serious condition. It may be incorrectly diagnosed at times, however, in many instances, it's very real. As mentioned, depression is more than just occasional sadness. It's a long-term mood disorder that can affect the way people see themselves and the world around them. It can affect a person's sleep: perhaps preventing them from being able to sleep, or just as likely, causing them to sleep excessively (as they seek to escape their perceived reality through sleep). Depression certainly affects a person's ability to have normal relationships with other people. Depression can also cause people to eat far too much or far too little, possibly further harming their self-image. Depression can affect people in many different ways, but the vast majority of them are extremely destructive.

The argument about what causes depression: nature or nurture, will wage on. As usual, my answer is: probably both. It is likely that chemical imbalances are very real. It's practically universally accepted in the medical world, at this point. However, environment also has an impact. If a person has a terrible family life or relationship. Or if they lose a loved one. Or have some kind of major problem with their physical appearance that causes them to get teased. Both nature and nurture can cause depression. It's when both come into play, at the same time, that things get extra dangerous. It's often when a person has a chemical imbalance (or some biological tendency to be depressed), and that imbalance is combined with a very destructive environment, that we find very volatile individuals capable of almost anything.

One of the main questions is "What is the best way to deal with depression?" A lot of people believe in medication. Others believe in therapy. Some in both. And for many people, these are likely very good options. But with regards to medicine, I've always gone back to the scene in "A Beautiful Mind" where John Nash believes that his pills affect his ability to think, feel, and act as he normally had. It would make sense that if you change one thing in the brain, it might affect another. Furthermore, some very special people might be mentally strong enough to deal with their mental health problems without medicine. And perhaps even without therapy. However, many (and most) are probably not. And the tradeoffs depressed people have to make (such as those that may come with taking meds) are necessary to make sure that they (and the people around them) are safe. One of the bad things about depressed people is they usually pull away from other people. This causes them to be even more isolated and feel even more depressed. People need to be careful when they see somebody who is showing signs of depression and try to get them help.

Why Many in the World Dislike Americans

I try to guess why Americans are the way they are. I want to say that they don't travel much, but some Americans travel quite a bit. But, I think you have to do more than just travel to other places to really understand them anyway. I think you have to live there. When you just travel to a place, you are able to see some of the effects, but not understand the causes. You might be able to get an idea of what kinds of things the people in a place think, but you have no real chance to learn about *why* they might think or act that way. In Europe, it's easy to travel to other countries and learn a lot about groups of people who are extremely different than you. However, in much of the US, you have to go quite far to encounter people from a truly radically different culture. And although Mexico is radically different from the U.S., the poverty and crime in Mexico make it far from an ideal place to go learn and experience another culture. And Canadian culture, other than not being overly aggressive and arrogant pricks, is pretty much the same as ours.

But many Americans don't seem to have virtually any interest in any culture (except for their own), anyway. They have to be forced to learn about new people and new ideas. In their minds, it's too hard for them to learn about other cultures...and really, they just don't care. And that's also two of the traits that cause many people in the world to dislike them: their laziness and self-absorption. Americans, as a whole, are intellectually lazy. In 2013, young Americans just want to party, get drunk, and have sex. School, work, and learning are all afterthoughts. I mean, how many Americans can locate the countries we've bombed on a map?

Americans can also be very selfish. They've been taught that nobody is going to look out for them other than themselves. And so many Americans only care about themselves. Spend a lot of time with Spanish, Africans, and a group of Asians, and you will typically see them share more than a group of Americans the same age. They are typically more polite. And they tend to show other people more respect.

Americans are also extremely aggressive and quick to resort to violence. People fight everywhere. However, people in some places seem to look to violence first whenever they have conflicts. This willingness to fight, which is actually eagerness at times, shows up in both individual Americans as well as in the way our government handles our foreign policy. With this kind of mentality, it's no wonder the U.S. has homicide rates that are third world. And much of the world is simply tired of Americans and their aggression.

But most of all, Americans are typically very arrogant. Humility is just not a trait that is strongly valued in American culture. This arrogance is a very noticeable trait when you go out to other places. One of the things you'll find if you travel a lot is that every place has a different way of doing things. It's okay (and very natural) to prefer your way of doing things. Sometimes, even I am like that. However, rarely is it an issue of "right" or "wrong." Sometimes. But not often. Usually it's just different. But many Americans often can't be convinced of that. Americans just *know* their way is the best way...even if they have no idea why (or even if they don't know how other people do things).. They just know they are the greatest, most important country in the world. But they have no real knowledge of history. They don't realize Thomas Jefferson was a racist and Benjamin Franklin was a drunken man whore. No, our Founding Fathers walked on water. Americans also know they are the richest country in the world. But perhaps if they weren't so busy basking in their own glory, they would notice their country starting to crumble before their eyes and start to change direction. But, they are far too arrogant for that. And that is ultimately why many people in the world dislike them.

The Return of the Roaring Twenties

America has entered into a crazy era in American history. It's a very serious time and a little bit of a scary time. Unemployment was as bad as it had been in decades. People are hurting, but at the same time, the federal government's budget has spiraled out of control. We are heading down a very dangerous path. And I can't help but notice so many economic and cultural similarities between the so-called "Roaring Twenties" and today. Is the next Great Depression right around the corner?

The "Roaring Twenties" was a booming economic time...much like the 90's. Marginal tax rates (high for the richest Americans during and directly after World War I) were lowered to encourage economic growth. Interest rates were also lowered. And guess what happened? A huge speculative bubble formed (the Stock Market). And that bubble burst in 1929 and led to the Great Depression of the 1930's.

But the Roaring Twenties aren't just similar to recent days because of economic and monetary policy. There were several aspects of the culture that are similar. For one, new technologies were rampant at that time. There were many, many new kinds of products that were coming out and every family wanted one. Consumerism was really growing and Americans were spending lots of money. People also began to liberalize some their views. Women began getting more rights in the 20's (which was one of the great things about the 20's). Gays also. People in the Roaring Twenties partied and hit it hard. They loved to drink, smoke, and party. Sexual mores liberalized as well. However, many Americans did become more conservative about immigration during the 20's. The Immigration Act of 1924 limited immigration from countries where 2% or more of the U.S. population were immigrants from those countries.

Many of the cultural and economic phenomena experienced in the 1920's are almost identical to what is going on today. Culturally, we have further liberalized our views towards both women and gays...which is a good thing. But we've also become very xenophobic and anti-immigrant like many in the 20's...which is a bad thing. New technologies are constantly coming out, driving consumerism. Furthermore, for the last decade, it seems like new asset bubbles have been forming and bursting. Monetary policy today isn't all that dissimilar from monetary policy in the 20's. Interest rates are practically at zero and have been for a long time. In the 90's under Clinton, the Federal Reserve kept very low interest rates which created the dot.com bubble that burst in 2000. The Federal Reserve then lowered interest rates very low again following the economic calamity that resulted from 9-11. And that, along with the low interest rates from the Clinton era, created the real estate bubble. And here we are, in 2013, still with the foot on the accelerator and artificially low interest rates. What bubbles and recessions/depressions are we creating now? (Think student loans and, globally, sovereign debt).

We must not forget what happened after the 1920's: the 1930's. And I think that is exactly where America is headed. We barely avoided it this last time after we deregulated Wall Street and they took crazy gambles. It cost the American taxpayers quite a bit of money, but we avoided the depression that would have ensued. But, we are still pumping tons of cheap money into the system. And it's not working. The economy is still struggling. And I think you're seeing America headed towards another very tough period like the 1930's. Those who do not learn from history are doomed to repeat it. A correction in prices will almost certainly come eventually. The only question is: how big of a correction will it be?

America's Future (Culture and Politics Collide): The Fall of Rome

America's days as the world's super power are numbered. Earlier, in chapter 50, we tied the first half and the second half of this book together, explaining how a society is a unique byproduct of its politics and its culture. In fact, these things are coming together in a perfect storm to destroy this country, which at one point, really might have been the greatest in the world. At some point, Americans will likely only have the memories of the good times…not because I want that to be the case, but because that's what happens when your country's cultural, political, and economic frameworks collapse.

This country's educational system is completely broken. Many of our kids are idiots. They don't care about learning. Sure, our parents' parents said the same thing about them (and maybe they were right…), but I'm looking at America's future…and it doesn't look pretty. Are there kids out there who are brilliant and motivated and all of those things? Absolutely. America is still capable of churning out some of the world's best and brightest. But more and more of our young kids are turning out to be stupid, lazy, good-for-nothing criminals. And that's not a good sign for Rome.

There's been a decline in the family and in morals. Divorce rates are still extremely high (starting right here with yours truly). When parents get old, they often can't rely on their kids to take care of them. Either the relationship has been broken entirely or the kids simply are in no shape to take care of them. A society needs a strong family structure. Children need a mother and a father. I'm not criticizing single parents who do the best damn job that most of them can. However, the reality simply is that a child is better off having two parents than one. However, at the same time, some of the "traditional" two-person households in this country are so dysfunctional, they're worse than only having one active parent. Our society is falling apart.

When you combine these cultural breakdowns with the economic breakdowns we've had, it ultimately results in violence. And we are a gun loving country that loses thousands and thousands of innocent people because of our stupid gun obsession. We have become jaded to it…watching the news of almost any U.S. city is more like watching the news in Iraq sometimes. We think other countries are dangerous, but like a frog in boiling water, we don't even recognize the violence that *we* commit...against each other.

These cultural problems are working with our political and economic problems to help ensure our destruction. Debt, both as a country and as individuals, was talked about frequently in this book. It can not be stated enough. We are broke. At some point, people will stop loaning us money and then the whole thing stops. Party over. Political corruption helped cause it. We were too stupid to see the wolves in sheep's clothing. We were too lazy to take responsibility for our government. We didn't understand what they were doing and just trusted our government not to screw up. But instead, government failed to control the major financial companies in this country who utilized the magic combination of loose monetary policy (cheap money) and deregulation to create massive bubbles that they used to enrich themselves over and over again. Housing prices soared. Money flowed. The whole country partied. But it wasn't real. The homes weren't RE-ALLY worth that much. And unfortunately, we all now have to bear the burden for years to come. Many people who bought their homes (or refinanced) at their peaks...their home is simply not going to grow in value. There are tons of homes that will probably continue to come on the market as more and more people get foreclosed upon.

As previously discussed, the United States has over $16 trillion in debt. This is over 100% of GDP. Each year, the U.S. has been spending over $1 trillion more than they earn. They spend $800 billion each year on Medicare and Medicaid costs. As more people become eligible for Medicare (due to the aging U.S. population) and more people likely become eligible for Medicaid (as the economy continues to stall, prices continue to rise, and more people reach the poverty level), federal expenditures for Medicare and Medicaid will surely continue to rise. We currently spend $700 billion on Social Security, and as more and more seniors reach the normal retirement age, those costs will also rise. Military spending is over $600 billion, with both parties either refusing or afraid to cut it. Add in annual interest payments of about $300 billion (extremely low considering the size of the debt), and you have mandatory expenses (plus the military) exceeding total annual revenue. Not to mention the other $1 trillion the U.S. government spends every year.

And here's the biggest problem of all. There's been much discussion of the dreaded sequester and "fiscal cliff" in the U.S. (increases in taxes and cuts in defense and other discretionary spending). These spending cuts and tax increases were scheduled to take effect if Congress could not reach a long-term budget deal to reduce the massive deficit. The concern was that if the tax increases and spending cuts happened, then they'd send the U.S. into recession. But you see, the U.S. is starting to experience the same exact problem that the debt plagued countries in the Eurozone have been facing. If they want to get their budgets under control (which is eventually necessary in order to ensure that people will keep loaning them money at affordable rates), then they must cut government spending. But, if they cut government spending, then it hurts the economy. What happens if they cut Social Security? Then old people will have less money to buy new TVs, go out to eat, etc. And it hurts the economy. What happens if they cut Medicare (or Medicaid)? Then some people will not go to the doctor (which will hurt the healthcare economy), while others will still go to the doctor, but will pay more out of pocket and have less money to spend on other things. What happens if the government builds fewer bombs and spends less on the military? Then those companies that make bombs will lay people off, further hurting the economy. America has enjoyed keeping its economy afloat by spending borrowed money, but those days are coming to a close. America must now choose between a path of fiscal sanity (and feeling even more pain now), or a path of more borrowing that will ultimately lead to a Greek style disaster later. I can almost guarantee you that none of our politicians have the balls to take the pain now and America will experience a disaster they haven't experienced in generations in the future.

The 90's seemed awesome (although much of it due to a boom created by low interest rates). Then that bubble burst and September 11th happened. We then decided that the best way to keep America safe was to go fight an insanely expensive war in Iraq (which just happened to enrich tons of Bush's and Cheney's friends). We have a broken healthcare system with costs spiraling out of control, which in combination with an aging U.S. population, is putting a severe strain on our social programs. At the same time, we continue to fund the largest military in the world (by a MILE). Our national debt has reached unmanageable levels so we can protect our empire and cut taxes for the richest Americans, some of whom are the same people who got us into the financial crisis that we're in. And neither Democrats nor Republicans are willing to step up and accept responsibility. And now the bill for all of this is coming due. It's about $16 trillion. When the world loses confidence in the dollar and interest rates rise, America will have the most horrible wakeup call it has experienced in decades. Many assume that the U.S dollar will remain the world's reserve currency forever, because in most of our lifetimes, that has been the case. Having the status as the world's reserve currency is one of the most powerful things a country can possess. However, history has taught us many, many times that a currency doesn't enjoy that status forever and the U.S. dollar will be no different. Many countries have already begun to engage in currency swaps and the U.S. dollar is falling quickly in terms of its usage in global trade. At some point, when countries continue to find alternatives to the dollar and when investors demand higher rates on U.S. bonds to compensate for the additional risk, America will be forced to choose between a Greek style depression (if they choose austerity) or African levels of inflation (should they choose to simply keep printing money). Remember the 1970's? That was nothing compared to the future.

It's not that I am rooting for America to fail. Far from it. Most of the people I love and care about live there. But the numbers are the numbers. I'm afraid the reality may be that America is like a tree that is rotten on the inside. Perhaps on the outside, it still looks strong and healthy. But on the inside, it is dying and rotting and a strong wind might actually knock it over. It may sound ridiculous to many, but if in 1980 you predicted the Soviet Union would cease to exist on the map just ten years later, people would have also thought you were ridiculous (but spending beyond your means is a powerful force). Hope it was fun while it lasted, America, because I'm afraid the party is probably almost over.

Endnotes

[1] CBO

[2] "That's the way the cookie crumbles." *Msnbc.com News Services*. 4 February 2005. Online.

[3] Barker, Tim. "Universal Fall Leads To Lawsuit." *Orlando Sentinel*. 5 January 2000. Online.

[4] Caulkins, Jonathan, **Angela Hawken, Beau Kilmer**, Mark A.R. Kleiman. *Marijuana Legalization: What Everyone Needs to Know*. New York: Oxford University Press, 2012.

[5] Perez, Evan. "Mexican Guns Tied to U.S.: American-Sourced Weapons Account for 70% of Seized Firearms in Mexico." *Wall Street Journal*. 10 June 2011. Online.

[6] FBI Crime in the United States 2009

[7] Noyes, Dan. "Hot Guns: How Criminals Get Guns." *PBS Frontline*. June 1997. Online.

[8] SSA Annual Statistical Supplement, released Feb 2011

[9] SSA

[10] Morgan, David. "Social Security, health spending to hit $3.2 trillion a year." *Reuters*. 5 February 2013. Online.

[11] "Consumer Credit." Federal Reserve Board. January 2013.

[12] "The Financial Crisis Inquiry Report." The Financial Crisis Inquiry Commission. January 2011.

[13] Teitelbaum, Richard. "Secret AIG Document Shows Goldman Sachs Minted Most Toxic CDOs." *Bloomberg*. 23 February 2010. Online.

[14] Schmidt, Robert & Phil Mattingly. "Bank Lobby's Onslaught Shifts Debate on Volcker Rule." *Bloomberg*. 26 March 2012. Online.

[15] **Bennett** Jeff and Jeffrey Sparshott. "GM to Buy Back $5.5 Billion in Stock From Treasury." *Wall Street Journal*. 19December 2012. Online.

[16] "Detroit 3–UAW Labor Contract Negotiations." Center For Automotive Research. 2011.

[17] **Yglesias, Matthew.** "CPI Unchained." *Slate*. 30 December 2012. Online.

[18] O'Driscoll Jr., Gerald P. "The Federal Reserve's Covert Bailout of Europe." *Wall Street Journal*. 28 December 2011. Online.

[19] "Federal Reserve System." Report to Congressional Addressees. United States Government Accountability Office. July 2011

[20] **Gutierrez, Carl.** "Fannie And Freddie Are Fine, Bernanke Says." *Forbes*. 16 July 2008. Online.

[21] Dixon, Kim and Kevin Drawbaugh. "Factbox: Half of Americans pay no U.S. income tax? Well, sort of .." *Reuters*. 18 September 2012. Online.

[22] BLS JOLTS (Job Openings and Labor Turnover Survey)

[23] Powell, Benjamin. "The Law Of Unintended Consequences: Georgia's Immigration Law Backfires." *Forbes*. 17 May 2012. Online.

[24] U.S. Energy Information Agency

[25] Shanker, Thom. "U.S. Arms Sales Make Up Most of Global Market." *New York Times*. 26 August 2012. Online.

[26] Stockholm International Peace Research Institute (SIPRI)

[27] Brush, Michael. "War Means a Windfall for CEO's..." *MSN*. 19 September 2007. Online.

[28] "Airline Travel Since 9/11." Bureau of Transportation Statistics. December 2005.

[29] "The Impact of September 11 2001 on Aviation." International Air Transport Association.

[30] United States Census Bureau

[31] Cartine, Mike. "EU GOVTS- Greece PSI looking at actual 78% NPV loss." *Reuters*. 9 March 2012. Online.

[32] Kessler, **Glenn**. "Why is the national debt $16 trillion?" *The Washington Post*. 04 January 2013. Online.

[33] Belloit, Jerry and Anthony Grenci. "The Impact of the Tax Reform Act of 1986 on the Real Estate and Savings and Loan Industries." *Association of Pennsylvania University Business and Economics Faculty (APUBEF) Proceedings*. October (2004): 9-16.

[34] "The 1981 US Air Traffic Controllers Strike." *BBC*. 11 April 2001. Online.

[35] Abrams, Burton A. "How Richard Nixon Pressured Arthur Burns: Evidence from the Nixon Tape." *Journal of Economic Perspectives*. Volume 20, Number 4 Fall (2006): 177–188.

[36] Richter, Bob. "Tonkin Incident Might Not Have Occurred." *San Antonio Express News*. 3 August 2002. Online.

[37] Berg, Raffi. "Why did Israel attack USS Liberty?" *BBC*. 8 June 2007. Online.

[38] "Redistricting: A Story Of Divisive Politics, Odd Shapes." *NPR*. 24 September 2012. Online.

[39] Federal Election Commission

[40] Center for Responsive Politics

[41] Banschick, Mark, M.D. "The High Failure Rate of Second and Third Marriages." *Psychology Today*. 6 February 2012. Online.

[42] Bronstein, Scott. "Another guilty plea in Mississippi pickup-truck hate- crime death." *CNN*. 5 December 2012. Online.

[43] "The State of Homelessness in America in 2012." National Alliance to End Homelessness. 17 January 2012.

[44] "Mental Illness and Homelessness." National Coalition for the Homeless. July 2009.

[45] Hsu, Spencer S. "FBI Papers Show Terror Inquiries Into PETA; Other Groups Tracked." *Washington Post*. 20 December 2005. Online.

[46] Smith, Chris. "The Most and Least Profitable NBA Teams." *Forbes*. 25 January 2012. Online.

[47] Gaines, Cork. "Sports Chart Of The Day: NFL Revenue Is Nearly 25% More Than MLB." *Business Insider*. 9 October 2012. Online.

[48] Kaufman, Marc. "Study Finds No Cancer-Marijuana Connection." *Washington Post*. 26 May 2006. Online.

[49] Gray, Kenturah. "Celebrity Worship Syndrome Abounds." *ABC News*. 23 September 2003. Online.

Book Recommendations

Here are some books that I would highly recommend to the readers of this book:

A Post-American World (Version 2.0) by Fareed Zakaria

The World is Flat 3.0: A Brief History of the 21st Century by Thomas Friedman

Every Nation for Itself: Winners and Losers in a G-Zero World by Ian Bremmer

That Used to Be Us: How America Fell Behind in the World It Invented and How We Can Come Back by Thomas Friedman and Michael Mandelbaum

A History of the Modern Middle East (Fifth Edition) by William Cleveland and Martin Bunton

The Quest: Energy, Security, and the Making of the Modern World by Daniel Yergin

Winner Take All: China's Race for Resources and What it Means for the World by Dambisa Moyo

Naked Economics: Undressing the Dismal Science by Charles Wheelan

The Real Crash: America's Coming Bankruptcy by Peter Schiff

Currency Wars: The Making of the Next Global Crisis by James Rickards

Dollarocracy: How Money and the Media Election Process is Destroying America by John Nichols and Robert W. McChesney

Rise of the Warrior Cop: The Militarization of America's Police Force by Radley Balko

The Smartest Kids in the World: And How They Got That Way by Amanda Ripley

From Jesus to Christianity: How Four Generations of Visionaries and Storytellers Created the New Testament and the Christian Faith by Michael White

Outliers: The Story of Success by Malcolm Gladwell

Steve Jobs by Walter Isaacson

Confidence Men: Wall Street, Washington, and the Education of a President by Ron Suskind

The Leadership Challenge: How to Make Extraordinary Things Happen in Organizations by Barry Posner and James Kouzes

The Seven Habits of Highly Effective People by Stephen Covey

How to Win Friends and Influence People by Dale Carnegie